The Warsaw Uprising of 1944

The Warsaw Uprising of 1944

Włodzimierz Borodziej

Translated by Barbara Harshav

THE UNIVERSITY OF WISCONSIN PRESS

The University of Wisconsin Press
1930 Monroe Street
Madison, Wisconsin 53711

www.wisc.edu/wisconsinpress/

3 Henrietta Street
London WC2E 8LU, England

Library of Congress Cataloging-in-Publication Data
Borodziej, Wlodzimierz.
[Warschauer Aufstand 1944. English]
The Warsaw Uprising of 1944 / Wlodzimierz Borodziej, translated by Barbara Harshav.
p. cm.
Includes bibliographical references.
ISBN 0-299-20730-7 (cloth : alk. paper)
1. Warsaw (Poland)—History—Uprising, 1944. 2. World War, 1939–1945—Poland—
Warsaw. I. Title.
D765.2.W3B57713 2005
940.53′43841—dc22
2005010202

Table of Contents

Acknowledgments

WHEN WALTER PEHLE OF S. FISCHER VERLAG suggested I write a book about the Warsaw Uprising, I immediately agreed; it was not altogether clear to me then what I would be getting myself into. As long as it was about the pre- and posthistory of the uprising, the narrative was within the range of the conventional. The political, diplomatic, and military aspects have been well researched. A survey in the last analysis concerns only the selection of the most important themes and facts.

Yet it was very difficult to make this selection to portray the period between August 1 and October 2, 1944. This part has led me into a brand new world where ultimately the only issue is whether one does not fail completely, for—as I am convinced—this world can be grasped only inadequately by a historian. I always had the feeling that I was missing the historical reality because the extent of human suffering was constantly beyond my ability to describe it.

In the summer of 2000, when the manuscript was complete, on a sunny afternoon in the New City of Warsaw, I caught myself thinking that I was seeing an unreal, double city: all around me, a multilingual mass of cheerful, suntanned tourists were strolling, while another reality was present in my mind's eye: In which house on which day, fifty-six years earlier, how many people perished and in what way? Ever since then, I have had even less understanding of my colleagues who deal with mass murder and mass death.

I also know now why I have grown up in such a desolate and nonurban city—what is annihilated takes a long time to be revived.

Thanks to Walter Pehle for his suggestion and the infinite patience with which he fostered the gradually emerging project. Thanks to Zygmunt Walkowski for contributing the photos and for his help with the captions. I thank my friend Andrzej K. Kunert for once again being able to answer several questions. Finally, thanks to the staff of the University of Wisconsin Press, for making possible the publication of the English version of this book.

Warsaw, June 7, 2001

Abbreviations

AK	Armia Krajowa (Home Army)
AL	Armia Ludowa (People's Army)
AOK	Armeeoberkommando (Army Supreme Command)
BIP	Biuro Informacji i Propagandy (Office for Information and Propaganda)
Gestapo	Geheime Staatspolizei (Secret State Police)
DiM	Dokumenty i materiały do historii stosunków polsko-radzieckich
GG	Generalgouvernement
KPP	Komunistyczna Partia Polski (Polish Communist Party)
NKVD	Narodnyj Kommissariat Wnutrennikh Del (People's Commissariat for Internal Affairs)
NSZ	Narodowe Siły Zbrojne (National Armed Forces)
OKW	Oberkommando der Wehrmacht (Supreme Command of the German Armed Forces)
PAST	Polska Akcyjna Spółka Telefoniczna (Polish Telephone Company)
PKWN	Polski Komitet Wyzwolenia Narodowego (Polish Committee of National Liberation
POW	Polska Organizacja Wojskowa (Polish Military Organization)
PPR	Polska Partia Robotnicza (Polish Workers' Party)
PPS	Polska Partia Socjalistyczna (Polish Socialist Party)
PZPR	Polska Zjednoczona Partia Robotnicza (Polish United Workers' Party)
RAF	Royal Air Force
RGO	Rada Główna Opiekuncza (Main Committee for Social Welfare)

Abbreviations

RJN	Rada Jedności Narodowej (Council of National Unity)
RONA	Russkaja Osvoboditelnaja Narodnaja Armia (Russian People's Liberation Army)
SL	Stronnictwo Ludowe (Peasants' Party)
SN	Stronnictwo Narodowe (National Party)
SOE	Special Operations Executive
SP	Stronnictwo Pracy (Labor Party)
SZP	Służba Zwycięstwu Polsce (Service for the Victory of Poland)
TL	Trybuna Ludu
UPA	Ukrajińska Powstańska Armija (Ukrainian Rebel Army)
VfZ	Vierteljahrshefte für Zeitgeschichte
WP	Wojsko Polskie (Polish Army)
ZO	Związek Odwetu (Retaliation Unit)
ŻOB	Żydowska Organiźlacja Bojowa (Jewish Fighting Organization)
ZPP	Związek Patriotów Polskich (Union of Polish Patriots)
ZWZ	Związek Walki Zbrojnej (Union for Armed Struggle)

The Warsaw Uprising of 1944

Introduction

JULY 24 IS KRYSTYNA'S NAME DAY. On the evening of July 24, 1944,
Krystyna Wańkowicz, born in 1919, student of history in the underground university of Warsaw, invited her friends over. The war kept
many of them away: some were dead or missing; others had been
taken to Germany for forced labor; others were in camps; a few were
serving in the Polish army in Italy and France. War and occupation had
left clear traces among Warsaw's youth, but life went on and the five
years stolen from the young people seemed to be coming to an end. On
that day, the front was perhaps 100 kilometers (about 62 miles) away and
constantly moving toward Warsaw. It was a fine celebration, concluding
with the sixteen young people dancing a mazurka.

Adam Grocholski, who led the mazurka's seventh couple, was shot by
the Germans even before the start of the Uprising. Romek Wańkowicz, the
hostess's cousin, fell on August 1; his sister Irena on the last day of the Uprising, along with Ewa Matuszewska, Grocholski's partner in couple
seven. The hostess, a communications messenger in the elite scout battalion "Parasol," in which several of her friends fought, died in the bitter
struggles for the Protestant cemetery on the sixth day of the Uprising—
like Magda Morowska, who had danced in couple five. Others who participated in the celebration also participated in the Uprising—as soldiers
or civilians. On October 3, 1944, when the remnants of the Armia Krajowa
(AK), the Home Army, marched out of the ruins of Warsaw into German
captivity, they lay under the rubble of the Old City, in the mass graves of
Żoliborz and Mokotów, in the collapsed first-aid cellars of the city center.[1]
Poland had lost a whole generation, along with its capital.

In the not exactly tranquil history of Poland of the last centuries, hardly
any event compares with the trauma of the 1944 Warsaw Uprising. It was

the last in a long series of national revolts against foreign rule—beginning in 1794 with the rebellion of Tadeusz Kościuszko, who wanted to annul the second partition of Poland of 1793. The clashes took place in what is now central, western, and southern Poland; Vilnius had also participated in this conflict for a while. More than half a year later, it was quashed by Russian and Prussian troops.

The seizure of power by Poles in Poznań and West Prussia after the defeat of Prussia in Jena and Auerstedt in October of 1806 is also sometimes called an uprising or "national revolution"; the events were indeed limited to the Prussian area of partition—but not all of it—and from the beginning were under the aegis of the victorious French troops.

On the other hand, there is no doubt about the significance of the November Insurrection of 1830–31 in the Polish national tradition. It also took place only in a part of the country—in the Kingdom of Poland established in 1815; but the length of the battles, and the human and material resources employed on both sides, went far beyond the dimensions of the Kościuszko uprising. Between February and September 1831, the events were more like a regular Polish-Russian war than a classical uprising, before czarist troops finally carried the day. The Russian repressions—convictions, deportations, property confiscations—marked the end of the cohabitation of the Polish elite with St. Petersburg, defined by the Vienna Congress; at the same time, they consolidated the memory of 1830–31 in the national tradition of the subsequent decades. Even in recent times, the question of the meaning and chances of the November Insurrection has been the focus of lively scholarly and journalistic controversy.

The years 1846 and 1848 play a smaller role in the national pantheon. Within a few days, in February 1846, Austrian troops suppressed an amateurish organized revolt in what was at least the nominally autonomous free city of Kraków, which was subsequently integrated into the Hapsburg monarchy. The conspirators of 1846 joined the "Springtime of Nations" of 1848 with hardly better results: Kraków surrendered by April to Austrian troops; Lwów only after the turning point of the revolution in November. In the Prussian area, the ruling troops forced the rebels to surrender in May after a few weeks of clashes.

The next big uprising included the kingdom of Poland in January 1863, when a nationwide conspiracy tried to surprise the Russian troops—the beginning of a long and bitter partisan war. Although the Russians were far superior in military terms, they initially overestimated the rebel forces and retreated to the big cities. It took a Russian army of 300,000 men more than 1,200 engagements to subdue a badly trained and armed rebel force of 25,000–30,000 men. The legends of the January uprising refer less to the barely victorious military campaigns of the Poles than to their success in the civilian realm: the underground succeeded in temporarily creating an efficient organizational structure that collected taxes for the uprising, published an illegal press, and posted announcements in such quantities that the police could not remove them fast enough. This so-called "underground state" dictated laws and proscriptions of the code of behavior for the Poles under Russian rule and operated its own criminal justice system in competition with the special courts of the occupier. However, the expected help from outside—especially from France and Great Britain—failed to materialize. In the spring of 1864, the uprising in fact collapsed and was followed by new convictions, deportations, and property confiscations. In partitioned Poland, forty years of "peace" then prevailed, where the memory of the trauma of 1863 pulled the ground out from further conspiracies.

In 1905, when this peace was shaken by violent debates between the police, the army, and the workers, the last uprising during partition began. Unlike its predecessors, this time hope for help from the Western powers did not play a role in the event, which focused on the social question. However, in the agitation of Polish, Jewish, and German socialists, the social issue merged with the unsolved national question into a powerful argument against the Russian autocratic system. The social revolutionary impact made the uprising in the kingdom of Poland part of the whole Russian revolution (in 1905, 29 percent of all strikes in the Empire were recorded in the kingdom of Poland, and 20 percent of political prisoners were held here), a factor that implied another distinction between 1905 and previous revolts: The Polish right was a crucial opponent of the social revolutionaries; thus the revolution of 1905–7 presents elements of a civil war. Despite the defeat, the strikes and struggles resulted in a clear progress in social legislation and civil rights, but once more Poland failed to win independence.

After 123 years of partition, this goal was achieved in November 1918 by the almost simultaneous defeat of all three partition partners in World War I. Since Russia had lost not only the war but was also pushed out of east-central Europe, and Austria-Hungary had fallen apart at the same time, the revolts of the Poles were directed only against Germany—the last power that could at least try to preserve the remaining stocks of its share in the partition booty. The revolt began in late December 1918 with an uncoordinated commotion in Poznań and led to the removal of German troops and authorities from most of the province a few days later. The military counteraction of the German units brought the uprising to the brink of defeat in February 1919. Yet, France enforced a truce between rebel and German troops; for a change, the hope for Western support was fulfilled. The boundary won by the uprising was by and large acknowledged in the Versailles Treaty. In Upper Silesia, whose fate was to be decided by a plebiscite, according to Article 88 of the Peace Treaty, there were strikes and armed conflicts with the German police in August 1919 and August 1920. With the so-called third Silesian uprising, which broke out in early May 1921, the Poles tried to pressure the allies to change the unfavorable result of the plebiscite (about 60 percent of the votes for Germany, 40 percent for Poland) into a partial success at the negotiating table. Struggles on both sides lasted for weeks with a harshness on both sides that resembled civil war. The result was the partition of Upper Silesia, which continued until 1939.

The events in Russian Poland and Galicia shortly before the battles in Poznań, which can hardly be called an uprising, are not so well known but have considerably more significance for our subject. Russian Poland, under Russian rule since 1815, was conquered by German and Austro-Hungarian troops in 1915. The weaker the Central European Powers, the greater were the Polish hopes for a definitive revision of the partitions and for regaining national independence. After the disintegration of Russia, the Poles now awaited the defeat of Germany and the Hapsburg monarchy. The semilegal Polish Military Organization (Polska Organizacja Wojskowa, POW), initially tolerated and even promoted by the occupation forces, slowly turned into a secret underground organization waiting for the collapse of the occupation. In early 1917 it numbered about 11,000 members and was entrenched among the workers and peasants. By October 1918 the POW had grown to about 20,000 members—including many women, as in the "underground state" of 1863. In mid-October, in a large-scale campaign, the POW tried to intimidate the authorities and police of the Central Powers with a series of assassination attempts. Railroad junctions and other logistically important targets were attacked. Yet, the real test followed a few weeks later. Even though the occupation troops were far superior in every respect to the relatively few irregulars, the Poles soon succeeded—with few losses—in penetrating barracks, occupying arms and munitions depots, and disarming small bases. Power went to the POW because, in the autumn of 1918, the war-weary German and Austro-Hungarian soldiers were hardly interested in starting a new struggle now in the last days of the World War. They simply wanted to go home and, if any officers were not inclined to go along with that—which was not the rule in the multinational Austro-Hungarian army—the soldiers simply refused to obey.

The image of Polish workers, students, and peasants sporting red and white armbands and easily disarming the previously invincible occupation troops was deeply etched in the minds of both participants and observers; after 123 years of partition and several failed attempts, the putsch that had been won with practically no losses was obviously regarded as a kind of miracle. The myth of the POW began to develop in the days right after the disarmament of the German and Austro-Hungarian troops, when it suddenly turned out that, for the time being, the newly emerging Polish statehood was to be in the hands of the troops of the youth organization that surfaced from the underground. No wonder the staff officers of the resistance movement in World War II, who studied the liberation of the country from the Nazi regime, often went back to the experiences of that memorable November in 1918, to the memory of events in which they themselves had often participated as young men. The consequences of narrowing the horizon to the key experience of 1918 will be discussed later.

Despite all similarities, the Warsaw Uprising of 1944 was clearly distinct from its historical predecessors. Naturally, this was also a struggle against foreign rule: The hope for help from outside played a great role; their own inferiority was once more to be compensated for by catching the enemy off guard; and the model of older uprisings made the stake of their own lives obvious, which would hardly have been imaginable in any other historical background.

But in no other revolt can a similar compression of political, military, and geographical factors be found. No conflict was planned and pre-pared for so long; no other was intended to produce such a radical change and improvement of basic conditions in such a short time. The mechanism set in motion on August 1, 1944, was meant to change the status of the "Polish question" in international policy with one bold stroke. The calculation was that, within forty-eight hours, a relatively small troop of 30,000 to 40,000 mostly unarmed soldiers of the resistance would end the Nazi occupation, renew the success of November 1918, and force the Soviets to revise their Polish policy. The possibility of es-cape—in case the attack on the German troops failed, in case Moscow was to make unanticipated military or political decisions—was not planned, for when the Warsaw resistance fighters emerged from the un-derground into open struggle, the possibilities of a retreat to the status quo ante vanished.

The enterprise of the Warsaw Uprising was concentrated in a small, densely populated space. Ever since 1831, Warsaw had in fact been a provincial city in the Russian empire. In the late nineteenth century, it had experienced a significant impetus to industrialization but had not undergone any phase of modern remodeling as a capital city with cor-responding prestigious boulevards and buildings. The considerable government investments of the short period in the 1930s between the end of the global economic depression and the beginning of the war had not been sufficient for a large-scale reorganization, so the capital remained infamous for its narrowness and its housing shortage. Those who know the constraints of present-day Warsaw (495 square kilometers and 1.6 million inhabitants) will recognize conditions before World War II: after the vast expansion of the city in 1916, and a few later incorporations, 1.3 million inhabitants lived in 144 square kilometers. Except for the few modern residential buildings constructed in the 1930s, most Warsaw residents in 1939 lived in cramped conditions.

Ever since the Middle Ages, the real city had developed on the left bank of the Vistula. Praga, on the right bank, received a town charter in 1648 and was united with Warsaw in 1791. During the industrialization of the nineteenth century, the eastern part of the city remained peripheral; aside from a few factories and railroad stations, there was hardly anything new there. On the left bank were the city hall, the Old City, and the royal palace; the prestigious north–south axis (Royal Road) Krakowskie Przedmieście Street—Nowy Świat Street—Ujazdowskie Avenue, with ministries, embassies, and hotels; the main railroad station, the university and the technical university, the national museum completed in 1938, the industrial quarter of Wola in the west, the modern residential district of Żoliborz in the north, and Mokotów in the south.

As the biggest city between Moscow and Berlin, Warsaw was an important junction. Traffic on the east–west axis crossed the Vistula on five bridges (three street bridges and two railroad bridges), two of which were north of the Old City (one street bridge and one railroad bridge). The Kierbedź Bridge for automobile and streetcar traffic was on the level of the royal palace, that is, on the southern edge of the Old City. Some 1,500 meters to the south, the so-called middle-line (railroad) bridge, completed in 1931, ran right next to the prestigious Poniatowski Bridge for street traffic. This link, opened in January 1914, was blown up by the Russian army in the summer of 1915, and reconstruction was not completed until 1926. In the bridges area, the Vistula is only 400 meters wide. The eastern bank in Praga is flat, and the western valley bank is covered by an overhang that rises some 20 meters above the river.

With Okęcie and Bielany, Warsaw had two large and a few small airports, one of them in Mokotów. "Unlike Paris," the military historian Hanns von Krannhals summarizes, "back then [1944], because of its confused, sometimes chaotic style of building, Warsaw was a city that was very suitable for an uprising. Indeed, except for the overhang and the river, it lacked practically all natural obstacles (old moats, water surfaces, steep stretches in the city), but since there are only a few main thoroughfares in the inner city, the firing range and field of activity of the Germans was limited, and the many crooked streets offered several advantages to the rebels operating on a small scale. The sometimes numerous subcellars offered many possibilities of escape and attack that were hard to see."[2]

After the beginning of the war, the number of residences and residents continually declined. During the siege in September 1939, some 10 percent of the inhabitable houses were destroyed; during the annihilation of the Ghetto and after the uprising in April 1943, even more damage (up to 15 percent) was inflicted. Some 25,000 Warsaw residents fell victim to the battles in the first month of the war; later tens of thousands were shot, sent to concentration camps, or deported to Germany for forced labor. Far and away the greatest losses in Warsaw under German occupation, however, were suffered by the Jews: of the roughly 400,000 Jewish inhabitants (in 1939, about 30 percent of the total population), only a few thousand fled in time or survived underground or in the last labor camps until the summer of 1944. The Ghetto was formed in the autumn of 1940 in the northwest part of the city center; by July 1942 some 100,000 people had died there and another 300,000 fell victim to the mass murder from July to September 1942. The last 60,000 Jews were murdered or sent to concentration and death camps during the Ghetto Uprising in April 1943, and in May the Ghetto itself was liquidated and destroyed.

In the summer of 1944, the Germans formed the second largest population group after the Poles. The German population in Warsaw—unlike Kraków—had not grown rapidly, and there was no real population increase; according to German data, in late 1943, Reichsdeutsche (Germans), Stammdeutsche (Germans by origin or descendants of Germans), and Volksdeutsche (ethnic Germans) altogether constituted about 3 percent of the total population (Reichsdeutsche more than 16,000; Volksdeutsche and Stammdeutsche almost 14,700). In the summer of 1944, Warsaw may have numbered some 900,000 inhabitants (aside from German troops and police); about three-fourths of them lived on the left side of the Vistula.[3] These people now became mass victims of the battles during the Uprising.

Along with the great population density, Warsaw was marked by a strong concentration of industry and educational and cultural institutions. The capital was a center, among other things, for heavy industry, mechanical engineering, armaments, electrical technology, chemistry, and foodstuffs—with 108,000 employees and workers (1938). Before 1939, about 40 percent of Polish students studied in the city and 52 percent of Polish books were published there; more than 40 percent of Polish theaters were located in Warsaw. After 1928 the city housed the National Library;[4] the image of the center—especially along the north–south axis from the Old City to Belvedere Castle south of the city center—was defined by memorials, aristocratic palaces, and churches (only

Kraków had more sights). The new, thoroughly prestigious administration buildings of the 1930s were also here.

The occupation had strengthened another feature of the capital. Even in 1938, with barely a fifth of those gainfully employed, the proportion of employees and officials was far beyond the average in the country. After 1939, this strata of the better-educated class experienced especially intense persecution as "intelligentsia"; they were murdered or imprisoned en masse, particularly in the areas of northern and western Poland annexed to the Reich. Those who could, escaped to the Generalgouvernement (GG), where conditions were more bearable. Some of these people survived the years 1939 to 1944 in Warsaw because both the legal and illegal labor market was relatively large there, and the anonymity of the big city and—later—the strength of the resistance movement offered the best chances for survival. The secret Uniwersytet Ziem Zachodnich (University of the Western Area), established and led by Poznań scholars, is the best-known example of the significance of Warsaw in the intellectual life of Poland under German occupation. Other data also indicate this process of concentrating the intellectual elite in the capital: between one-third and one-half of the underground press appeared there, and almost all—after 1942 all—conspiratorial organizations were directed from here. Krystyna Wańkowicz's guests were also members of the underground, either as soldiers of the resistance or students of the secret universities. If the Uprising had succeeded, they would have formed the elite of the resurrected republic.

Contemporaries did not disagree about what the defeat of the Warsaw Uprising meant for the history of Poland: the landscape of ruins of Warsaw was not only an impressive symbol of Poland's enormous loss in those last five years but also represented the greatest "single item" in the long list of national revolts. On the day after the surrender, the *Biuletyn Informacyjny,* the main organ of the AK, warned against judging the last sixty-three days hastily; "the accounting" should be left to history.[5] In the first session of the Council of National Unity (of the underground "parliament") after the Uprising, one of the leading socialist politicians of the resistance admonished his colleagues that the urgent task was "setting the moral aspect of the Uprising": "We need to oppose every criticism of the Uprising. Our task is to elevate the moral dignity of the Uprising."[6] Those present knew that the problem with such categorical statements was not likely to be solved: the Uprising, for which the old elites in the underground bore responsibility, constituted a disastrous break after five years of both heroic and ostensibly promising resistance. Now, with Warsaw, not only had the biggest and strongest military center of the resistance dropped out, and links with other regions been broken, but the defeat in the decisive battle against the occupier undermined the legitimacy of the former leadership of the "underground state," which considered itself the continuation of the Second Republic.

In 1946, Kazimierz Wyka, a literary historian and essayist from Kraków who had spent the war years in a small town in the General-gouvernement, formulated the thesis that, for the Poles, the Warsaw Uprising had been a shock, not only because of the outward appearance of the extent of the catastrophe. After the trauma of September 1939 ("first autumn") when a supposedly strong state collapsed within weeks, the "second autumn" of 1944 revealed a repeated, basic failure "from the top," which now shaped the social perception of the old elites. The period of the occupation, those years of political abstinence when decisions were entrusted (because of the extraordinary circumstances) to the unknown leaders in the underground, now gave way to a massive refusal to obey. This disappointment led to both internal emigration as well as migration to the social revolutionary camp.[7] After the Warsaw defeat, the way to a Soviet-dependent Poland without Lwów and Vilnius seemed programmed in advance, not only in the view of the Kraków intellectual. On the other hand, the Communists—short-term beneficiaries of the mood described by Wyka—were undoubtedly also largely responsible for the catastrophe, which gave the whole question another dimension of political relevance.

It is on the background of these debates, which we shall examine in the conclusion, that the historiography of the Uprising has developed. Even in 1945–46, many small articles appeared, mainly individual memoirs of battles and events of the summer of 1944. This flow of first accounts broke off in 1947–48. In the shadow of the political trials against the prewar elites, dominated by the defamation and criminalization of the officer corps in Stalinist Poland, from 1948 to 1956 not a single work was published that would have met basic scholarly standards. The military historian Adam Borkiewicz, who tried to write a treatise on the Uprising between 1948 and 1950, incurred the disfavor of the authorities, and his documents were confiscated by the security police. His wife, Anna Borkiewicz, also a former member of the AK, was sentenced to seven years in prison for "collecting and preserving material that glorifies the AK and disparages the [Communist People's Army] AL."[8] Only one scholarly volume defending the good name of the non-Communist resistance against the widespread "black legend" appeared in exile—along with a few memoirs of prominent combatants.[9]

This changed with the de-Stalinization of 1956, which was particularly violent in Poland. In 1957 Roman Bratny published the novel *Kolumbowie. Rocznik 20*, which presented the fate of the AK youth in the crucial years between 1943 and 1947 (the book was not allowed to appear in East

Germany until 1981 [!]). Prior to 1976, this cult novel, whose key scenes took place in the summer of 1944, went through fifteen editions in Poland. Another classic, *Kamienie rzucone na szaniec* by Aleksander Kamiński, went through nine editions by 1979. This work was also devoted to the youthful Warsaw resistance fighters, and in 1956 it was included in the list of obligatory readings for grammar school students. On April 29, 1957, the premiere of Andrzej Wajda's *Kanał* (The Channel)—perhaps the most important media event in connection with the Uprising—took place. For the first time, the film told the history of the meaningless deaths of the young rebels, the battle, the degradation, the hopelessness and fear. The most impressive part was set in the sewer, where a group of AK soldiers try to reach the center; in the end—instead of before the saving exit—some stand before a German guard, others before bars, which was generally understood as a metaphor for the Soviet failure to help. The film evoked controversial reviews that accused the director of defiling the national pantheon—which had been defiled often enough since 1944. Nevertheless, the work received the most important Polish film prize in 1957[10] and soon attained the status of a classic, all of which transmitted an image of the Uprising to the next generations of Poles.

De-Stalinization also created the framework for research into contemporary history in the country. The comprehensive military histories of Adam Borkiewicz and Jerzy Kirchmayer, from 1957 and 1959 respectively, are the first standard works still read today.[11] Hundreds of other publications followed: on the early history of the Uprising as a subject of international policy; on battles and individual parts of the city; on the assistance of the Allies and crimes of the Germans; on individual underground organizations, units, and emergency services; and on civilian population, surrender, losses, and destruction. Half a century after the Uprising, the bibliography for this subject fills three volumes,[12] and more has been added in recent years.[13]

It is neither meaningful nor possible to discuss this mountain of specialized literature here. Instead we shall note a few of its features that have also shaped this book. First, most of the publications are of a documentary nature. Thousands of individual events from the military and civilian area have been reconstructed in the past decades. On the one hand, these usually contain little that is interesting for noncombatants; on the other hand, they reproduce a dense image that is probably exceptional and not just in contemporary Polish history. Second, this quantitative mainstream has little to do with the spectacular discussions about the Uprising: the debate about whether the Uprising was necessary and inevitable or a superfluous product of a amateurish policy has no direct connection with the real events after August 1, 1944. Had the Red Army attacked and occupied the city, the Uprising might have been rescued and the meaning of the decision of July 31, 1944, would have been quite different in an historical perspective. Third, there is an internal political discussion and expertise that is hardly known outside Poland: with few exceptions,[14] especially in the area of diplomatic history,[15] non-Polish publications have hardly played a role in the debate about the Uprising.[16]

This book is limited to conveying the essential features of the expertise. The interested reader has to seek the countless details in the monographs, for this is a deep introduction to the subject, not a comprehensive "last word," which will never be given anyway. Because the reader is not necessarily an expert in contemporary Polish history, the representation of the Uprising is presented in two introductory parts: on occupation policy and resistance from 1939 to 1944, and on the "Polish question" in this period. The next chapters deal with the origins of the Uprising from July 20, 1944, before the insurrection itself is examined. The concluding chapter examines the history of the effect of those sixty-three days in 1944 on Polish society in the postwar period.

1

Occupation and Resistance

THE POLISH DRAMA OF WORLD WAR II began with the German attack on September 1, 1939. The defeat of the Polish armed forces in the struggle against the Wehrmacht was apparent by September 17, when the Red Army marched into eastern Poland. On September 28 Warsaw surrendered, but a few Polish units continued to fight; in Moscow, the foreign ministers of Germany and the Soviet Union signed a border treaty, considering "it as exclusively their task, after the disintegration of the former Polish state, to reestablish peace and order in these territories and to assure to the peoples living there a peaceful life in keeping with their national character." In the "Confidential Protocol" Ribbentrop and Molotov committed themselves to redefine the "spheres of influence" agreed upon in August[1]: as a result of the new arrangement, the Reich received almost the entire ethnic Polish area, while the Soviet Union received eastern Poland, where the "Slavic minorities" (Ukrainians and Belarusians), allegedly needing protection against Poles and Jews, formed the majority. Germany thus occupied 48.4 percent of the Polish national territory with 63 percent of the population; the Soviet Union 51.6 percent of the territory with 37 percent of the Polish citizens. The eastern zone of occupation was annexed to the Soviet Union in 1939, enforcing an alleged plebiscite. As for the German Reich, it annexed the northern and western Polish provinces; central Poland was combined in the so-called Generalgovernement (GG) under Generalgouverneur (viceroy) Hans Frank. According to the supplementary protocol, "neither side will permit on their territories any sort of Polish agitation affecting the territory of the other country. They (will) abort such agitation on their own territories and will inform each other as to effective measures to accomplish this."

The occupation powers obviously assumed they could solve the "Polish question" by partition and thus remove it from the agenda of European policy. However, Russian and Prussian experience prior to 1918 left no doubt that the Poles would not accept this lying down—and precisely because of that, it seemed advisable to the Nazis and the Soviets to fight the predictable Polish underground together. To this day, little is known about the cooperation between the NKVD and the Gestapo before the German attack on the Soviet Union.

In many respects, German and Soviet occupation policies were similar, but also different in many areas. In the territories incorporated into the Reich, a policy of germanization was immediately introduced, which began by depriving Poles of all basic civil rights. Members of the Polish elite—from politicians, church representatives, and well-to-do citizens to teachers—were dispossessed, taken to camps, or expelled if they hadn't already fled in September and October or been shot by the task forces of the Security Police and the Volksdeutsche "Self-Defense." Altogether, probably more than 900,000 people were banished from their homes in territories incorporated into the Generalgouvernement or were sent off for forced labor in the Reich. Moreover, the Germans introduced the obligation to work in the annexed territories, closed Polish schools (in the "Reichsgau Wartheland," along with most of the Roman Catholic churches), and dissolved Polish offices, even the self-governing bodies. Property of any value was transferred to Germans and Volksdeutsche who had settled there. In the course of germanization, place and street names were "germanized," German was introduced as the official language, and—in some of the incorporated territories—speaking Polish in public was forbidden. Terror and mass deportations dissolved a massive resistance in Poznań, Pomerania, and Upper Silesia, where every conspiratorial activity involved great risks, claimed many victims, and thus seldom succeeded at enlisting the masses. There were also espionage, sabotage, and other specialized forms of resistance in this area, but resistance in the incorporated territories shifted to military actions for once, in 1944.

The radical sovietization of eastern Poland had similar results.[2] The Soviets dissolved Polish governmental and local administration organs, forbade all social federations, abolished Polish as an official language and sometimes as the language of education, stripped the churches of all effective activity, nationalized industry, and changed agricultural relations—first through land reform and soon after through forced collectivization. Legal, cultural, and socio-political conformity was accompanied by massive terror. Shootings, imprisonment, convictions, and—from early 1940—deportations to the east and south of the USSR became an everyday experience for the population in the occupied territories. Discrimination and terror under Soviet occupation mostly affected those Poles who formed the majority of the "target groups"—landowners, officials, intellectuals, priests, settlers, forest rangers, and police. Nevertheless, the core of sovietization was not nationalist: a Polish Communist could have a career in the "Western Ukraine" just as well as a Ukrainian "nationalist" could be arrested; wealthy Jews were dispossessed of their property as well as wealthy Poles.

In this respect, sovietization differed essentially from germanization, which had a racist orientation from the start.[3] The roughly 2.5 million Polish Jews who had come under Nazi occupation in 1939 were first to be concentrated in ghettos, which were then established in the incorporated territories and the GG (the largest were in Warsaw and Łódź). The "final solution" began with the mass deaths of ghettoized Jews, who fell victim to starvation and illness by the hundreds of thousands, and it continued with the industrialized mass killings in the death camps in occupied Poland created to gas Jews from all of occupied Europe.

The second "race" that was ultimately "to disappear" in the process of the "ethnic reallocation of the land" in the east, destined for germanization, were the Poles. Yet during the war different principles were to apply to the incorporated territories and the GG.

The GG initially covered 95,000 square kilometers with about 12 million inhabitants; after the formation of the district of Galicia on August 1, 1941, it covered 142,000 square kilometers with about 17 million inhabitants. The Poles constituted the large majority; only in Galicia were they numerically inferior to the Ukrainians. The "enormous manpower reservoir" was to be treated as a colony and at first not opened to German settlement. In agriculture, the old property rights largely remained in place, the Roman Catholic church was allowed to continue, and primary and vocational schools were maintained with a few cutbacks. At first, it was mainly members of the "ruling class" who were terrorized, killed, or sent to concentration camps, as well as all those who resisted debasement to the status of an underclass without rights or culture, and who were forced to work. Yet, in the first years, "ethnic reallocation of the land" through expulsion failed to materialize, and even later was pursued only tentatively (by expelling more than 100,000 Poles from the area of Zamość in 1942–43). Another important characteristic of this colony in the middle of Europe was that the Poles were indeed deprived of their rights, but the local administration, economy, transportation, and health systems could not manage without Polish community officials, auxiliary police, engineers, railroad workers, and physicians. For the resistance, the significance of the support of these groups was as significant as the numerical superiority of the Polish population vis-à-vis Germans and Ukrainians.

Economic exploitation was the short-term goal of the occupation policy; at the same time, it was to prepare the ground for the new order after the war, which was also envisaged in other areas. "The Poles may have access only to such possibilities of education that show them the hopelessness of their national existence," explained Hans Frank, the newly appointed viceroy, about his educational policy, which was expressed most succinctly in the dissolution of high schools and middle schools, as well as in the deportation of the professors from Kraków's Jagiellonian University to Sachsenhausen-Ovanienburg concentration camp.[4] The various measures of making slaves of the Poles were held together by such unprecedented terrorism, unknown until the attack on Yugoslavia and the Soviet Union: "In Prague, for example, big red posters were put up saying that seven Czechs were shot today," the viceroy told a journalist in February 1940. "I tell myself if I wanted to have a poster hung up for every seven Poles shot, there wouldn't be enough forests in Poland to produce the paper for such posters."[5]

Special courts and special criminal law, the principle of collective imprisonment and whippings, deportations to concentration camps, and mass shootings of members of the Polish intelligentsia (especially in the "exceptional campaign of pacification" in the spring of 1940) characterized the German exercise of power—but despite its high intensity and ubiquitous presence, terror in the GG did not fill its intended function. Trusting the effect of their brutality, the occupation force waived all legitimation of its rule in advance and thus thwarted the emergence of even a rudimentary loyalty of the oppressed population from the start. But at the same time, despite great losses, the masses and social ties of Polish society in the GG remained intact. Abolishing the principles of European law did enable the rulers "to brand all opponents—even putative ones—as criminals in principle." The outcome was paradoxical though: "This principle created ideal growth conditions for the resistance movement because the need for protection from such criminalization was beyond the possibility of defense of the individual and consequently forced a crossover to organized groups of the underground movement."[6] In other words, many advantages could result from the obviously illegal and dangerous membership in a resistance organization under the especially threatening conditions of life under occupation: emotional support and security, potential support from the personal environment, or material assistance in the broadest sense of the word.[7]

Finally, one important motive for the individual to join the underground was the traditional pattern of relations. As outlined in the introduction, resistance against a foreign authority was nothing new in Polish history. This tradition was conveyed to the youth in school and family,[8] and many older people were familiar with resistance from their own experiences. Thus, members of the generation born between 1880 and 1900, who were dominant among the underground decision makers, had in their youth partaken in nearly every form of resistance that would resurface more intensely after 1939. Secret schools and high schools, economic boycott, other forms of civil disobedience, political and military conspiratorial organizations, armed struggle—all these had already existed in Poland between 1900 and 1918, and countless undertakings in the period between 1939 and 1944 bore the stamp of these predecessors.

The first attempts at organized resistance emerged as early as September 1939, during and immediately after surrender negotiations of individual troop units. Along with professional officers, civil officials were also active, providing secret organizations with money, blank identity cards, and the like. The frequency of such occurrences supports the conclusion that many officers and officials considered the path to the underground as their duty, as a natural continuation of their prewar activity. Between 1926 and 1939, it was precisely these groups that had formed the backbone of the authoritarian dictatorship established gradually after Józef Piłsudski's coup d'état in May 1926, under the motto "return to (political) health" (Sanacja). The Polish state that had once won their loyalty still functioned—contrary to the expectations of the occupiers—as a point of reference for the self-conception of the elite. On the one hand, this position was registered as proof of the patriotism of the former rulers; yet more importantly, the activities of the old ruling class clashed with the massive refusal of the whole prewar opposition. That is, the former opposition, repressed by the regime until 1939, saw the behavior of the Sanacja supporters mainly as an attempt to reproduce in the underground the conditions that had characterized the dictatorship.

From 1926 to 1939, Poland was ruled by a military dictatorship. The authoritarian regime did indeed behave with marked civility compared to its eastern and—after 1933—western neighbors; yet, following the usual pattern of those days from Estonia to Greece, it plagued the opposition with censorship, preventing and forging elections, limiting freedom of assembly, and so forth. In the last years before the war, repressions against the Ukrainians became especially aggravated, and relations with other minorities were also tense. In the summer of 1939, under the pressure of the German threat, this internal political rift seemed to lose significance. The regime successfully insisted on the legitimating function of patriotism and won broad support by demonstrating presumed strength. But, when the Polish army was smashed within a few weeks by the Wehrmacht, social frustration over the unexpected defeat was manifested in a radical rejection of the Sanacja regime and its representatives who were still in the country. The beginnings of resistance after the September defeat can be seen against the background of this mood: in 1939–40, nearly all parties established their own political—and military, if possible—underground organizations in order to forestall the presumably threatened takeover by the Sanacja elite. The race for political dominance in the resistance had begun.[9]

Naturally, there were various deviations from the plan of a quasi-political foundation of the resistance sketched here. Thus, during the defense of Warsaw in September 1939, soldiers, the city administration, and former members of the opposition worked closely together. The decision to go underground was made from both sides; however, after the Germans had marched in, the emerging conspiracy network of the parties was not subordinate at first to the military organization. We know the history of the emergence of the conspiracy in Warsaw better than in other places; but then it was marked by another characteristic, which is especially emphasized in more recent literature. Aside from officers, officials, and opposition politicians, countless people of other professions were involved, whose immediate commitment to resistance cannot be explained by political motives in the narrow sense. Hundreds of underground organizations—not only in Warsaw—were established "from below" in conjunction with existing ties of family, job, friendship, and neighbors.[10] Protective associations and other paramilitary groups, scouts and athletic federations, simply all social bonds, proved to be rallying points. Hundreds of conspiratorial networks thus emerged as an expression of a spontaneous rebellion against this humiliation, and were not created "from above," as a result of a party political calculation.[11]

The numerical ratio between the two types of organizations will never be clear: many processes are known only fragmentarily, sometimes a person worked in several connections, others left no verifiable traces. The extant reports of the organizations need looking at carefully, since the number of their members on paper was often quite exaggerated. Two circumstances, however, should be emphasized as irrefutable: first, the intelligentsia, who were trained as reserve officers, played the crucial role in the first phase of the resistance. Second, the activity of this group fell on fertile ground by 1940. In the reports to the government-in-exile, the leadership of the Union for Armed Struggle (Związek Walki Zbrojnej, ZWZ), established in late 1939 to early 1940, repeatedly asserted the great difficulty of recruiting new members because of the existence of so many other organizations. These reports seldom talk about the passivity of the population, as would have been thoroughly

19

conceivable after the shock of September 1939; and in the few cases when the reports discover passivity, they point at the failure of the politically active social groups, which should have been able to mobilize the "lower classes" for the struggle.[12]

If the entire Polish national territory of August 31, 1939, is considered as a potential field of activity of the resistance, certain distinctions emerge. In 1939, a third of Polish citizens belonged to the national minorities: Ukrainians, Jews, Belarusians, and Germans (in Warsaw, the Jews, with 30 percent, constituted the only large minority). For various reasons, none of these nationalities participated in the Polish resistance to any relevant extent: the politically active Ukrainians wanted their own state, the Jews were separated from the Poles by the occupation policy, the Belarusians could be mobilized only here and there for the Polish resistance, and the Germans generally could not. That meant that this resistance could be active only in those areas where the Poles constituted a majority. The different forms of occupation policy of Berlin and Moscow achieved such a divisive effect that the underground as a mass phenomenon was limited to the Generalgouvernement and—after 1941—to a few eastern districts (the area around Vilnius and also Volhynia in 1943–44).

Thus, the differences between the GG on the one hand and the western and eastern territories on the other were significant, yet no genuine collaboration would have occurred—and not only because all prerequisites for it were lacking on the part of the Germans.[13] In the first year of the war, in the GG—unlike most occupied countries in Europe—there was a clear division between political collaboration and loyalty to the occupied state. In the "Basic guidelines for the relationship of the society to the occupiers," of November 1939, the government-in-exile explicitly allowed the continuation of work in the autonomous administration and all nonpolitical branches and organs of government—as long as this cooperation did not involve political obligations. Charitable organizations could also cooperate with the occupation power if necessary. But, in the private sector, the social and political boycott was anticipated from the start, and at that time, the "guidelines" promised death to spies and provocateurs.[14] From 1942 on, the underground courts did indeed issue hundreds of sentences against individual collaborators— V-men (police informants recruited from the local population), informers, denouncers of Jews (*szmalcownicy*), overenthusiastic police—thus making steps toward treason even more risky.

The underground justice system was only one of several areas of activity of civilian resistance. Since December 1940, civilian authorities were led by what the government-in-exile (until June 1940 in Angers, later in London) called the "delegate of the government in the country," who held the additional title of Deputy Prime Minister in 1944. Fifteen departments were subordinate to the Delegatura, whose jurisdiction stretched from taking stock of foreign political changes, through social welfare in the broadest sense and organizing acts of resistance, to planning for the postwar period. The department of the interior gradually constructed a new Polish administration, which—like the police-style organization in this department—showed up in 1944 in several territories as support for the rebel troops and as a symbol of the new government. The department of press and information included a publishing organization that—sometimes in competition with the military publisher—produced hundreds of books and brochures, as well as several newspapers. The department of education and culture organized a secret school and college system.[15] Information about the individual centers of civilian resistance can be derived by examining the distribution of the money smuggled in from London. In 1942, the budget of the Delegatura amounted to 400,000 British pounds. Of that, 30 percent was allotted to social welfare, 20 percent went to social, political, and youth organizations in the underground, 18 percent to the secret school system, 15 percent for the machinery of the civilian resistance, 5 percent was used for defense, and 12 percent was registered as loss from confiscations and other unanticipated events. The structure of expenses in subsequent years may have been similar. From 1942 to 1944, the civilian positions got roughly less than a third of the $27 million earmarked for the resistance from exile.[16]

Especially in the first year, the government Delegatura found itself in a tense relationship with the leadership of the military resistance. Both were working for the common goal of building an underground state that could repeat the miracle of 1918. After the experiences with the authoritarian military dictatorship from 1926 to 1939, however, politicians naturally responded with extreme distrust to every activity of the military. In the first year, the ideas of both sides collided over who really had the final word in all possible issues. Thus, it was a preprogrammed conflict to a certain extent, since, before 1939, the opposition had hardly any representatives in the officer corps, while the political party basis of the dictatorship had almost completely broken away in 1939. Moreover, the conflict between the military and the politicians took place on a field where separate party interests concerning the so-called consolidation (*scalenie*) of military underground organizations clearly violated the government demand for unity, represented by the military.

By October 1939, the major parties of the pre-1939 opposition merged into one secret Main Council of National Defense (Rada Główna Obrony Narodowej). Until 1944, the group changed its name several times; in the last year of the occupation, it acted as a Council of National Unity (Rada

Jedności Narodowej, RJN), but its nature remained the same: leading representatives of the Peasants' Party (Stronnictwo Ludowe, SL), the National Party (Stronnictwo Narodowe, SN), the Socialists (Polska Partia Socjalistyczna, PPS), and the Christian Democratic Labor Party (Stronnictwo Pracy, SP) formed an advisory board to the Delegate and considered itself a substitute for the Parliament that had been dissolved in 1939. The natural rivalry of the politicians with the military returned with a vengeance in the party committee because the parties, as mentioned earlier, had established their own military organizations at the beginning of the occupation and did not want to subordinate them to the central military leadership. If hard-to-prove data can be believed, two of them, the moderate SL and the rightist SN, succeeded in uniting several tens of thousands of members in 1943. Since the ZWZ and its successor, the AK (Armia Krajowa, the secret army, or the home army, granted appropriate authority by the government-in-exile), understandably considered one of their main tasks to be consolidating the whole military underground, the conflict was both inevitable and protracted: Despite the support of the government-in-exile, it was not until 1943–44 that the AK succeeded in integrating most of the party associations into the troops. At this point, the AK had 300,000 to 350,000 members throughout the country, but only a fraction of these soldiers were armed: in early spring of 1944, the total number of active partisans in the AK in the forests could hardly have been more than 20,000.

Aside from the AK, in 1944, after drawn-out negotiations with party leaderships and local organizations, basically only two segments of the underground remained—the extreme right and the extreme left. In 1942, the National Armed Forces (Narodowe Siły Zbrojne, NSZ) emerged from a consolidation of splinter groups of the SN who did not want to join the AK, and organizations of the extreme right of the prewar period, who mostly also rejected subordination to the resistance loyal to the government. The NSZ developed regionally into a strong organization. Especially in the district of Radom, a few of their functionaries were proven to have collaborated with the Germans in the fight against the Communists, for one thing. In Warsaw, however, the extreme right did not play a big role.

Relations between the underground loyal to the government and the Communists were even more complicated. In the 1920s and '30s, the Polish Communist Party (Komunistyczna Partia Polski, KPP) was illegal. They rejected the parliamentary (and definitely the authoritarian) system and advocated revising the borders both in the west and in the east in favor of the neighboring states. Excluded from the established parties and from the state because of this platform, the KPP developed into a reservoir for radical antirepublican forces; among them, the national minorities, particularly the Jews, played a big role. In 1937–38 the Polish Communist Party was dissolved by the Comintern, and most of its functionaries living in Moscow or summoned there were arrested by the Soviet secret police, murdered, or sent to camps; only one single member of the old leadership survived. Between 1939 and 1941 the Polish Communists hesitated to go underground, not least because of the German-Soviet pact. Therefore, the Communist resistance began only with the arrival of Polish Comintern functionaries in the GG, who parachuted from a Soviet plane in December 1941. In January 1942, they established the Polish Workers' Party (Polska Partia Robotnicza, PPR)—to the disapproval of older comrades, the new party avoided the word "Communism" in every form, just as the party denied its dependence on the Comintern. The main goal of the PPR was the radicalization of the armed resistance against the occupiers. Fear of the Germans drove new supporters into the arms of the Communist underground, which acted under emphatically national solutions. In 1943 and 1944, in a few areas of the GG, especially the district of Lublin, it became a genuine rival to the resistance loyal to the government; in Warsaw, the Peoples' Army (Armia Ludowa, AL), the military organization of the Communists, remained a small group.

The PPR was an important phenomenon in the total picture of the Polish underground. It was the only party to interpret the principle of self-determination of peoples in the sense that the Ukrainians, Belarusians, and Lithuanians had rights to join the Soviet republics of the same name. Thus, unlike all other forces in exile and underground, which insisted on the principle of the integrity of the territory of the state of 1939, the Communists sided with Moscow in the debate about the future Polish borders. In February 1943, when discussions took place between representatives of the underground loyal to the government and the PPR, it turned out that the gap between the two groups could not be bridged. The Communists could not withdraw their agreement on the transfer of the eastern area any more than the "Underground State" was willing to see the Communists as anything other than dangerous agents, guided by the Comintern. As expected, the discussions failed,[17] and the PPR remained some kind of an essentially smaller opposite pole to the "bourgeois" camp. Relations between individual partisan units of the AK and the AL developed in various ways; there was both cooperation and conflict. The latent opposition did not lead—as in Yugoslavia or Greece—to an outbreak of mass hostilities; but, to the end, namely in the summer of 1944, the split between the majority loyal to the government and the growing Communist minority remained a crucial feature of the Polish resistance.

2

The "Polish Question"

1939–1944

H AD THERE BEEN NO HITLER-STALIN PACT of August 23, 1939, there would have been no Polish Question in World War II. In terms of military might, the Third Reich was so superior to the Polish Republic that the Wehrmacht would not have needed any Soviet support; by September 17, when the Red Army crossed the eastern Polish border, the campaign in the west had been decided. But when eastern Poland was occupied by the Soviets and formally incorporated into the USSR, a very complicated situation emerged: Poland was divided between the officially neutral Soviet Union and the Reich. On September 3, the Western powers had declared war against Germany without actually coming to the aid of the Polish ally. Now, France and Great Britain were hoping for a German-Soviet conflict, which would have entangled Germany in a two-front war. After the unexpected defeat of France in June 1940, this hope became even stronger in London. Great Britain was now fighting against Germany without one single strong ally, while Berlin occupied a large part of western and central Europe, and later southern Europe as well, and had two important de facto allies in Italy and the Soviet Union.

In this situation, the British scrupulously avoided even asking the Soviets about their ideas for the future of Poland. A good pretext for that was provided by the course of the Soviet-German border, which resembled the so-called Curzon line in places, that is, the line British foreign policy had been willing to accept in 1920 during the Polish-Soviet war as the future western border of Russia.

On June 22, 1941, when the German attack on the Soviet Union began, the disastrous alliance of the old and new partition powers shattered. The British now pressed for an immediate treaty between Moscow and the Polish government-in-exile in London led by Prime Minister General Władysław Sikorski. As the conflict spread in the east, the Polish ally, which had always been relatively insignificant strategically, now became even more unimportant for the real outcome of the war. On the other hand, a great deal now depended on Soviet Russia. The collapse of the Stalinist empire and the occupation of European Russia by German troops—in the summer of 1941 there were important reasons to consider the real possibility of this worst-case scenario—would mean a new turn in the war and thus crucially weaken Great Britain's strategic situation. Therefore, the first priority was to strengthen Moscow's will to hold out; moreover, the Polish government-in-exile had to be moved to accept a compromise acceptable to Stalin.

In the preceding months, this question had been discussed under several guises. In terms of national rights, it was extremely problematic: by occupying eastern Poland, the Soviet Union had broken several bilateral and multilateral treaties. The government-in-exile trusted in the principle often confirmed in London (and later in the Atlantic Charter) of the nonrecognition of any territorial changes made during the war and hoped that the Polish-British Agreement of Mutual Assistance of August 25, 1939, in which the British had promised Poland "all the support and assistance in its power"[1] in case of an attack, represented a binding commitment. The Poles extended this obligation to the Soviet invasion, contrary to the secret Polish-British supplementary protocol of August 25, in which Germany was named unambiguously as a potential aggressor. The foreign policy committee of Chamberlain's cabinet had made this specification of the protocol two days after the conclusion of the Hitler-Stalin pact, since Britain otherwise had to grant Poland a guarantee against an aggression from Russia.[2]

Between September 1939 and June 1941, the British made several attempts to get the Polish allies to accept such an interpretation of the treaty of August 25, which left all possibilities open to them in case Moscow relented. In October 1939 Chamberlain and his foreign minister Edward Halifax had explained to the amazed Polish foreign minister August Zaleski that Poland was to abstain from all anti-Soviet activities. The expectation of a British declaration of war against the Soviet Union was unrealistic. As for the roughly 12,000 square kilometers west of the Curzon Line, Poland could hope to have them returned only "in negotiations with Soviet Russia at a future peace conference"; this meant that, in the British view, too, Moscow was simply going to keep more than 90 percent of its loot (193,000 square kilometers). Along with London's hope of Moscow's about-face in the international play of forces, was the already hinted-at motive of the Curzon Line. The reference to the British border proposal of 1920 was to demonstrate that Great Britain also considered the essentially more eastern Polish-Soviet borders that were established in the Polish-Soviet treaty of Riga in 1921, and thus recognized by Moscow, as unwarranted.[3]

This British position had a long prehistory: the Polish Republic, as it emerged in 1918 after over a century of partition, enjoyed little sympathy in public opinion in England. It was unpopular because its territorial claims against its two big neighbors went too far, according to the British view. With the left, the Polish war against the Soviet Union in 1920 played an additional role; in that year the later doctrinaire anti-Communist Ernest Bevin was active in the Hands-Off-Russia movement. With the right, there was also hope for Russia, which made the Poles look like an interference factor. Labor and Conservative parties agreed on rejecting the Polish dictatorship, after 1926.[4] Then, in the early phase of the war, it turned out that the Polish question was regarded merely as a kind of function of British-Soviet relations by the most influential organs of the British press—the *Times* and the *Daily Express*. Along with the Russian historian and *Times* commentator E. H. Carr, Lord William M. Beaverbrook, press czar and owner of the *Daily Express* and a member of Churchill's cabinet was the most influential exponent of an explicit pro-Soviet direction that always subordinated Polish arguments to Russian ones.[5]

Only in the leadership of the Special Operations Executive (SOE, the British center for support of European resistance movements), which had held the Polish underground in high esteem from the beginning, did pro-Polish voices usually prevail. In the Foreign Office, on the other hand, criticism of the "irrational" policy of the Poles dominated.

The fundamental pro-Russian option was weakened after the Soviet attack on Finland in late November 1939, when sending a Polish expedition corps—according to later plans a mixed corps—to the new theater of war was considered for a short time. Yet, opposition to the position of the government-in-exile proved to be irreconcilable: the Poles maintained that they were in fact in a state of war with the Soviet Union, and a *restitutio ad integrum*, meaning a return to the territorial situation of 1939, was still the fundamental war aim. This dissent prevailed even after a cabinet crisis about a policy memorandum regarding Russia in July 1940 (after the defeat of France and the annexation of the Baltic republics to the Soviet Union). The next endurance test of British-Polish relations was thus preprogrammed, and it erupted in November 1940. In his speech to the House of Commons on September 5, the new Prime Minister Winston S. Churchill had repeated in a conspicuously artificial format that His Majesty's government recognized no territorial changes made since the beginning of the war. Still, he left the back door open by claiming as an exception those border changes that take place with the "free consent and goodwill of the parties concerned."

The British ambassador in Moscow, Stafford Cripps, was much clearer in a memo he presented to the Soviet Foreign Ministry on October 22: Moscow's benevolent neutrality in the current conflict deserved London's recognition of the "de facto sovereignty of the USSR" in the Baltic republics, Bessarabia, northern Bukovina, and "those parts of former Poland now under Soviet control." The overeager ambassador had certainly ventured too far with the "former Poland"—after all, Great Britain found itself in the war precisely because it had tried to prevent the disappearance of Poland. Cripps had no doubt been authorized by the War Cabinet to make a presentation that was essentially a de facto British recognition of the Soviet expansion of 1939–40 in exchange for dissociating Moscow from Berlin.[6] The issue got into the press, the Poles protested, the British washed their hands of it, and the official correspondence stopped until January 1941. One remaining result was that, anytime there was talk of Russia in the BBC Polish broadcasts, they were censored in advance by the Foreign Office.

On June 22, 1941, new possibilities of negotiations about eastern Poland opened for all actors in the diplomatic circle. The British were primarily interested in including Moscow in the anti-Hitler coalition; the Soviets wanted international recognition of the annexations they had been served on a silver platter in October 1940 and had not accepted. Naturally, the situation of the government-in-exile was the most complex issue. In a written declaration of foreign policy principles of the cabinet in the summer of 1940, the consequences of a possible British-Soviet alliance were outlined with the formulation that "the necessity of revising our point of view in the sense of moving the discussion with the Soviet occupiers to a further level can result." This is exactly what happened after June 22: dependent on its British hosts in every respect, the government-in-exile had to submit to a certain extent to the internal constraints of the anti-Hitler coalition—but without losing sight of its main objective, the preservation of the territorial integrity of the Republic. In addition to the border problem, there was the question of the Polish prisoners-of-war, internees, deportees, and convicts—approximately more than 700,000 people who had disappeared since the autumn of 1939 into the Gulag, the Far East, and Kazakhstan in prisons, camps, and construction battalions of the Red Army. The fact that most of the captured officers had already been murdered by the Soviet secret police in mass shootings in the spring of 1940 was not yet known, nor was the name "Katyn."[7] But quite independent of that, the simple knowledge of hundreds of thousands of displaced persons meant that the government-in-exile could be blackmailed. On the other hand, it must have been important to the Soviets to transport the tens of thousands of Polish noncommissioned officers and soldiers (of the barely 10,000 imprisoned officers, according to later Soviet data, exactly 1,658 had survived) as Allied troops from the Gulag to the collapsing western front, which was hardly conceivable without a compromise with the Polish side. This implied that Moscow must have backed off at least from its thesis about the disintegration of the Polish state, with which it had once justified its invasion of eastern Poland.

On June 23 Prime Minister Sikorski said in a radio address that the "Polish-Russian question" had now disappeared from international politics, which meant the return to the old border treaty of 1921. The Russians did indeed have a quite different conception of coexistence in this coalition, into which they were being pushed by Hitler: The Soviet ambassador Ivan Maiskii, in his first discussion with the British Foreign Minister, who quickly assumed the role of a very active intermediary, referred to a Poland in "its ethnic borders." That could only have meant the boundary line established by the Soviets with the German Reich in the border treaty of September 28, 1939, and which Maiskii's interlocutor preferred to call the Curzon Line. Furthermore, the Soviet ambassador spoke of the formation of "national committees" in Moscow—a Polish one, a Yugoslavian one, and a Czechoslovakian one—which were obviously to act independent of the governments-in-exile and to whom, in the case of Poland, the released prisoners-of-war were to be delivered.

In subsequent weeks, Maiskii backed off from the postulate of a brand new determination of the eastern border of Poland and the formation of a countergovernment in Moscow. During this time, the British put increasing pressure on the Poles to sign. The government-in-exile resisted because it correctly sensed an ambush in the formula now under discussion, which resulted in the Soviets declaring the Hitler-Stalin pact invalid. Moreover, it was not convinced that the Soviet Union would withstand the German attack and, despite their clear interest in a Polish-Soviet balance, the British finally avoided everything that could be understood as a confirmation of the territorial integrity of Poland concerning the August 1939 borders. At the last minute they resorted to repeating the formula of nonrecognition of territorial changes made in Poland since the outbreak of the war.

The treaty was signed on July 30, 1941. In Article One, the Soviet government declared that "the Government of the Union of Soviet Socialist Republics recognizes that the Soviet-German treaties of 1939 relative to territorial changes in Poland have lost their validity." In the supplementary protocol, the Soviet Union now granted "amnesty" "to all Polish citizens who are at present deprived of their freedom in the territory of the USSR, either as prisoners of war or on other adequate grounds."[8] Both states committed themselves to a common struggle against Germany. Thus, at least at first glance, the clauses of the treaty consisted of pure self-evident truths. But in the course of the negotia-tions and even into August, there was increased opposition within the government-in-exile to the ostensibly unambiguous text of the treaty: Sikorski's opponents warned that, by a special interpretation of the in-dividual articles, the Soviets could reach a conclusion that would be un-desirable for the Poles. It was only with considerable effort (and British support) that the Prime Minister succeeded in overcoming the resis-tance of several cabinet members. Thus, in exile, the Peasant's Party played an important role, while in the underground all parties saw the agreement as the only chance for releasing their fellow countrymen from Soviet camps. Now, however, the value of the new Polish-Soviet comradeship-in-arms was still uncertain.

By the autumn of 1941, there were increasing indications that the treaty of July 30 offered no practicable basis for Polish-Soviet relations even within the war coalition. Although the release of the prisoners dragged on, the originally anticipated maximum number of 25,000 sol-diers was soon exceeded; along with them, thousands of civilians grad-ually arrived in the army camps. The road that the starving—and often sick—released prisoners took to Buzuluk, where the staff of the emerg-ing Polish army was functioning, was full of obstacles that could not all be explained by the war and the deplorable condition of the railroads. The welfare and hygiene of the troops was catastrophic, and the Soviets explained that, in view of their defeats on the front, they were unable to arm the Polish units.[9] Gradually it turned out that the Soviet inspectors had let only some of those released from the camps go toward the army. On November 10 the Polish embassy protested that only Polish citizens of Polish nationality were allowed to get through. On December 1, 1941—right before Sikorski's arrival for his first and, as it turned out, last visit to Stalin—the Soviet foreign ministry replied that it was only be-cause of "the good will and compliance" of the Soviet authorities that the Polish citizenship of persons of Polish origin was not questioned. The other inhabitants of the former eastern Poland—Ukrainians, Bela-rusians, Jews—were Soviet citizens on account of the decree of the Presidium of the Supreme Soviet of November 29, 1939. Thus, what the bitterest Polish critics of the treaty of July 1941 had prophesied had hap-pened: Moscow now referred to internal legislation to produce a legal basis for the annexation of eastern Poland.[10]

Discussions between Stalin and Sikorski on December 3 and 4, 1941, were inconclusive concerning the border question. The Wehrmacht were positioned outside Moscow, and the Polish government-in-exile gave the Soviet Union few chances of surviving the winter. Still treated with hostility by London opponents, even if Sikorski had wanted to and if the constitution had allowed him, Sikorski did not dare take any great risk in the border question, because an agreement with the existentially threatened Moscow would have cost him his head in internal politics.[11] Moscow, on the other hand, remained consistent even at the moment of greatest threat. This time, Stalin did state that he wanted to change the borders only *"ĉut ĉut"* (a little),[12] but after the experiences of the last two years, this was much too little to break down the reserve of his Polish negotiating partner. The Polish-Soviet summit revolved mainly around questions of the Polish army in Russia. It concerned problems of welfare that were vital in the winter, the unsolved question of armaments, the future transfer of the troops into the supposedly healthier climate of the Central Asian Republics, and their strength. (Those numbers were determined by the level of Soviet food supply, which had to be shared with the Polish civilians assembled in the military camps.) The missing officers who could not be found were hardly mentioned. Finally, there was agreement on increasing the numbers of those serving in the army to 96,000 soldiers and moving some of the troops (25,000 members of the marines and air force, as well as soldiers in tank units) to Polish units in the Middle East and the west. Questions of the border and hence of citizenship remained unsolved, and Sikorski set off on an inspection of the Russian army.

On December 7 the Japanese attack on Pearl Harbor pushed the United States into the anti-Hitler coalition, which now assumed a brand new form. The Poles—who had hoped for the friendly relations they had traditionally enjoyed with the U.S. President—were hardly aware that, with the Soviet victory near Moscow and the American entry into the war, the importance of the government-in-exile within the coalition had been reduced to practically nothing. British Foreign Minister Anthony Eden arrived in Moscow a few days before Sikorski, and in his first conversation with Stalin, the Soviet dictator demanded the signing of a secret protocol recognizing the Soviet borders of 1941.

After his return to London, Sikorski tried several times to commit the Allies to the Polish point of view. This became even less likely during the course of 1942 than it had been in the second half of 1941. Visits to the United States (March 1942, December 1942–January 1943) did not produce the hoped-for results; moreover, the Americans made it clear that they accepted the British line of nonrecognition without territorial guarantees. The British rejected the arguments of the government-in-exile as steadfastly as before, and not only for pragmatic reasons, as they kept insinuating.[13] However, neither London nor Washington was willing to agree officially to the Moscow demands, particularly in relation to eastern Poland.[14] Meanwhile, relations of the government-in-exile with the Soviet Union grew worse from one month to the next. In March and April, part of General Anders's army (33,000 soldiers, accompanied by

11,000 civilians) left the Soviet Union for Iran; in subsequent months Moscow gave up the hope that the Polish troops would strengthen its western front. The Poles did not want to fight beside their erstwhile prison guards; anyway, up until Stalingrad, many did not believe the Soviet Union could win. Moreover, there was always the vivid fear that the Polish divisions would be used as cannon fodder; and, considering the way the Soviets treated their own losses, that would have been tantamount to a suicide of the relatively small Polish army.[15] The mere existence of the Anders troops and the system of social welfare for Poles in the Soviet empire caused countless problems and tensions: Moscow correctly saw this special exclave (with its own widespread support network) as a stronghold of virulent anti-Communism, and ultimately it wanted only the rapid withdrawal of the intractable allies.

Soviet consent to the concept of transferring all the troops also had an internal coalition component. Churchill, who had proposed the transfer of the Anders Army to the Caucasus and Iran as early as October 1941 in talks with Stalin, now hoped this would free British troops in the Middle East, who were needed in North Africa. At the same time, the withdrawal offered the Soviets the opportunity to implement a general adjustment of relations to the government-in-exile to suit itself. Nine of the twenty branches of the embassy, involved mainly with social welfare for deported Poles in various parts of the country, were closed in July, and the staff of the remaining ones were stripped of diplomatic immunity. Moscow now officially approved the withdrawal of the Anders Army; in subsequent weeks the whole Polish social welfare network was dissolved, and 130 staff members were arrested. In August, scarcely 45,000 of General Anders's soldiers and about 25,000 civilians left the Soviet Union—the "inhuman country," where tens of thousands of their family members had perished and other hundreds of thousands had to remain because they had not reached the base of the Anders Army garrison. After a long period in Iran and the Middle East, while troops and civilians gradually recovered from the diseases and hunger of 1939–42, the army went to the Italian front in 1944, as part of the Allied forces. After 1945 very few of the soldiers decided to return to Poland, which had meanwhile become Communist.

After the withdrawal of the army—which normal, that is uninformed, Soviet citizens could have experienced as faint-hearted at best, especially during the initial stages of the battle for Stalingrad—tensions did not subside. On January 16, 1943, the Soviet Foreign Ministry confirmed what had been the practice of Moscow Polish policy for months, namely, that the 1941 promise to treat Polish citizens of Polish nationality as actual Polish citizens, in fact, no longer applied. A TASS communiqué of March 1 made it perfectly clear that the announcements of the

Polish government proved "that, in these issues [borders and citizenship], current Polish government circles do not represent the real opinion of the Polish nation." Also in March, the Communist Union of Polish Patriots (Związek Patriotów Polskich, ZPP) was founded in Moscow; since the cabinet in exile was still recalcitrant on the boundary issue, Stalin publicly resorted to the alternative of a countergovernment declared by Maiskii in July 1941. Polish protests could not change anything in this policy.

The announcement on Berlin radio (April 13, 1943) of the discovery of mass graves in the Katyn forest ushered in the final stage of the permanent Polish-Soviet crisis. The Germans claimed to have found some ten thousand corpses, which matched the number of missing Polish officers whom the Polish embassy in Russia had been searching for in vain since 1941. The Poles knew the signs that pointed to Moscow as the perpetrators and were sure that this time—for a change—German propaganda only had to tell the truth to put the government-in-exile in an impossible situation. The officers—all of them prisoners-of-war—were victims of a mass murder; the government could neither keep silent nor, against their better judgment, endorse the Soviet version that the Germans were the perpetrators. The British tried to prevent the Poles from appealing to the International Red Cross, since they understandably feared that Stalin would use every such step as an excuse to break off diplomatic relations. On April 16 the government did take this step, which was impossible pragmatically but the only possible one for all other reasons. On April 25, in an official note, Molotov accused the Poles of "contact and arrangement with Hitler . . . to force Soviet Russia to make territorial concessions at the cost of the Soviet Ukraine, Soviet Belarus, and Soviet Lithuania," and announced the "interruption" of diplomatic relations with the government-in-exile.

The "interruption," which could also be interpreted as a suspension but was really a break, represented another maneuver of deception in the Soviet game about Poland; it suggested that a resumption of relations was indeed within the realm of possibility. In reality, preparations for the establishment of a Communist regime in Poland were carried out openly, since as far as Moscow was concerned, the government-in-exile was no longer a participant in the conflict. On May 8 Moscow indicated officially that it had approved of the establishment of a Communist Polish infantry division in Russia. Until the actual takeover of power in the summer of 1944, exploratory talks were to be conducted with the Polish government-in-exile, but they did not change the pace of implementation of the new concept.

Basically, the agreement of the other big powers was necessary, which was why the Polish question constantly became an object of negotiation of the Big Three, while the government-in-exile gradually dropped to the status of a supernumerary. This loss of significance was encouraged not only by the Soviet military successes of 1943 and 1944 but also by the mysterious death of Prime Minister Sikorski in an airplane crash in Gibraltar on July 4, 1943. His successor, the former head of the Peasants' Party in exile, Stanisław Mikołajczyk, was a capable politician and, if need be, a tough and clever negotiator. Yet, his authority both at home and abroad still had to be built up, and circumstances were quite unfavorable for that.

In the spring of 1943 the British had no doubt who was behind the murders in Katyn; the most important paper on this question by Ambassador Owen O'Malley, which had been done at Churchill's request, left no doubt about that. The addressees in the Foreign Office were helpless; ultimately the document was made accessible only to the smallest circle of initiates since "this evidence cannot affect our course of action," as the highest official in the Foreign Office noted dryly.[16]

In fact, in 1943 the British and Americans had essentially more important things to discuss with the Soviets than a massacre of Polish officers in the middle of Belarus three years earlier. On the agenda were the "second front" in Europe and the postwar order on the continent, the future world organization and the fate of Germany's satellites, and ultimately the partition of Germany itself. Like Yugoslavia, Poland was a complicated chapter of interallied relations. It did have a higher strategic significance than the kingdom of Serbia, Croatia, and Slovenia—especially in view of the advance of the Red Army to Belarus—and could indirectly influence several votes in the United States. Nonetheless, it remained a regional problem, and—according to the tacit agreement of the Big Three—regional problems might be solved by the directly affected big power, perhaps not on its own but under the clear priority of its interests. This principle found its full expression in the infamous Moscow percentage settlement of October 1944, when Stalin and Churchill defined their zones of influence in southeastern Europe, but it was essentially applied back in 1943—if not before.

The informal definition of spheres of interest was used as early as 1941, when the British began to coordinate their aid program for continental resistance movements with the Russians. The Polish underground disappeared from the British lists of potential receivers of arms immediately after June 22. The agreement between the SOE and the NKVD (Narodnyj Komissariat Wnutrennich Del) of September 30, 1941, established that the problem of possible cooperation between the Soviet authorities and the diversion organizations in Poland and Czechoslovakia would be a subject of discussion between the USSR and the corresponding governments of those countries. In subsequent years, the central administration of the SOE in London was not very happy about this ambivalent formulation, which Moscow interpreted as an exclusive right to support—or ignore—east-Central European resistance. Yet, the SOE could not prevail with regard to the Foreign Office and, even in 1943, the British commitment to the resistance in Poland loyal to the government remained dependent on British-Soviet relations or on the actual or feared reactions to British actions.[17]

At the Foreign Ministers' Conference in October 1943, Molotov clarified the Soviet position regarding the AK. At the preparation for the meeting, there was a violent Polish-British quarrel over the support plan for the AK. Eden now showed Molotov the reservations of the British side—they did not know if they should help the AK with large supplies of weapons. Thus invited, the Soviet Foreign Minister first had to be assured "that the weapons will get into the right hands"; the Polish government-in-exile gave no "guarantee of friendly feelings toward the Soviet Union." At the same time, the SOE admitted openly to the Poles that consideration for Moscow forbade any great support for the AK.[18] The results of these British tactics in the question of conveying weapons were catastrophic—the lack of weapons made it difficult for the AK to manage in the crucial year of 1944. From 1941 to 1944 the Allied air force dropped some six hundred tons of material for the AK; it is not known how much of that ever reached its proper target. The Greek resistance received about ten times as much material, the French about 10,500 tons. On one single day, July 14, 1944, Allied planes dropped about three hundred tons of material for the Resistance over southern France—half of what the AK got in more than three years.

The Moscow Conference of Foreign Ministers and the failure of the plans for arming the AK, which the British justified officially with technical problems, was only the prelude to the actual preliminary decision of the "Polish question" in Tehran a month later. Before the summit meeting, Mikołajczyk warned Churchill and Roosevelt that there was no leeway on the question of the eastern borders. Eden's answer to the memorandum was an equally categorical statement that the British government was thus deprived of any chance of a successful mediation. Churchill himself even refused a direct discussion with the Polish Prime Minister. Despite these tensions in the preliminary stages, the British fought in Tehran for a reasonably honorable solution of the border question—in favor of Moscow but with written guarantees for Poles concerning compensation in the north and west at the expense of Germany. Churchill used matches to demonstrate how he imagined the western extension of Russia and the western shift of Poland and Germany. While the British were really convinced of this solution, Roosevelt indicated in a discussion with Stalin that, for him, it was simply a matter of American Polish votes in the next election. This diplomatic slip of the president—no one had forced him to weaken his negotiating position so pointlessly and gratuitously—must have delighted Stalin. The decision on the western shift of Poland then clearly turned out to suit Moscow: Stalin merely gave up about a tenth of his captured property in the northern section of the border, but with Lwów and Vilnius—which had been ceded to Lithuania for a few months in 1939—he got the lion's share of what had been annexed by the Soviet Union in 1939 (180,000 square kilometers out of 201,000). Nearly as grave as this substantial determination was the fact that the decision of the Big Three was kept secret from the government-in-exile. Until the fall of 1944, the Poles believed that only a general exchange of opinions without any resolutions had taken place in Tehran. Indeed, the government-in-exile should have trusted their own ears more: on February 22, 1944, when Churchill made a speech in the House of Commons declaring himself in favor of the Curzon Line, they still did not want to believe it.

On January 4, 1944, the Red Army crossed the old Polish-Soviet border in Volhynia. The official Soviet announcements now no longer referred exclusively to the Curzon Line as a future national border; a reorganization of the government-in-exile (by removing "anti-Soviet members") was also mentioned more clearly as a prerequisite for the assumption of any negotiations. The British tried once again to mediate. They advised the Poles to be reasonable and recognize the Soviet claims and thus remove the most conspicuous opponents of such a "compromise"; Churchill, on the other hand, indicated to Stalin that the Soviet demands went too far. Even so, British-Polish and British-Soviet negotiations came to nothing. A direct Soviet exploratory discussion with the government-in-exile also ended inconclusively on June 23—the day after the beginning of the big offensive of the Red Army in Belarus, which crushed the German army group "Mitte" within a few weeks and moved the remnants hundreds of kilometers to the west. In this way, the acts of war shifted into an area where the AK had a few considerable partisan units available. The Soviets increasingly accused the Polish resistance openly of collaboration; evidently, they were willing to give up military cooperation with the underground loyal to the government. Now, the AK itself confronted a genuine dilemma. The Soviets were beating the German troops and liquidating the German occupation—the main goal of the resistance—but as the Red Army was moving into former eastern Poland only as an ally of the Allies, its future relationship to the AK was completely uncertain. In early summer 1944, the Polish resistance therefore found itself in a situation where the risks and consequences of either solution could not be calculated.

3

Planning the Uprising and
First Attempt of Transition

FROM THE START, the Polish resistance saw itself as a continuation of the Second Republic, thus subordinate to the government formed by General Władysław Sikorski, which emerged on September 30, 1939, in French exile. A few days before, on the night of September 27, shortly before the surrender of the capital, the soldiers in besieged Warsaw established the underground organization Service for the Victory of Poland (Służba Zwycięstwu Polsce, SZP). In exile, representatives of the prewar opposition were dominant; in the underground, on the other hand, high officers of the Sanacja regime dominated. It took weeks to connect Paris and Warsaw and allow the government to take control of the resistance from a distance. The exile politicians distrusted the officers, especially the founder of the SZP, General Michał Karaszewicz-Tokarzewski. Therefore, the government-in-exile dissolved the SZP and sent the former commander to a suicide squad in the Soviet zone of occupation, where he was promptly arrested. In January 1940 the SZP was replaced by the Union of Armed Struggle (Związek Walki Zbrojnej, ZWZ).

In exile the ZWZ was controlled by the supreme commander and prime minister, General Sikorski, and by General Kazimierz Sosnkowski, a fellow traveler of Józef Piłsudski at a time, however, when the dictator had no political functions and was thus relatively uncompromised. Sosnkowski now chaired the committee for national issues of the government-in-exile and was theoretically commander of the resistance organization in the country. The commanders of the six regions of Warsaw, Kraków (GG), Toruń, Poznań (incorporated territory), Białystok, and Lwów (Soviet occupation zone), were subordinate to him. Given the wretched knowledge of the government-in-exile about the situation in the country—news was brought by couriers who often took months to go through neutral states into occupied Poland and come back—this quasi-federalist structure hardly had any chance to prove its worth and can be explained only in terms of the political distrust of the government-in-exile. On December 4, 1939, Sikorski and Sosnkowski sent "Instruction no. 1" to the former chief of staff of the SZP, the politically unhampered professional officer Colonel Stefan "Grot" Rowecki. This "Instruction" set rules for the fundamental issues of constructing and using the resistance organization. The ZWZ was defined as a secret and military organization built on "ruthlessly obeyed principles of hierarchy and discipline." It was to be the only organization in the occupied country, "pan-national, above parties and classes," and its ranks were to unite all Poles "who want to fight the occupier conspiratorially with weapons in hand, regardless of differences in political and social convictions." The goal of underground activity was to reconstruct the government and prepare for an armed uprising "behind the lines of the occupation army in Poland," which was to break out as soon as regular Polish units marched in. But, before that, armed struggle was out of the question: "In no case does the Polish government permit belligerent actions on the territory of the homeland because at present the political goal of such action seems unclear, and secondly, because in the current beginning stage, a military action would turn out to be weak and could capture only a few points of the country. The result of such an action would most likely be disproportionate to the reprisals they would bring upon the country by giving the occupier an excuse to destroy Poland mercilessly. For now, stay away from diversionary acts and wait for relevant directives from the supreme commander."[1]

Rowecki assumed the leadership of the most important Region One, based in Warsaw. In February 1940, after Tokarzewski was removed, he became the real commander of the ZWZ under German occupation, and in effect, the two sections under Soviet occupation were also subordinate to him. After the defeat of France, the fiction of the six equal regions was abandoned, and Rowecki was officially promoted to general and made commander (Komendant Główny) of the entire underground force. In the prewar Polish army, Rowecki, born in 1895, was considered one of the best officers of the younger generation. He was known, among other things, for works on military theory and history (like street battles, fortifications, propaganda, the Red Army). For a professional soldier, his interests were unusually broad, and that may have given the commander of the ZWZ (who had led one of the two Polish tank brigades in September 1939) few illusions about the future use of underground troops: even under optimal conditions, irregular partisans and urban guerilla units had little hope of success in battle against regular army troops. As a twenty-three-year-old first lieutenant, Rowecki had disarmed an entire German company in November 1918 with just a handful of volunteers; but he did not forget that such daring feats were possible only in a struggle with troops who were reluctant to fight.[2]

On this issue, there were no differences in principle in the correspondence between the government-in-exile and Rowecki as commander of the military resistance—it was only known more precisely in exile that Allied support for a Polish uprising would turn out to be much more modest than was generally hoped in the underground. London and Warsaw were in complete agreement on the precise separation of the tasks of the resistance for "now" and "later." The country was now to provide espionage work for the Allies, sabotage German armament and transportation, and be ready for reprisals against especially brutal actions of the occupier; but the real goal—the Uprising—was still in the unforeseeable future. The resistance, wrote Rowecki in November 1939, could appear openly only when Germany collapsed "or at least when one leg buckled. Then we should be able to cut through veins and tendons in the other leg, and bring down the German colossus."[3] Unlike the overwhelming majority of his subordinates, Rowecki was hardly convinced that the outbreak of a "real" war on Germany's western border would automatically introduce such a development. After France fell, which confirmed his skepticism, the prospect of a German collapse became more remote and that of an uprising thoroughly uncertain. The subsequent months, characterized by general pessimism and helplessness, were the only ones in the history of the underground when the number of soldiers sworn in decreased rather than increased.[4]

The staff officers of the ZWZ began planning the Uprising precisely in that phase of general hopelessness, namely, in the second half of 1940.[5] The corresponding memorandum was sent to London in February 1941 as "Operative Report no. 54," and arrived there only after the outbreak of the German-Soviet war, which rendered it thoroughly obsolete; nevertheless, as a first plan of uprising and indication of the way the staff of the resistance was thinking, it deserves attention. "Operative Report no. 54"[6] dealt with several variants of situations that could promote or prevent the outbreak of the Uprising in one form or another. The one uncertainty was the condition and position of the Soviet Union. Resistance would be hopeless in case of a Soviet attack on a Germany crushed by the blows of the Western Allies, or in case of a new German-Soviet agreement in which Moscow would take over the GG from Berlin. In the unlikely case that the Soviet Union would be attacked by the German Reich, hold out against this aggression, and repel the Wehrmacht back to Polish national territory, *"it would be lunacy to offer military opposition to an opponent who was strong enough to beat the German army"* [emphasis mine—W.B.]. Therefore, "our role would be limited to remaining underground with the whole machinery and postponing planning for the Uprising to that moment when the Soviet system and state start to collapse." Yet, the possibility was considered more likely that, in case of a German attack, the Soviets would suffer several severe defeats and the Wehrmacht would penetrate deep into Russia. Under these circumstances, the Uprising would be a genuine attack on the Germans, which essentially simplified the planning.

The other cornerstones were the geographical data. The resistance was to concentrate on the occupation of traffic junctions, especially the big railroad stations and bridges of the Vistula, in order to be able to control the withdrawal of the German troops; these were not to be attacked but forced to hand over their weapons. West and north of the GG (in Poznań and Pomerania), the Uprising had to be supported by a direct involvement of the Polish paratrooper units from the west; the landing of Polish troops on the Baltic coast, at best in the bay of Danzig, was generally seen as optimal for any large military campaign. The planners considered Allied air support—the other cornerstone of the Uprising plans—as an essential condition for the success of the entire endeavor. Even in the big cities of the GG like Warsaw and Kraków, where in all probability the underground could assemble the strongest forces, even in 1940–41, several parts of the city and targets like airports or barracks were considered impregnable without Allied support.

However, the most important prerequisite for military victory was the collapse of German combat morale. "Our active appearance against the Germans in the country can take place only when the German nation collapses under the effect of military defeats, hunger, and propaganda, which break the discipline of the troops who are demoralized and no longer hope for victory, and are ready to abandon their posts and withdraw to home and family." It was important that both phenomena take place at the same time: "Every attempt at an action against an adequate troop—aside from its numerical strength—even if revolutionary agitation spreads in Germany, would certainly be smothered in blood by ground and air action. Also vice versa, namely, if an obvious collapse of discipline in the army and occupation administration occurs, but the German nation is not caught up in revolution, starting to fight could turn out to be too risky. Only the coincidence of both indications of German collapse—internal turmoil at home and the decline of discipline in the army—gives us the possibility of an effective military action. This is the most important, even the only important prerequisite." Obviously, the planners of the underground were guided strongly by the memory of the autumn of 1918; in fact, the scenario amounted to a repeat of the configuration of that time, only this time, the quantitatively and qualitatively increased possibilities of the Allied air forces were to guarantee success to the Polish revolt. How realistically the professional soldiers of 1941 assessed the chances of the underground in battle against regular troops is also clear; the ZWZ was to direct its military actions against police, party, and administrative machinery, disarm the demoralized Wehrmacht or let it go west through corridors but not fight the regular troops. Direct attacks on the troops were not anticipated.

After "Operative Report no. 54" had been outdated by the outbreak of the German-Soviet war, the staff of the ZWZ continued to plan for the Uprising. In the spring of 1942, it received at least two clarifications from the supreme commander, in which Sikorski clearly rejected all ideas of the underground about the extent of assistance hoped for from the Allies (landing on the Baltic Sea, bombing and support flights, use of the Polish paratroopers and other troops) as unrealistic. The resistance now had to enlist its own resources as bases for planning much more than ever.

Ever since the second half of 1940, these possibilities had increased enormously. From the beginning, Rowecki had limited the direct struggle to attacks against collaborators and members of the police machinery, and promoted sabotage in transportation and the armaments industry. The acts of damage and arson "were to appear to be accidents, so that no reprisals are taken against the population; instead, these incidents are to incriminate the Germans themselves and evoke doubt in them [. . .] about their own people on the assumption that the sabotage came from their own ranks."[7] According to ZWZ data, there were thousands of these targeted acts of sabotage and assassinations: damaged and burned locomotives and train cars, defective machine tools, radios, gun barrels, motors and munitions, burned warehouses, poisoned people and animals. By the first months of 1941 the resistance could point to results that represented an important contribution to the Allied war effort and also produced no reprisals because the perpetrators were usually anonymous.[8]

The calculation of at least not provoking the scourge of the occupying power by strictly limiting sabotage did not work. The constant terror perpetrated on the Polish population mainly had other roots: the economic exploitation of the human and material resources of the GG increased from one year to the next, primarily in the form of mass deportations to Germany for forced labor and a constant increase of the agricultural quotas. Passive resistance against these and similar measures was broken with brute force: mass shootings and arrests and deportations to concentration camps were the ordinary methods. In this situation it was increasingly harder for Rowecki to maintain his reserve in the area of direct armed struggle, especially when the Communist party, reactivated in 1942, soon leveled an important argument against the ZWZ/AK "at-the-ready" position of the resistance loyal to the government. In 1941 acts of sabotage were carried out by a specialized unit of the ZWZ, the Retaliation Unit (Związek Odwetu, ZO). In 1942 the elite organization Wachlarz emerged and carried out several actions—typically—east of the old Polish-Soviet border to avoid reprisals against Polish citizens. Even against the background of the civilian resistance that had begun to spread widely, these measures could not make up the deficit resulting from the principle of restraint in direct battle in the GG: after years of conspiracy, the underground loyal to the government (for the sake of its legitimacy) had to prove that the Poles had not become completely defenseless to the terror of the occupation. In August 1942 Rowecki sent a worried cable to London that "the principle followed by the Germans of collective responsibility and mass terror as preventive measures has meant that the nation under occupation has suffered great losses despite passive behavior and even though it has avoided provoking these blows." A passive mindset was spreading, but more dynamic, active people were joining the Soviet partisans.

Ever since the autumn of 1942, the AK had increasingly turned to active counterterror. At the beginning of the new year, there was a lot of action around Zamość, where the Germans had introduced the biggest expulsion action in the GG; the resistance of the AK and the military associations of the Peasants' Party prevented much of the planned recolonization by Volksdeutsche of the farmlands of the expelled Poles. In January, the Leadership of Diversion (Kierownictwo Dywersji, Kedyw) emerged, combining the fighting units of the AK and entrusting them with new missions (expansion of sabotage and diversionary tactics, and reprisals). These ingenious acts prepared both the soldiers and the civilian population for the Uprising.[9] In March 1943, Rowecki issued a new order that—renouncing the previous tactic—provided for the formation of partisan units. From now on, the actions of the AK were to be characterized by the abbreviation "WP" (Wojsko Polskie, Polish Army), as a clear sign of the presence of the resistance.[10] In the spring and summer of 1943, the "security situation" in the GG changed rapidly because of this shift in AK behavior—terror and counterterror escalated to an unprecedented degree, and respect for the increasing presence of the "underground state" grew. Warsaw played a special role in 1943–44, when Kedyw carried out its most spectacular assassination attempts and attacks. Several notorious Gestapo officers were shot on the street. On February 1, 1944, the Warsaw SS and police chief was assassinated.[11]

Planning for the Uprising in 1942 and 1943 can be seen against the background of this development. In September 1942 Rowecki presented "Operative Report no. 154," which specified seven major goals of the Uprising:

1. Crushing the German occupation by destroying administration, party organs, and German population, and by removing German troops by means of a "voluntary or forced evacuation."
2. Securing weapons and other armaments through the voluntary or forced surrender of relevant stocks.
3. Resistance against "Ukrainian claims" (southeast of the old state territories).
4–6. Restoration of law and order, reconstruction of the regular army, support for the new civilian administration.
7. Occupation of areas within the old state territory which could not be occupied in the initial stages of the Uprising, as well as new areas "whose occupation is imperative for a strong future Poland."

The September 1942 plan contained essential elements of the 1940–41 plan, specified a few tasks and assumptions, yet clearly shifted the emphases. One major problem, the Soviet Union, seemed more calculable now. Either—in case of a German victory, which was still considered quite likely in September 1942—the Soviet Union would no longer play any role at the beginning of the Uprising, or it would defeat the Germans and enter Poland at their backs. "Given such a situation," commented Rowecki, "we have no chance to offer resistance. I assume that the quarrel between Russia and Poland shifts to the political level, where our most important trump would be the exile army, which is outside Russian access. In such a case, I think that the fighting forces in the country are kept underground and brought to light only if the supreme commander needs them in the crucial game against the Russian invasion."

The relationship between the geographical and demographic facts, Allied help, and the potential of the resistance itself could be calculated better after three years of war and occupation. Realistically, the staff of the AK counted only the areas of the GG settled by a Polish majority and a few neighboring regions (including parts of Upper Silesia and Łódź) as essential areas for the Uprising, which was outlined by the cities of Warsaw, Łódź, Kraków, Rzeszów, and Lublin. In most of the incorporated areas, eastern Galicia as well as the eastern provinces now subordinate to the German Reichs Commissariat, the Uprising could be brought in only from outside, since the local forces (or the support of the civilian population) were too minimal.

Compared with 1940–41, hope for direct Allied help—after Sikor-ski's corrections—clearly declined. Since the Polish air force and para-trooper brigade would most likely be used by the Allies themselves in case of an Allied landing on the continent, the AK could count only on its own units in the direct struggle. The ideas of the hostile force they confronted resulted from that. As in "Report no. 54," the underground assumed that the major opponents were the party, police, administra-tion, and German population, and only finally the Wehrmacht units sta-tioned in the GG. To be successful, the Uprising had to be implemented throughout the entire targeted area simultaneously and unexpectedly. After the area of the uprising was under the control of the AK, it was to assume an important role for the whole anti-Hitler coalition, since Ger-man troop transports could be moved westward out of the east only through eastern Prussia, possibly through southern Poland.

"Report no. 154" was an expression of the clearly heightened self-awareness of the staff of the AK. Direct Allied support was no longer seen as an imperative condition for action; the fundamental doubts of the military ability of the underground, which existed in 1940–41, had given way to the idea that the German occupation machinery could be crippled under certain conditions, so that occupying central Poland, at least, would be possible. For mysterious reasons, respect for the combat effectiveness of the Wehrmacht had disappeared; all these develop-ments were to play an important role in the planning of 1943.

"Report no. 154" did not reach the government-in-exile in London until March 1943, and by then the crucial turning point on the eastern front had been an obvious fact for weeks. Shortly thereafter Stalin broke off relations with the government-in-exile; both destroyed the founda-tions of the second plan for an uprising. Rowecki had certainly antici-pated this since, in the winter of 1942–43 in his reports to Sikorski, he had often examined Polish-Soviet relations again and again in connec-tion with plans for the Uprising. The commander of the AK clearly saw the threat by the victorious Soviet Union as a key problem of the final phase of the war in Poland.[12] That did not require any clairvoyant abili-ties: after Rowecki's arrest by the Gestapo on June 30, 1943, the "Russian problem" soon became critical for his successor, General Tadeusz "Bór" Komorowski. In the correspondence with London, this issue received increasing attention.

In the final dispatches between Rowecki and Sikorski, a consensus gradually emerged to give up the idea of a single, simultaneous revolt against the German occupation in the GG in favor of several local, stag-gered uprisings in the old eastern area. The commander of the AK and the prime minister agreed that, given Soviet claims to the eastern areas, a demonstration of Polish rights to these provinces was urgently necessary, and hence from the beginning, the focus was on the two big cities of Vilnius and Lwów, which, according to the Soviets, were parts of the Lithuanian or Ukrainian Socialist Republic. In February 1943 Rowecki proposed setting the first phase of the Uprising in the eastern areas in motion, focusing on Vilnius and Lwów; the second phase would concentrate on Białystok, Brest, and the areas around the Bug and San. Only afterward would central Poland be included: "It is imperative that we demonstrate to the invading Russians our will to protect our rights and our assets in the eastern areas. This can be achieved by starting open battles against the Germans at a given time and by the immediate restoration of Polish rule of these areas." This fundamental conviction was approved by Sikorski. Until "Black Week"—from June 30, 1943, when Rowecki was arrested until July 4 when Sikorski perished—there was no decision about what was to happen to the soldiers and functionaries of the resistance who would have to come out of their secret undergrounds during the battle if no compromise on the border issue were found by that time and the Russians insisted on exercising their sovereignty over the disputed areas.

In the autumn of 1943 Komorowski and Sosnkowski, who was appointed supreme commander after Sikorski's death, came back to this question. The new commander of the AK, born in 1895 like Rowecki, and a professional officer like his predecessor, had been active in the underground from the start and was promoted to general in May 1940. Until June 1943 Sosnkowski had worked as Rowecki's deputy but was not especially prominent. Unlike his predecessor, he was hardly considered an impressive personality. The "Man without Qualities" was to be much more receptive than Rowecki to outside influences. A firm political line, seen clearly in the dispatches in the first half of 1943, was no longer visible after Komorowski took command of the AK. His direct superior in London, on the other hand, had absolutely clear intentions but preferred to propose them in the form of long memoranda, which were fairly useless as the basis for orders. In the summer of 1941 Sosnkowski had resigned from the cabinet in protest against the Polish-Soviet agreement of July 30; and in 1943 he was considered by both the Russians and the British as a firm opponent of compromise in the border question. Moscow liked to use his name to point to the allegedly "fascistic-reactionary circle" in the Polish government-in-exile. While Rowecki had set the tone of the correspondence between Warsaw and London prior to June 1943, after that summer the focus shifted to the other side; Sosnkowski, certainly a clever political mind, could, however, hardly use his formal and actual predominance. First, his possibilities of action were limited, and his relations to new Prime Minister Mikołajczyk were extremely bad from the start. Second, making decisions was never one of his strong points. The new supreme commander liked to think in big contexts, broad alternatives, and options, but over and over again he shrank from issuing a simple order.

In the underground, the planning went on despite the crises of the summer. On October 14 the new commander of the AK reported on his intentions to the political leaders of the resistance. Komorowski replied only indirectly to the question of whether an uprising was possible at all given the strength of the enemy—he said that the risk was essentially greater today than in the past. Therefore, five basic prerequisites had to be fulfilled: the outbreak had to be coordinated with the course of the war on the front; it (meaning the outbreak) must be triggered at the right moment; it needed to be protected against the enemy air force and tank units and had to be executed in a modern fashion; and finally, the Uprising absolutely had to be "simultaneous, general, abrupt, and of short duration." On the basis of his knowledge of the situation on the front and political relations, Sosnowski would be expected to order a transition to alert status. Bór-Komorowski would then determine the concrete date of the attack "in the area of ethnographic Poland" (namely, in the GG inhabited by a majority of Poles), and from that moment on, there was no return. The attack would be aimed only at the most strategically important targets, and Warsaw was the first. Supported by Allied airstrike forces, the Uprising had to protect central Poland from the invasion of the Red Army; then there was the question of the relationship of the Soviets to the AK, as well as the question of the rapid restoration of internal order and security.[13]

It was not by chance that Sosnkowski began the dialogue with Bór-Komorowski—in two detailed dispatches on October 5 and 21, 1943,—with completely different ideas. His diagnosis mainly concerned the political risks: The government-in-exile must be careful not to fall victim to a new Munich, for the Western Allies tended to recognize the Russian territorial claims and to satisfy their eastern ally at the expense of Poland. That was why it was necessary to remain strong and insist on the principle of the inviolability of the borders—as long as no agreement was concluded with Russia, a purely military and unconditional cooperation with the Red Army was unacceptable. Therefore, the Uprising was to break out only when the Allies had expressed their full support for the line of the government-in-exile.

Among other reasons, because of the arguments of the supreme commander (Sosnkowski), after several weeks of negotiations the cabinet-in-exile adopted a government order for the Uprising dated October 27, 1943: Depending on the political and military situation in Europe, the resistance was either to provoke an uprising or to implement a "heightened campaign of sabotage and diversion." The Uprising was anticipated in two scenarios—if the Allies in the West achieved the crucial breakthrough and could come immediately to the aid of the Polish underground, or if the Wehrmacht collapsed in the East. In both cases, any outbreak was to demonstrate the Polish will to fight and contribute clearly to the victory of the anti-Hitler coalition. The real decision-making power—and thus responsibility for the choice of time—was reserved for the government-in-exile and the supreme commander. The "heightened campaign of sabotage and diversion" was to be implemented if neither of the situations mentioned occurred. This concept meant primarily a reinforcement of the previous clashes of the AK. On this point, the government order remained vague; clearly the central idea here was for the battles to have the least possible detrimental effect on the civilian population.

Instructions on behavior vis-à-vis the Red Army were similarly fuzzy. The resumption of diplomatic relations before the invasion of the Soviets was treated as the one possible variant. In this case, the AK in the territories occupied by the Soviets was to remain underground and not emerge before the return of the government-in-exile; only then could military cooperation also be accepted. If the Soviets insisted on adding the eastern territories, the government-in-exile would request the intervention of the United Nations. A similar protest was anticipated for the second case, that is, if the Red Army occupied the former eastern Poland without resumption of diplomatic relations. The AK would then implement the "heightened campaign of sabotage and diversion" and would go back underground and move to "self-defense" in case of Soviet reprisals. Finally, as a third variation, the cabinet-in-exile dealt with a German-Soviet agreement that would complicate the situation of the resistance even more; then the resistance would have had to wait for decisions from the government-in-exile.

The government order of October 27, 1943, represented an important break in planning for the Uprising by mainly bypassing reality, and it must have reinforced the impression in the underground leadership that, despite its insight into the grand strategy of the Allies, the London cabinet really had little to offer. In the case of the most likely scenario at that time—that the Red Army would enter the former eastern Poland before diplomatic relations were resumed—the government-in-exile proposed a practically impossible procedure and trusted to the effectiveness of its protest. How the AK in the Soviet-occupied provinces could return underground after a phase of heightened activity, and how it could disguise itself from the Soviets, was not clear at all.

This was really too much. On November 26 Komorowski cabled back that he had ordered the AK units (those that would be in Soviet-occupied territories right after the end of the fighting) to stop conspiratorial activities. The preceding armed campaigns of the underground would thus be attributed only to the actual inciters, namely, the resistance loyal to the government, and it was hardly conceivable that the extensive conspiratorial network of the AK could be kept secret from the Soviets. Only a small, completely reorganized and camouflaged part of the resistance was to remain underground under Soviet occupation. Bór-Komorowski did not mention the goal of this anti-Soviet conspiracy. Yet, the construction of a new resistance now working against Moscow corresponded with the logic of the previous development; as in the years from 1939 to 1941, the Soviet Union had once again become the enemy of Poland, and there was little hope that this conflict would be resolved in the foreseeable future. The anti-Soviet conspiracy was considered an instrument of the government-in-exile had it become a Cold War or even a third World War, when any solution of the border issue acceptable to the Poles would have been rejected by Moscow, and the problem could be reopened in the framework of a global debate between the United States, Great Britain, and the USSR. For the present, in the final phase of World War II, both the United States and Great Britain refused to send Allied observer missions to Poland.[14]

The order of November 20, which Komorowski referred to in his dispatch, concluded the previous discussion of the uprising by prescribing the Burza (Thunderstorm) plan as the guideline for the entire AK in the East and the GG. In case of a German retreat on the whole eastern front, Warsaw Center was to use a coded radio broadcast to arrange for the AK commanders in the various regions to begin the campaign. Initially, large cities were excluded, as Burza was to erupt primarily in the countryside. In case there was no general and simultaneous retreat of the Wehrmacht from Polish territories, the local commanders could decide the timing themselves: At the moment when the German retreat from a certain territory was immediately impending, the local AK was to shift to attacks on the withdrawing troops. Coordinating these attacks with Soviet staffs was not anticipated. Only when the battle was over was the Polish commander to confront the Red Army "as a host" and, along with representatives of the Polish civilian administration, agree on cooperation in practical matters.

The practical expression of the distinction between an uprising and "heightened campaign of diversion," extrapolated by the Burza order, remained unclear. Basically, Komorowski envisaged a series of local campaigns like uprisings, in which an enormous responsibility would be imposed on the individual commanders, especially in what used to be eastern Poland: the relatively weak AK units, which could not rely on an ethnic Polish population in the rural areas, had to mobilize quickly and conduct a surprise attack, despite an anticipated confusion of the situation on the front. A premature beginning of an uprising threatened to lead to a catastrophic defeat, because the German troops were generally far superior to the partisans in numbers and munitions as well as experience and discipline. If the right moment were missed, the whole thing would have been in vain—for four years the resistance had promised its mostly young members and the entire society to prepare the great strike for liberation. For it now to be steamrollered by events seemed like a nightmare.

The hopelessness faced by the leadership of the AK in early 1944 was seen by no one as clearly and unequivocally as its supreme commander. In several dispatches to Komorowski, Sosnkowski referred to the military and political problems of the Burza planning: The Allies had left the Poles in the lurch, and the Soviets had no intention of discussing the affiliation of eastern Poland. The Soviets would arrest the exposed members of the resistance and, at best, force them to integrate into Polish Communist troops; the whole undertaking was a "desperate invitation to an auto-da-fé of the country." However, the supreme commander had nothing definite to propose to solve the problem, so Poland and the AK were to insist on the former principles and wait for the great inter-Allied conflict after the defeat of Germany. As a practical transitional solution, Sosnkowski proposed removing AK troops from the eastern territories in Soviet hands by transferring them south—to western Galicia, possibly Hungary, perhaps through Slovakia. Naturally, in practical terms, the idea could not be carried out and was rejected by Komorowski.

Meanwhile, the problem of the Red Army invasion into eastern Poland assumed concrete form. The first testing ground was Volhynia.[15] Prior to 1939, Volhynia, with over nine percent of the entire area of the country, had been the second largest Polish province in terms of area but with only 6 percent of the national population. Twenty-three percent of the territory was covered with forests and altogether agrarian; a quarter of the population lived in mostly small towns and a few mid-sized cities. Volhynia was backward and poor; ethnically, it had a Ukrainian majority. The Poles were only about one-sixth of the Volhynian population, whereas the Ukrainians were over two-thirds. In 1939 the area was integrated into the Ukrainian SSR as Northern Ukraine; in the summer of 1941 Volhynia and Podolia were added to the Reichskommissariat Ukraine (Ukranian Reichs territory). More than in the GG, German occupation forces here resorted to the cooperative Ukrainians, who believed initially that they could establish the nucleus of their independent state (Samostijna Ukraina) under German rule; from 1942 on, more Poles were also accepted in the administration; there were both Ukrainian and Polish police units and auxiliary troops.

The Nazis tolerated and promoted the increasing anti-Polish radicalization of the Ukrainians but did not comply with their crucial requirement of establishing a sovereign state. This and the general brutality of the occupation regime strengthened the Ukrainian resistance, an expanded part of which was combined with the Ukrainian Rebel Army (Ukrajińska Powstańska Armija, UPA) after October 1942. In terms of priority, the first enemy of the UPA was the Soviet Union, for the time being the Soviet partisans; the second were the Poles who initially had been commanded to desert Volhynia; and the Germans were only in third place. In March 1943 some five thousand members of the Ukrainian police—sometimes whole departments—went over to the partisans, followed later by most of the remaining seven thousand. After this reinforcement, the UPA had some thirty thousand soldiers in their units, some of them well armed and well led. Occasional talks between moderate Polish and Ukrainian politicians in the underground were inconclusive, since the Poles insisted on the territorial political status quo ante, while the Ukrainians wanted the inclusion of Volhynia into the future Samostijna Ukraina.

The first attack by Ukrainian partisans on Polish villages took place in November 1942, a large wave of attacks followed in February 1943, and the first climax of the violent "de-Polonization" was achieved the following summer. The UPA attacked everywhere; it captured Polish villages and expelled or murdered the population without regard for age or gender. The extent of the violence of the "bloody nights" in Volhynia and, for the most part, the treatment of the civilian population, were reminiscent of the worst civil wars of southern and eastern Europe. Approximately thirty to fifty thousand Volhynian Poles perished in these bloodbaths; the number of victims in the neighboring district of Galicia may have reached about twenty thousand and was considerably lower (about five thousand) in the Lublin district, where "de-Polonization" began later. The number of Ukrainian victims of Polish counterterror, which also began later, was estimated at fifteen to twenty thousand altogether. Here, too, especially in 1944, entire villages were murdered. The German administration initially supported the Ukrainians and later Poles and Ukrainians in turn, and originally may have seen an effective instrument in this "divide and conquer" strategy; but in view of the raging civil war since the second half of 1943, the administration was virtually helpless. The Germans held their own only in the cities; Volhynia broke down as a supplier of agricultural quotas.[16]

Defense of the villages against the UPA attacks was borne by local units of the AK. In early 1943, as a result of the Soviet deportations of 1940–41, Nazi terror, and the flight to the neighboring GG, the Polish rural population of Volhynia had shrunk to less than half of the prewar level, that is, to 5 to 7 percent of the inhabitants. The minimal support in the population was certainly a major reason why the organization of the resistance guided from Warsaw made practically no progress in the first years. Under Soviet occupation, all officers sent to Volhynia were arrested by the NKVD. A new group was sent to Volhynia in November 1941 but they were arrested and shot by the Germans. After several attempts to rebuild the AK had been unsuccessful in 1943, Volhynia was eliminated from the AK section of Lwów and was placed directly under Warsaw Central in the second half of the year. At the same time, the remaining Polish rural population organized local self-defense units, which withstood their first tests in battle against German—and increasingly—Ukrainian attacks. They were reinforced by members of the Wachlarz elite fighting groups, who often assumed the rank of officers in the emerging Volhynian units of the AK. In February 1944 Lieutenant Colonel Wojciech Kiwerski from Warsaw took command in Volhynia. The Twenty-seventh Volhynian Infantry Division of the AK (this had been the name and number of the prewar infantry division stationed in Volhynia) was formed from local units and initially numbered some 6,000 soldiers, about 7,300 by the spring.

Kiwerski had come to Volhynia to lead the first Burza action. On January 4, 1944, the Soviets had crossed the old eastern border of Poland at Sarny in Volhynia. On February 2, 1944, units of the First Ukrainian Front occupied the eastern Volhynian town of Równe and Łuck in the central part of the region. The Twenty-seventh Division had withdrawn to the German occupied western part, south of Kowel; the starting conditions for a general test of the Burza scenario seemed optimal in February 1944 for several reasons. With its bad roads and railroad connections, extensive forests, and swamps, Volhynia was best suited geographically for partisan fighting. After the losses of the last months, the Fourth Tank Army of the German Army South did not seem able to withstand the attacking Soviets. Moreover, the Twenty-seventh Division and the Polish resistance in Volhynia had relatively good experiences with Soviet partisans; since the UPA also fought against them, large groups of Poles went over to the Soviets in 1942 and 1943 or formed Polish-Soviet partisan groups. Thus, relations between the Soviets and the AK lacked that tension that had often led to clashes in the area of Vilnius. Finally, after battle experience against Ukrainian partisans, the units of the Twenty-seventh Division had a considerable military value: the number of combatants was over 40 percent of the prewar strength (measured by other partisan "divisions" and "brigades," this was high), and the ratio of light weapons looked similar. In contrast, the division's supply of mortars, grenades, and artillery was only 9 to 20 percent of prewar strength.

In January and February, individual AK troops moved successively from fighting the UPA to fighting the Germans. They cooperated with Soviet partisans in several skirmishes. On March 18 the Twenty-seventh Division made contact with regular Soviet troops and carried out more extensive attacks with them; at this time, the Germans tried intensively but unsuccessfully to win over the Polish units for a common fight against "Soviet and Ukrainian gangs." On March 20 the AK joined a Soviet radio troop. On March 21 a first meeting with high officers of the Red Army took place, which was regarded as an agreement on the operative plans and also proceeded smoothly as did previous contacts with Soviet partisans—the AK received Soviet munitions. On March 26 a meeting took place between Kiwerski and Soviet General Sergeev, who was introduced to the Poles as the commander of the army attacking in the direction of Kowel. Sergeev proposed integrating the Twenty-seventh Division into the Polish Communist units under General Zygmunt Berling, but obviously he did not insist. However, he did demand the complete tactical subordination of the AK division to the Soviet high command.[17] According to Kiwerski's description, Sergeev was willing to acknowledge—as a countermove—that the Volhynian division was subordinate to London or Warsaw and could maintain unhindered radio communication with their superiors. Sergeev also demanded that all local AK units be incorporated in the Twenty-seventh Division because the Soviets did not want any partisan units in their rear; after filling up a normal army division, the Twenty-seventh was to be reorganized. Kiwerski promised to give an answer within four days after consulting with his superiors. On their own, Kiwerski and Sergeev agreed to coordinate operative tasks for the following days.

The conditions posed by the Soviets to the commander of the Twenty-seventh Division were completely outside the framework of recent Polish-Soviet relations. None of the points was unacceptable. Sergeyev's conditions were—as we know now—coordinated with Moscow, but gave the Polish troops a certain amount of leeway. It is possible that the Soviet general simply interpreted the directive falsely.[18]

We do not know how long it took the dispatch to get to the desk of the Warsaw commander of the AK. On April 5 Komorowski reported to London about the unexpectedly positive news from the east, and informed Sosnkowski that he approved the basic conditions of the cooperation for Kowel. Strangely, Komorowski's answer did not reach the staff of the Twenty-seventh Division until April 12. Not only was the four day deadline negotiated on March 27 long past, but the telegram appeared in a radically different form, which now had nothing in common with the optimistic assumptions of the second half of March—except for geography. In a more peaceful phase, the Wehrmacht had been

51

able to regroup: a new army group (North Ukraine) had been formed under Field Marshall Walter Model; they had mastered a situation that had just recently been hopeless; and they stabilized the front, with the help of reinforcements. The railroad junction of Kowel was held by the Wehrmacht. The Germans gradually went on the offensive, which included purging the area west of the city of Soviet and Polish partisans. On April 4 the Soviet ring around Kowel broke, and the Red Army pushed eastward. This straightening of the front followed a series of operations against the partisans, which were carried out with the support of tanks and airplanes. The Twenty-seventh AK division, along with a few Soviet units, found itself suddenly engaged in several battles with regular troops superior in every respect and fighting for its bare survival. On April 18 the division commander fell; on April 20–21 the badly decimated Polish troops succeeded in escaping the attack and breaking through northward to Polesia. Weeks later, a smaller part of the division got through with great losses for the Soviets. Most of the units crossed the Bug, joined the AK section of Lublin, and fought there against the Germans until July 26, 1944, when they were disarmed by the Soviets.

From the perspective of the Warsaw AK staff and the government-in-exile, the Burza campaign in Volhynia had taught several lessons. First, the total concept had worked neither militarily nor politically. Despite optimal starting conditions, there was no quick victory over the retreating German troops, not to mention time for the restoration of the Polish administrative machinery in the disputed eastern territories. The second important lesson was that the Soviets were surprisingly ready for military cooperation at the front, even though it turned out that, for technical reasons, this cooperation had not been successful. Third, after the battles for Kowel, the propaganda value of Burza in rural areas was clearly nil: Even the relatively strong Twenty-seventh Division was barely visible among the Soviet partisans and frontline troops in the week-long battles; and abroad, a few Volhynian villages were not exactly familiar territory. If the AK wanted to put on an effective demonstration of its strength, it had to find another stage. In June the central AK staff probably decided, against the original Burza plan, to shift the next phase of the struggle to the big cities of eastern Poland.

After the Volhynian experiment, there remained some doubt. Were Sergeev's conditions really a bellwether for the future behavior of the Soviets? How could the weaknesses in communication within individual AK units, between them and the Red Army, or between them and Warsaw, be overcome? And—could the resistance in general fill the military and political role assigned to it?

4

The Dress Rehearsal

Lwów, Lublin, Vilnius

T HE ONLY BIG CITIES in the old Polish eastern provinces were Lwów
and Vilnius. Lwów, until 1918 the capital of the Austrian "Kingdom of Galicia," transportation junction, and site of the local parliament and the university, had about 315,000 inhabitants before the war.
About half of them were Poles, one-third were Jews, and 16 percent were
Ukrainians. Vilnius, since 1919 a university city but a significant regional center, numbered about 200,000 inhabitants, two-thirds of them
Poles and 28 percent Jews; the rest were mainly Belarusians. The ratio of
nationalities in the surrounding countryside looked quite different: in
the province of Lwów, the official results of the census of 1931 showed
over one-third of the population were Ukrainians (in the neighboring
duchies, this rose to even 45 or 72 percent); in the province of Vilnius,
Belarusians amounted to 38 percent.

Between the wars, both cities were important centers of culture and
scholarship, and after September 1939 they experienced several waves
of migration. In Vilnius the population rose by a third with the influx of
Polish and Jewish refugees as well as Lithuanian immigrants, to at least
270,000 people by June 1940. After the annexation of Lithuania, Soviet
deportations began here too, while the first wave of them had already hit
Lwów in February 1940. These deportations, along with arrests, con-
scriptions into the Red Army, and other sanctions of the Soviet authorities, may have reduced the population of Lwów and Vilnius by tens of
thousands. Most of the victims were Poles, but Jews, Ukrainians, Lithuanians, and Belarusians were also affected. At the same time, according
to the terms of the German-Soviet agreement, Volksdeutsche were re-
settled "home in the Reich." In June 1941 the Soviets were driven out by
the Wehrmacht; the Holocaust began immediately afterward and within
the next years, the Jews in eastern Galicia and the Vilnius district were

nearly all annihilated. As a result the population structure of Lwów and Vilnius radically changed in the spring of 1944. Despite all losses under Soviet and Nazi rule, the relative proportion of the Poles may have risen, and the same applied at least to a similar extent for the Belarusians and Lithuanians in the Vilnius district and for the Ukrainians in eastern Galicia. Since the summer of 1941, all three groups had raised their own armed troops under German occupation—the Lithuanians raised one legal police force collaborating with the Germans, and the Ukrainians gathered a police force and partisan groups. The Poles supplied some police units in eastern Galicia, but were mainly protected and represented by the resistance loyal to the government. The development of this resistance occurred in distinct stages.

In Vilnius, in 1939–40, when the enemy was "simply" the political police of the authoritarian Lithuanian regime, which found little support in the established population, several underground organizations emerged, whose members numbered in the thousands.[1] After the Soviet annexation of the city in the summer of 1940, the NKVD crushed most of these organizations. The reconstruction began in the second half of 1941. By 1942 the first partisan units emerged in the neighboring district of Nowogródek, and after 1943, in the Vilnius district itself. They did fight the Germans but their main enemy was the Lithuanian police recently established by the occupation power; moreover, since the summer of 1943, violent battles were fought in several circles of Polish and Soviet partisans.[2] Belarusians kept deserting the Lithuanian police for the AK.[3] In this all-out struggle, the AK, concentrated in early 1944 in three big "brigades" and a few smaller units, achieved significant successes in the spring. In several battles in April and May, the "Lithuanian special units" (Vietine Rikitne), just established by the Germans under General Povilas Plechavicius, were beaten and disarmed, which led to their rapid dissolution; the captured weapons considerably increased the fighting capacity of the Vilnius AK. At the same time, negotiations between the occupying forces and the Polish resistance continued; in at least two cases, the Germans managed to persuade AK units that were constantly fighting against Soviet partisans to accept a cease-fire agreement, which held until June.[4] A vigorous intervention of the Warsaw high command of the AK ended any further rapprochement with the occupation forces, who clearly preferred to have the AK rather than the Lithuanian police on their side.

On June 1 the district of Nowogródek was subordinated to the AK commander of Vilnius, Colonel Aleksander ("Wilk") Krzyżanowski, which meant that he commanded the AK in a territory of 52,000 square kilometers with almost 2.3 million inhabitants. Even before that, German control of the area had shrunk to the cities and the most important transportation junctions; now the countryside was ruled partly by Soviet and partly by Polish partisans. Clashes between the groups that had been hostile since 1943 were incessant. Not until early June 1944 did "Wilk" manage to negotiate a truce with the Soviets as well as a partial cooperation for the impending battle against the Germans.

Krzyżanowski had learned only very late, on June 12, that the united forces of the AK districts of Vilnius and Nowogródek had been assigned to take the city of Vilnius according to the Burza guidelines—modified after the experience of Volhynia—before the invasion of the Red Army. On paper, "Wilk" had ten thousand to fifteen thousand soldiers in more than thirty partisan units, most of whom were relatively well armed, and some had considerable battle experience. The landscape of Vilnius offered another advantage: Thickly forested, with only a few bad roads, it protected the concentration of even large partisan units in the area around the city. The weakness of the Germans was equally advantageous—in late June and early July they seemed to be fully preoccupied with stabilizing the front after the defeats of recent weeks. Therefore, the plan of attack on Vilnius (code name Ostra Brama),[5] signed by Krzyżanowski on June 26, started from the same premise as the whole Burza planning: The AK would attack just as the occupying forces evacuated the last positions in the territory in question. On July 3 the AK units of the districts of Vilnius and Nowogródek were ordered to be on alert outside the city shortly before midnight on July 7.

Operation Ostra Brama, however, turned out to be a failure. First, a few units of the AK were to carry out smaller actions in eight rural circles in the northeast, at the same time as the attack on the city; they were thus lost for Vilnius. Second, the Red Army moved to the city faster than "Wilk's" staff had assumed; on July 4 they crossed the old Polish border not far from the city, and thus the attack had to be pushed forward twenty-four hours. Third, the hasty assembly of the partisan units, sometimes operating dozens of kilometers from Vilnius, turned out to be a nearly hopeless undertaking. In only a few cases did radio contact exist—news and orders were normally brought by couriers or riders. In addition, the road to Vilnius for the units that now numbered hundreds of soldiers was anything but simple. The marching routes often collided with those of the German troops streaming back, the partisans engaged in battles, and there were delays of hours or days, so that on the evening of July 6, no more than four- to five thousand completely exhausted soldiers were finally ready for the attack on Vilnius. However, the most important reason for the failure was probably the changes in the city itself. By July 4 Lithuanian collaborators, German officials, and civilians of both nationalities had fled the city; in the second week of July, Vilnius was inhabited by about seventy- to eighty thousand people, mainly Poles.

Nevertheless, the regionally important transportation hub—despite the calculation of the AK—was constantly reinforced by the Germans as a "stronghold" (back in May, an AK report spoke of "Fortress Vilnius").[6] By July 6 several small units of the Wehrmacht and the police were assembled in the city from the surrounding area; the half-finished fortifications could be half-occupied. Above all, the Germans had been expecting the AK attack for days; a surprise attack was out of the question.

The AK attack on Vilnius began on July 7 after midnight and was stalled almost immediately by the barrage from the defenders. After a few hours the partisans withdrew to their morning starting positions. On the same day, the first Soviet tank units of the Third Belarusian Front appeared outside the city. On July 7 the German garrison was still reinforced by more than seventeen thousand soldiers. Led by General Rainer Stahel, they defended Vilnius until July 13. Only a small minority led by the commander of the "stronghold" managed to break out of the closed city and get through to their own lines.

Meanwhile, the AK, with a force of some six thousand soldiers, fought on the Soviet side from July 7 until the surrender of the remnants of the German garrison on July 13. From July 9, two liaison officers of the Third Belarusian Front worked under "Wilk's" orders. There was occasional tension when some Soviet commander demanded the Polish partisans join the Polish-Communist troops at once; but on the whole, cooperation clearly prevailed. On July 14 one of Krzyżanowski's subordinates reported to London: "Vilnius captured with great participation of the AK, which is in the city. Great losses and destruction. Relations to the Soviet Army correct at the moment. Talks are conducted. Vilnius has experienced freedom for a very brief but joyous moment. 14 VII—the Polish character of the city is evident (bije w oczy)."[7]

The "moment of freedom" was indeed "very brief." The Polish commander—like most of his subordinates—feared that the correct relations would soon come to an end and made a futile demand for sending a mission of Western Allies to Vilnius.[8] On July 14 Krzyżanowski negotiated with the staff of the Third Front over the fate of the Vilnius AK; relations remained calm, the Soviets did not threaten, intimidate, blackmail—they simply treated the AK like allies. At least no irreconcilable oppositions in these talks surfaced in the Polish report: the establishment of an AK division, organizationally independent, operatively subordinate to the Red Army, was to have been arranged in common. But on the same day, Moscow headquarters of the Red Army issued Directive no. 220145 on the unconditional disarming of the AK in Lithuania, western Belarus, and western Ukraine. Ivan Sierov, deputy to the head of the secret police, Lavrentii Beriia, was sent to Vilnius to "guarantee the necessary Czechist acts according to Directive 220145."[9] As a result, at the next meeting on the seventeenth, the commander of the Third Front rescinded the agreement of July 14. "Wilk" and most of his officers were disarmed and interned. AK troops outside the city, who resisted disarmament, were crushed by NKVD units, with dozens of fatalities—the experiment came to and end even before it had begun.[10] Warsaw immediately received news of the Vilnius disaster.

The hasty progress of the offensive of the First Belarusian Front in the days after the battle for Vilnius surprisingly led to another big city becoming the touchstone for relations between Moscow and the Polish underground. On the Red Army's road to Warsaw, about two-thirds of the way from Lwów, was Lublin. The city differed from Vilnius and Lwów because—despite the Catholic university founded in 1918—it was not considered one of the traditional and significant centers of the country. Additionally, Lublin was west of the Bug River, thus on the other side of the Curzon Line claimed by the Soviets and in a territory with a majority of Poles. In 1939 the city numbered 130,000 inhabitants, a third of them Jews who were murdered in the following years; so that in the summer of 1944, aside from a few Volksdeutsche and Ukrainians, Lublin was inhabited almost exclusively by Poles. From the beginning, the underground was relatively strong. Aside from the AK, there was a widespread network of military organizations of the Peasants' Party and, since 1943, the Communists and the National Armed Forces; large units of Soviet partisans also operated in the thickly forested areas around Lublin. All of them fought against the German occupation power, and at the same time, extremely different relations formed between Polish-Communist and Soviet partisans on the one hand, and the other organizations on the other, from tactical cooperation to barely suppressed hostility. Since 1943, the German occupation authorities had considered the district of Lublin the most dangerous part of the GG. The expulsion and resettlement campaign in Zamość, in which 100,000 Poles were driven out to make room for 10,000 Volksdeutsche settlers, had provoked massive resistance; since then, the police had increasing trouble controlling the "security situation." In the first half of 1944, the underground activity intensified: of some 2,150 armed actions carried out from the beginning of the conspiracy until June 1944, more than two-thirds took place in the winter and spring of the last year of the occupation. On June 18 the Germans launched a counterattack: 1,200 partisans of the AK and the military organization of the Peasants' Party, 1,900 Soviets, and 700 Communist partisans were surrounded in the forest of Biłgoraj in Operation "Whirlwind II." The AK units were crushed; the Soviets and the Communist AL were able to escape from the encirclement with some losses.

On July 14, the Burza order was issued to the Lublin AK. In the next two weeks, the Third, Ninth, and Twenty-seventh AK Divisions, which were active in the district, took part in the liberation of several cities; they occupied a few smaller ones in the phase between the withdrawal of the German troops and the invasion of the Red Army. The Soviets reached and crossed the Bug on July 20. On July 22 they liberated Chelm—the first big city west of the river. The Manifesto of the Polish Committee of National Liberation (see chapter 5), proclaiming the takeover of national force in the liberated territory by the Communists, was issued on that date and in that place. On July 23 the Soviet Second Tank Army occupied Lublin, where it hardly encountered any resistance, and within the next few days the entire district of Lublin was liberated. On July 25, on an open radio broadcast, the Twenty-seventh Division reported from the area north of Lublin to the Warsaw headquarters of the AK that they had been disarmed by the Soviets. A few days later, the Third Division reported cooperation with the Soviets, and the Lublin commander of the AK even wanted to start discussions with General Berling. But, on July 30, the Third Division was also disarmed by the Soviets; given the hopeless situation, the Lublin AK commander had issued an order at dawn to dissolve the division and hand the weapons over to the Soviets.[11] Thus, the experiment west of the Curzon Line had produced a result similar to that in Vilnius. The news from the area of Lublin arrived in Warsaw central command at the same time as the reports from Lwów.

Like Burza in Lublin, the battle for Lwów began some two weeks after the Vilnius operation. In the capital of eastern Galicia, things had been extremely rough for the Polish underground in the initial phase— until June 1941. The Soviet secret police was even more successful there than in Vilnius.[12] In 1939, of the first three eastern Galician commanders of the Polish underground, two were arrested and one was shot. At the end of that year, two separate organizations of the ZWZ existed in Lwów, both of which were probably infiltrated from mid-1940; arrests continued. Only after the withdrawal of the Soviets did the Warsaw officers succeed in "purging" the Lwów district of the ZWZ: Three leaders were shot as NKVD agents, and the two previously rival factions were combined under a unified command in May 1942. Despite arrests and sometimes considerable losses, the underground in Lwów loyal to the Government developed relatively fast; in the city alone, in March 1944, there were over 17,000 members of the AK, but only a fraction of them—about one-fifth—had weapons. Outside the city, since 1943, the AK units had fought first against the Germans, and after February 1944, increasingly against the Ukrainian UPA. After the success of their de-Polonization campaign in Volhynia, that group had focused its activity in early 1944 on eastern Galicia. The battles here between AK and UPA were like those in Volhynia—the Ukrainians attacked, drove out, and murdered the Polish civilian population; the AK defended and fought back, often uniting with Soviet partisans. Since April, the Allies occasionally dropped weapons for the eastern Galician AK; the few deliveries had considerably improved the former catastrophic equipment.

On April 14 the Red Army reached Tarnopol in eastern Galicia, some 80 kilometers southeast of the local capital. Ten days later the AK in Lwów received a new order about implementing the Burza campaign. The attack on the retreating German troops was to be carried out by all units of the district; special emphasis was placed on the mission to take over the administration right after fighting the rearguard of the Wehrmacht and "placing our own big forces on display [. . .] especially around Lwów and Drohobycz." In the order of July 5, the district command of the AK in Lwów specified that cooperation with the Soviets was to be limited to matters "resulting from the common fight against the Germans and the need for appropriate help." On July 14 the Red Army began its offensive on Lwów. The next day, the "determinations of implementation" of the Burza plan for the eastern Galician AK stated that battles in the city were to be entered only if the German or Ukrainian SS began exterminating the inhabitants of the city. In the first phase, the AK attack was to be pursued in a circle of ten kilometers outside Lwów; in the second phase the southern and western periphery of the city was the target. Yet, the development went far beyond these plans. By July 18 the first Soviet tanks stood six kilometers north of Lwów. Some of the German administration left the city; the AK was involved in several small battles in the countryside and amassed 11,000 badly armed soldiers for the crucial attack. On July 22 units of the Fourth Soviet Tank Army managed to penetrate the city with some surprise. Individual troops of the AK accompanied the attack, and these units now joined the advancing Soviets in battles inside the city. Soldiers of the AK hoisted the Polish, American, British, and Soviet flags on city hall as a sign of liberation. In fact, German resistance was minimal, and the Soviets fought through individual parts of the city without any trouble. Since the way to the next target of the offensive—Przemyśl—was already free, ousting the German troops from the northern district lasted until July 27–28, when the Wehrmacht's last rear guard left the city. The AK took part in all the fights, the Soviets praised the cooperation, and until July 31, two liaison officers each worked on the staff of their new partner-in-war. From July 22 or 27 the commander of the AK district, Colonel Władysław Filipkowski, and the Government delegate for Lwów, Dr. Adam Ostrowski, were no longer underground and made their activities known to the Red Army. The Soviets did indeed change their attitude about the underground state even during the fighting. A General "Ivanov"—at least later on Sierov, as already mentioned the highest-ranking and also most effective representative of the NKDW in Poland, used this code name—demanded that the AK lay down their arms or join the Polish Communist troops. The units in the city did in fact lay down their arms on July 28. Filipowski got an invitation from General Michał Żymierski, the commander of the Polish troops under the command of the Soviets, for discussions in Żytomierz.

Warsaw headquarters was badly informed about events in Lwów when it issued the order for the Uprising to begin in the city two days later. In eastern Galicia, Burza had proceeded successfully on the whole in military terms—the AK had demonstrated its presence without big losses. This military and psychological success resulted from the fact that the Germans—unlike Vilnius—had practically given up Lwów right at the start and simply wanted to gain time. In political terms, here, as in Vilnius, Burza was a partial success. In both cities, the Poles did not manage to greet the Soviets as "hosts"—the AK was too weak to capture a big city by itself and had to wait for the Red Army. Nevertheless, there was a brief phase of a normal cooperation with the eastern partner, the Polish presence, and the red and white flags flew on public buildings. That the outcome of this situation would be similar to that of Vilnius was anticipated on July 29.[13] But in the end result Vilnius, Lublin, and Lwów seemed to have given arguments to both sides, to both the critics of the Burza plan and its advocates. Because of this experience, the former could assert that partisans and urban guerillas had no chance without support by a regular army and, except for uncovering the underground fighters, the whole campaign had produced no real results. Clearly, transferring Burza to the big cities had brought no "effective publicity": the English and American media had taken as little note of Vilnius, Lublin, and Lwów as of Volhynia, and the same was true of the governments. The advocates of the campaign, on the other hand, could point to the partial military and political success, and to the collectively minimal losses.[14] Thus, ultimately it turned out that the dress rehearsals in Vilnius, Lublin, and Lwów were as unsuitable as an element of the decision-making process in Warsaw as was the campaign in Volhynia three months earlier.

5

On the Way to the Decision

July 20–31, 1944

I N MARCH 1944 Warsaw was taken out of the planning of the Burza campaign. The city was too big to be captured independently, the German garrison too strong to avoid long battles, and the hundreds of thousands of civilians would of course be affected. In the spring the AK high command assumed that, when the Germans retreated from the capital, the Warsaw units would be concentrated in the surrounding forests as partisan units to attack the German rear guard.[1] The city itself was to be spared in case it was declared an "open city" by the occupiers and thus protected from further war damage. In July hundreds of machine guns were transported to the rebels in the east from the central underground depot in Warsaw, which made the precarious armaments situation of the capital AK much worse.

On July 14 Bór-Komorowski reported to London that the violent Soviet conquest in Belarus and the crushing of the German army group "Mitte" threatened the whole northern section of the German front. The way to Warsaw was now open. At the same time, he noted that even under these ostensibly favorable starting conditions, an uprising would not be very promising: "In the current situation of the German forces in Poland and the preparations against the Uprising, which consist of fortifying every building and offices of the departments in them with bunkers and barbed wire, the Uprising has no chance of success. We can only rely on the case that the Germans collapse and the army falls apart. In the current situation, carrying out the Uprising would entail big losses, even with sufficient weapons and the participation of [Allied] air forces and paratroopers."[2]

In the following days, nothing happened to cast doubt on Komorowski's appraisal. German troops—beaten, clearly demoralized, and exhausted—marched west through Warsaw. They were joined by civilians, mostly the so-called Volksdeutsche from the territories east of the Vistula, with sheep and cows, on horse-drawn wagons, and on foot; many asked for water, some had lost their shoes on the way—like the troops, they had little in common with the previous image of the victorious Germans. Soviet troops stood outside Lwów in the southeast; the First Belarusian Front under Marshall Konstanty Rokossovskii began its offensive from Kowel to Lublin on July 18. The decisive event, however, apparently did not take place on the front but in the East Prussian "Wolf's Lair": on July 20, the bomb planted by Colonel Claus Schenk Graf von Stauffenberg that was to have killed Adolf Hitler was detonated there. As we know, the assassination attempt failed, but its psychological effect should not be underestimated. Ever since 1939, the leadership AK had thought of repeating the scenario of autumn 1918. The German troops, increasingly pressed by the Allies in the west, would gradually lose both faith in their victory and thus their fighting strength. For years the AK had promoted this process with the help of the so called "N" propaganda ("N" as in Niemcy, the Polish word for Germans). Hundreds of thousands of German fliers, newspapers, appeals, and the like, allegedly signed by German opposition and resistance fighters, were distributed among the German civilian population and mainly among members of the Wehrmacht. In these documents, Communists and Social Democrats called for "decent" soldiers and officers to fight against "reaction" and for resistance against party bosses, SS, and police.[3] The impression left by the remnants of the German army group "Mitte" marching through Warsaw was now multiplied as it were by news of the assassination attempt; all of a sudden, the enemy really seemed to be beaten.

On July 21, 1944, three high-ranking officers of the high command of the AK met in a secret apartment on Warsaw's Niepodległości Avenue: Bór's deputy and chief of staff of the AK, General Tadeusz Pełczyński (code name "Grzegorz"), his deputy for operations, General Leopold Okulicki ("Kobra"), and the director of Department One of the high command, Colonel Józef Szostak ("Filip"). Only Szostak was an average and unknown professional officer. Pełczyński (born 1892) had fought in Piłsudski's legions from 1914 to 1917, had remained in the army after the war, and had risen rapidly from 1926 after the coup. From 1927 to 1932 and from 1935 to 1938, he was head of Department Two of the general staff, thus responsible for military espionage and counterespionage, a position generally considered key within the informal decision-making structure of the military dictatorship. He was in the SZP-ZWZ-AK from the beginning, since late 1941, as chief of staff of the high command, and since September 1943, as Bór-Komorowski's deputy.[4]

Okulicki (born 1898) had also joined the legions as a volunteer in 1914. His career in the Polish army was less spectacular, but in 1935 he rose to the general staff, where, in April 1939, he assumed the office of deputy chief of Section Three. It was he who, on the night of August 31–September 1, 1939, as officer on duty in the general staff, received the first reports of the outbreak of war. He participated in the defense of Warsaw as a frontline officer and went underground right after the surrender. In the autumn of 1940 Okulicki was entrusted with the hopeless task of reconstructing the resistance in the Soviet occupation zone. The NKVD arrested him a few weeks after his arrival in January 1941, but he was released in August of that year after the Polish-Soviet agreement provided for the construction of a Polish army. Okulicki was General Władysław Anders's chief of staff and as such took part, among other things, in two discussions with Stalin. In the Polish general staff in London since the summer of 1943, he volunteered for work in the underground. On the night of May 21, 1944, he parachuted into Poland and two weeks later became Pełczyński's deputy and "chief of operations" of the AK. On July 27 he was also appointed leader of the organization "Nie" by Bór—a parallel conspiratorial structure within the AK, which was to be active in case the underground was dissolved by the Soviets under the new occupation.[5]

Unlike their commander and most of the staff officers of the AK, Pełczyński and Okulicki had true political mentalities. Their biographies are representative of that group of young officers of the prewar period who identified with the Sanacja dictatorship and the idea of the "armed act" according to the model of 1914–18. Okulicki, a dynamic and charismatic person, was also shaped by experiences with the Soviets in 1941–42; he saw the fight against the Germans unambiguously as a political signal, whose meaning would ultimately be defined and determined by relations with the Soviets: only a fighting Polish underground that had given the Germans serious difficulties could impel the Allies to represent the Polish question offensively with the Soviets. Now, on July 21, 1944, in Szostak's presence, Pełczyński and Okulicki decided—contrary to the March decision—to include Warsaw in planning for the Uprising. The guiding thought was to undermine the German defensive action against the Soviets by a military campaign in the city, thus keeping the fighting and destruction to a minimum, in order to be able to greet the Soviets as "hosts." Szostak later reported that he had presented several operative misgivings about this sudden change of course—the Warsaw AK was too weak, and first there had to be guaranteed a substantial air support by the Allies—but Pełczyński and Okulicki apparently ignored these objections.

On the same day, Okulicki and Pełczyński went to Bór-Komorowski.

The commander, a colorless cavalry officer without much charisma or political experience,[6] must also have been impressed by the attack on Hitler. He seems to have immediately accepted his subordinates' proposal to chuck out all previous planning games and concrete plans. On July 21 he cabled London: "I estimate that the Germans have suffered a defeat on the eastern front. Three armies of the middle front section have been crushed, the OKW [Oberkommando der Wehrmacht] cannot replace them with fresh forces in sufficient number to stop the Soviet army. The delay of the Soviet advance on this section is probably not to be attributed to a strengthened German resistance, but rather to a temporary weariness of the Soviet forces [. . .] As far as I can foresee, the Soviet movements westward on this section will be fast and, without a great and effective German counteraction, they will soon cross the Vistula going west [. . .] Altogether, it seems certain that the Germans can no longer take back the initiative on the eastern front from the Soviets and can no longer defend themselves. Recently, we have often observed manifestations of the internal collapse of the German army, which is very tired and shows no desire to fight.

"The latest fact about the attack on Hitler, along with the war situation of Germany, can at any moment lead to the breakdown [of Germany]. This forces a constant [. . .] readiness for the uprising.

"Therefore, I have given the order to be prepared for the uprising as of midnight July 25, without interrupting the previously implemented 'Burza' campaign."[7]

The preliminary decision given by Komorowski's order of July 21 was definitely not irrevocable. The commander could cancel the order of readiness for uprising at any time. The first Soviet troops were still more than a hundred kilometers southeast of Warsaw; it was not yet clear whether the OKW had in fact no response to the collapse of the German army group "Mitte." On July 22 the Soviets captured the first big city west of the Bug (Chełm near Lublin). The "Manifesto of the Polish Committee of National Liberation" (Polski Komitet Wyzwolenia Narodowego, PKWN) was dated on this day and in this place, as already mentioned, but in reality it had been formulated in Moscow by a group of Polish Communists under Molotov's supervision on July 20. To a large extent, the manifesto avoided social revolutionary tones and instead emphasized the national solidarity of the Poles in the struggle against the Germans; on the other hand, it did promise comprehensive social reforms and the continuation of the partnership with the powers of the anti-Hitler coalition. Yet, the crux of the statement was unmistakable: the government-in-exile in London and their agents in the country were accused of being "usurping powers, illegal powers," since the Communist "national assembly" was the only "legitimate source of power in

Poland," the committee "appointed" by it the only "legitimate executive force."[8] Radio Moscow broadcast the news of the formation of the committee on July 22 at 8:15 P.M.; strangely enough, the AK leadership did not become aware of this information until the next day.

Nevertheless, on July 22, more preliminary decisions were made. In a long dispatch to London, Komorowski explained the political background of his order of the previous day: the Soviets wanted "to liquidate independent Poland or [. . .] at least subordinate Poland politically." The British and the Americans would then help only if "all means [available to Poland] were brought to bear." Therefore, the fight against the Germans should be carried on unconditionally (among other things to deprive the Soviets of arguments in international circles) and should proclaim wide-ranging social reforms (land reform, socialization of industry, reevaluation of labor committees). Moreover, this was not the first time the commander of the AK, who was considered a moderate conservative, had gone beyond the Communists' demands at the same time in his socio-political program;[9] the "turn to the left," which Polish society had taken under the occupation and which was expressed here, was not to be confused with sympathy for the Soviets. To this day, there are no indications that the Soviet Union of 1944 had become attractive as a model for relevant groups of Polish society—except for a minority even among Polish Communists, who wanted to turn Poland into a Seventeenth Republic. The far-reaching popularity of "leftist" solutions and the natural gratitude for liberation from Nazi occupation did not result in an increased popularity of the eastern neighbor, which had September 17, 1939, and Katyn on its conscience.

On July 22 Komorowski also informed the AK staff of the decision to make Warsaw the site of the Uprising. Decades later, one of the participants in the meeting reported that there was no doubt in the group. Instead, those present assumed that "it was to be a police action, protecting the population and the city from marauders, lagging troops, and the rear guard, as well as from special units that were to carry out annihilation."[10] There was no resistance among the staff to such an action, or more precisely, to such a plan. On the same day, Komorowski discussed the new development with Jan Stanisław Jankowski, the highest representative of the government-in-exile in the underground. Jankowski promised to convene an immediate meeting of the most important parties of the resistance, that is, the Council of National Unity (Rada Jedności Narodowej, RJN); Komorowski and Jankowski immediately agreed on two questions for the representatives of the parties. The first was "whether the occupation of Warsaw by the AK was to precede the invasion of the Red Army." The second was somewhat more complicated: "How much time should there be between this AK occupation and the invasion?" The RJN answered the first question, as expected, with an unequivocal yes; in reply to the second, the answer was "at least twelve hours." Thus the position of the civilian representatives of the underground was established. A few days later—the date is not known precisely—the government delegate, in the presence of other high-ranking officers, ostentatiously gave the commander of the AK the order to begin the fight "under appropriate conditions and at an appropriate time," so that the civilian administration had their twelve hours for organization between the fighting and the invasion of the Soviets.

In the last week of July, there were clearly several meetings of the highest-ranking AK officers; regular staff meetings took place every day at 10 A.M. (in the last days of July, in the afternoon as well), and there were also unofficial discussions of different groups, in which the advocates of the Uprising tried to persuade their hesitant colleagues. Three decades later, Jean-François Steiner compiled a collage of various testimonies about these days, which shows plausibly how many human emotions clashed with one another—"old" against "young," former officers of the Czarist army against "Legionnaires," and always Okulicki against several others.[11] On July 25 Komorowski decided, contrary to the original plans, that headquarters would be constructed not in southern Mokotów but in the working-class quarter west of the center;[12] he made no more decisions.

On the same day, the head of Section Two, Iranek-Osmecki, warned that the situation on the eastern front was not clear and that a battle east of Warsaw could possibly be expected. Once again the decision was deferred. Colonel Kazimierz Iranek-Osmecki (born 1897), like Pełczyński and Okulicki, was a "Legionnaire" from World War I and a professional officer in the Second Republic. Since 1939 he had lived the life of a movie hero: he traveled twice between London and occupied Warsaw as a courier, parachuted back to the underground in 1943, and since early 1944 had been head of AK espionage.[13] More important than his Sanacja political origin was that he clearly gave professional knowledge priority over political calculation. The AK reconnaissance network was known among the Allies as a masterpiece of the Polish resistance; railroad workers in particular constantly supplied precise information about German troop movements. From this perspective, it clearly did not look as if the Third Reich was at death's door. In the next two days, the stream of German troop remnants retreating or fleeing through Warsaw dried up—a fact registered by the AK staff in the hectic last days of July, but it clearly did not entail any fundamental change of plan.

On July 26 Komorowski delivered an ultimatum to London to send the Polish paratrooper brigade that was ready for battle in England and waiting to be deployed. If he had known what losses the British and

Polish paratroopers were to suffer a few weeks later in a battle that took place in the rear of the western front, his optimism about the deployment of airborne troops in Warsaw—which could hardly be carried out in 1944 in any event—would certainly have been dampened. In the same dispatch, Komorowski reported that the AK was ready to fight for Warsaw at any moment: "I will immediately report the beginning of the battle," read the last sentence of the brief communiqué.[14]

On July 26 the high command of the AK met in the presence of the government delegate. A basic consensus emerged that a campaign was to be carried out in Warsaw—but apparently a lively discussion ensued as to "when" and "how."[15] Iranek-Osmecki repeated his warning of the previous day that the situation east of Warsaw was still unclear. On July 23 Rokossovskii's First Belarusian Front had captured Lublin—140 kilometers southeast of Warsaw—and moved farther west and northwest. At the same time, the arrival of the first big German tank units around Warsaw was reported. The head of the Warsaw AK district, Colonel Antoni Chruściel ("Monter"), emphasized on the other hand that the German defense east of the Vistula was weak. He also reported on the equipment of the units in the city under his command. After the Gestapo had tracked down several caches, and the Warsaw AK had sent significant shipments to the east in recent months, the AK still possessed only minimal arms. They probably had no more than 39 heavy MGs, 130 light MGs, over 600 MPs, 2,400 rifles, 2,800 pistols, 4 mortars, 21 British Piats (antitank guns), and 36,000 grenades.[16] The ammunition supply looked catastrophic—100 cartridges per MG, 30 per pistol. Monter's commentary on the arms situation was that the Warsaw AK could hold out three to four days in offensive fighting and up to fourteen days in a defensive position.[17] He hoped for the capture of German stocks of weapons and for Allied drops.

It is hard to comprehend today how the Warsaw district commander wanted to conduct an extensive attack against the Germans with the weapons available to his units. Nevertheless, on July 26, the plan he presented was miles away from a "police action": the attack in the city itself was to concentrate on the strategically important (thus necessarily most strongly defended) points (bridges on the Vistula and railroad stations), and at the same time "strong partisan actions" were to take place west of Warsaw, along with attacks on the German rear guard to the east.[18]

On July 27 Komorowski cabled London that, given the unclear situation east of the Vistula, he made every action in Warsaw dependent on the success or failure of the German attempt to stabilize the front. He also reported that the Soviets had begun disarming the Twenty-seventh Division of the AK in the area of Lublin:[19] "This fact, as well as the hostile attitude to our forces in the Vilnius region, clearly indicates that the

Soviets want to destroy the AK, which, as a Polish force, is not subordinated to them." And this, concluded the commander of the AK, could force his troops to self-defense.[20]

On the same day, in Warsaw, there were also quite different events. The German governor, Ludwig Fischer, called on the population to be calm and to work; the Wehrmacht would destroy the Red Army as the Polish army had done east of Warsaw in 1920 [!]. In the afternoon, he used public loudspeakers to call the people of Warsaw to work on fortifications. 100,000 people were expected to appear; virtually no one showed up. Just as German reinforcements discharged in the city and the surrounding area marched in ostentatious unity through the main streets of Warsaw,[21] police patrols were strengthened—the occupier showed that his period of weakness had passed. The Germans had known for some time that the AK was ready to launch an attack; now they were trying to prevent the eruption of the uprising with a demonstration of strength.[22]

The leadership of the AK feared massive reprisals from the boycott of Fischer's July 27th appeal; however, the occupation authority had never yet been confronted with open passive resistance on such a massive scale. On July 28 Monter put his troops on a state of alert. According to eyewitness reports, this mobilization of several thousand young men took place semipublicly, and the police reacted neither on July 28 nor on the 29th. Because of the curfew, the Warsaw AK soldiers could not go home, and 80 percent of them spent the night of July 28 at the secret gathering places. The young soldiers must have been frustrated; they wanted to fight, not to wait crowded in secret places and then be sent home.

The pressure thus emerging "from below" on the AK leadership was reinforced by the pressure from outside. London was sending unmistakable signals that the policy of fait accompli pursued by the underground leadership—the mobilization in the capital implemented without an order from London—was ultimately in the interest of the government-in-exile. After Mikołajczyk's trip to Moscow had been arranged (see chapter Seven), the cabinet decided to give the Warsaw decision-makers a free hand. On July 25 the ministerial council decided "to authorize the government delegate [namely, Jankowski in Warsaw] to make all decisions necessitated by the pace of the Soviet offensive, if need be without contacting the government in advance." In the dispatch to Jankowski, this carte blanche was even clearer.[23] Apparently, it was not known in London that Government authorization of its decision-making responsibility had already been ceded to the commander of the AK. Even had it been known in London, very little would have changed: completely misjudging the power relationships in place, Mikołajczyk hoped to strengthen his negotiating position with Stalin by an uprising in the capital. Other important dispatches of the authorities in exile—

under circumstances that are not fully explained to this day—were lost at this time or reached Warsaw only days after the Uprising erupted. Indeed, they would have made little difference in the situation.[24]

At the same time, the Warsaw leadership of the resistance was under pressure from new Moscow successes. On July 27 the Second Tank Army continued its attack along the Lublin-Warsaw road; the Eighth Guards and the First Polish Army started fighting around the bridgeheads west of Lublin, on the heights of Puławy (some 120 kilometers south of Warsaw). Radio Moscow announced an agreement between the Soviet Union and the PKWN. Stalin thus demonstrated that he wanted to enhance the status of the Polish Communists and their organization to an equal executive organ, able to conduct international negotiations for the liberated part of the country. On July 29 Radio Moscow announced that Soviet troops were a few dozen kilometers southeast of Warsaw; at the same time, it broadcast an appeal "to Warsaw" in Polish, "to join in battle against the Germans as in 1939 [!], this time in a decisive action." The next day, the Polish-language Moscow radio broadcast repeated the appeal, but without the embarrassing allusion to 1939.[25]

In those hectic days, there were still differences of opinion about a possible uprising within the AK high command and among the leading politicians of the underground. Many warned, others urged; Komorowski waited. On July 29 a definitive decision could have been made. On this day, Jan Nowak appeared before the commander of the AK and a few high-ranking staff officers. Nowak was an emissary from the government-in-exile in London and had arrived in Poland four days before. Despite his youth, Nowak (born 1913) was not an unknown quantity. Until 1943, he had played a leading role in the "N" campaign and had made the Warsaw-London trip as a courier three times before 1944.[26] His latest mission was certainly the most important: acting as a living tape recorder, he was to convey the arguments and intentions of the London government-in-exile and of Supreme Commander Sosnkowski—in a detailed manner that was rare under the conditions of coded radio communication.

Nowak's debriefing on July 29 became a four-hour meeting. The emissary made it clear that the planned military and political demonstration might help the prime minister in his Moscow talks—but only if the AK were in fact able to occupy the city. Hope for substantial support by the Allies was a chimera; the Polish paratrooper brigade was preparing for deployment on the western front, and the release of Polish bomber groups for Warsaw was not very likely either. At the Allied air base in Brindisi, Italy, where flights also left for Warsaw, there were currently six entire Polish plane crews who had nine aircraft. On the international stage, there would hardly be any changes, for the Soviets had long ago agreed with the West on their occupation zones.

Nowak's remarks were interrupted several times by couriers bringing news from the front. He heard place-names southeast of Warsaw: Garwolin, Otwock, Falenica, the first one sixty kilometers from the city, the last twenty. Nowak got the impression that his report was "a purely academic lecture. [. . .] Those present were pondering whether to start now, or to wait. It was clear that the die had been cast. . . ."[27] In the discussions that interrupted the lecture, this time the second deputy of the AK chief of staff, Colonel Janusz Bokszczanin (born 1894), broke in. He was a coauthor of the Uprising plans, one of the "hesitant ones" in the AK high command who now insisted on keeping to the ground rules of the military profession.[28] The attack might begin only at the moment when the Soviets had occupied the eastern part of the city, Praga, and would move to attack the "real" Warsaw, left of the Vistula. Whether this scenario was viable would be known only when the Red Army started the artillery barrage of Warsaw's left bank. A chain of observation posts, manned by experienced soldiers of the artillery surveyor troops. would be built and thus report routinely on the targets the Soviets were shooting at. The warning worked; once more the AK leadership dispersed without making a decision. Nowak's "academic lecture," which could have raised definitive arguments against the idea of an uprising in Warsaw, apparently sank in the general frenzy.

On July 30 the battles in the east could be heard more clearly in Warsaw than on previous days. The Second Tank Army now moved north and took the whole area east of Warsaw. The Soviets were now standing exactly on the place where they had suffered a crushing defeat in August 1920. But this time they fought successfully for the bridgeheads on the west bank of the Vistula in Puławy and Magnuszew. The military problem of the Red Army in late July 1944—like that of its predecessor twenty-four years before—was that the victories of the last weeks had taken the advancing troops far from their supply units; problems with fuel and munitions especially made it hard for the tank units of the Second Army. They operated in a constantly expanding area and pursued the goal, which only a few weeks ago had been a very abstract one, of crossing the Vistula, possibly even near Warsaw. According to this latest plan, the Second Tank Army was set to attack Praga on July 30, but on that day, its commander warned his superior Rokossovskii: "I'm running out of breath." In fact, the Second Tank Army now came upon an unexpectedly strong counterfront: east of Warsaw five German tank divisions, including the Fourth SS Tank Corps ("Viking" and "Death's Head" Divisions) as well as the elite "Hermann Göring" Division stood at the ready. Even if the German troops were as weak as the tank corps of the Second Army, they were still strong enough to force the Soviets into an immediate battle on July 31. On August 1, at 4 a.m., the Second

Soviet Tank Army went on the defensive. Of the 810 tanks it had on July 18, only a third could still be deployed on August 4.[29]

The battle in the east could be heard clearly in the city. The *Biuletyn Informacyjny,* the best-known press organ of the AK, had changed its agenda to a daily newspaper the previous day (July 30) and on July 31 put out an edition of allegedly 100,000 copies, with an article about the impending "day of retaliation." After years of occupation, contempt, and ubiquitous terror, the article openly expressed the idea of collective responsibility—previously used by the Germans as justification for the public shooting of hostages: "Now they [the Germans] will know what the idea of 'collective responsibility' is. No nation in Europe has deserved the translation of this German principle like the Germans. There are no good Germans. There are only German criminals or Germans who tolerated and supported the criminals. Where were the good Germans when innocents by the hundreds were shot on the streets of Warsaw? [. . .] The German nation is a nation of rabid dogs. Those we find can expect no mercy from the Poles. [. . .] The race of rabid dogs must be taught a lesson that it will preserve in its memory for more than one generation."[30] The threats applied to the German functionaries, officials, and uniformed men along with the Volksdeutsche, who made up the majority of the German population of Warsaw. After five years of occupation, these were no longer original thoughts in underground journalism. The dehumanization of the enemy, which had been pursued by Nazi propaganda against the Poles since the summer of 1939, now turned into a dehumanization of the image of the German enemy;[31] it was an expression of hatred and a desire to retaliate that seemed to be waiting backstage of the cannon-thunder in the east shortly before the explosion. On the other hand, even on this July 31, there were no signs that the young soldiers would follow the implicit appeal of the *Biuletyn* and not their officers. Responsibility for the decision had shifted from London to Warsaw, and here it remained in the hands of the underground leadership.

The participants of the morning meeting of the AK high command on July 31 naturally knew little about the tank battle beginning east of Warsaw. Once again there were controversies. Okulicki vociferously demanded a decision from the commander, but the head of Section II warned that the situation was unclear, and the commander of the Warsaw AK again spoke of the insufficient armament of his troops. Strangely enough, these controversies seem to have been resolved through a regular voting procedure: three of the present members of the AK high command supported the Uprising while four were against.[32] In the early afternoon, Komorowski conferred with the politicians of the RJN who were not prepared to take any risks at all—the decision remained suspended in this committee too.

It was made in the late afternoon of that same day. At 5 P.M., Komorowski, Okulicki, Pełczyński, and Major Janina Karasiówna (who did not take part in the following discussion) were in the apartment. The commander of the Warsaw AK, Chruściel, suddenly appeared with the news that Soviet tank troops had captured a few suburbs and entered Praga—the time had come. Komorowski immediately sent a messenger to the government delegate. After a few comments by the soldiers present and a few questions, Jankowski was to have said to Komorowski: "Let's go!" The commander of the AK subsequently instructed the commander of the Warsaw district to begin the Burza campaign in Warsaw on August 1 at 5 P.M.

After 6 P.M. a few other members of the high command came to the apartment. At least one of them—according to some statements, the head of Section II Iranek-Osmecki—made no secret of his amazement about the sudden order and doubted whether the situation did in fact look the way Chruściel had described it. "Too late," Komorowski was supposed to have answered the doubter. "The order is given. I will not change it."[33]

Since then, discussion of the circumstances and motives of the decisions of July 21–31, 1944, have filled volumes. Advocates of the Uprising put forth the most diverse arguments: that it could not have been known in July 1944 that the Soviets would let the Uprising bleed to death; that the pressure on the AK leadership "from below" had left no choice; that doing nothing would have had the same bad results as the decision of July 31. None of these arguments is sound, or more precisely, none can be verified, and some are obviously wrong—like the one that cites the allegedly overpowering pressure "from below." Until August 1, no examples of the breakdown of discipline in the ranks of the AK were known. And, according to this argument, the people of Warsaw, who had passively watched the defeated German troops march through their city during the week of July 26, would have had the spontaneous desire to rise up against the occupier (how they might have done so remains an open question) when that occupying force demonstrated strength.

For opponents of the Uprising, the main adversary was Okulicki, who admitted his position in the days after the catastrophe: "If a political error was made, the politicians, who were supposed to have taken care of relations with the Soviet Union, are responsible for it. The leadership and the soldiers of the Home Army only did their duty in service for their nation, when they started the battle for Warsaw and conducted it for sixty-three days. They could not have done otherwise, it would have been fainthearted and cowardly."[34] General Leopold Okulicki wrote these lines in the spring of 1945 in a Moscow prison; even as the anti-Hitler coalition continued, this highly decorated officer of the anti-

German resistance of Poland waited for a sham trial from the Stalinist prosecutor. He knew he would not leave the prison alive. The official death certificate, issued by the NKVD, is dated December 24, 1946. In July 1944, his son had been killed on the Italian front as a noncommissioned officer. That Okulicki staked his life for Poland according to his best opinion and paid the highest price for it—neither his contemporaries nor subsequent generations could find any fault with that. But did this have to mean deciding to accept a battle that was more than dubious from a military standpoint, in a city with several hundred thousand inhabitants?

6

Attack and Mass Murder

LOOKING BACK, it seemed to many eyewitnesses of August 1, 1944, as if an extraordinary number of young people in Warsaw had rushed across the city, some with bundles under their arm, others in coats, their expressions distracted, looking somehow military despite their civilian clothing. These soldiers in disguise went unnoticed by the police posted across the city, and in retrospect the German city commander, General Rainer Stahel, thought regretfully that all the reports coming in from the patrols stationed in the city had turned out to be worthless.[1]

Nevertheless, this was not a complete surprise. Before 5 P.M. (code word: "W" Hour), there was a lot of shooting—that afternoon, a group of armed socialists was surprised in the boiler room of a cooperative settlement in Żoliborz. Twenty-one soldiers, including the company leader, fell in the fire fight. The local police troops were now fully mobilized; tanks and tank carriers drove ostentatiously through the main streets of the quarter. In the Kamler factory northwest of the city center, where the leadership of the AK was holed up during the Uprising, fights also broke out before "W" Hour. By nightfall, the high command of the AK was surrounded in the factory by German forces (who could not know whom they were dealing with).[2] When the massive attacks on the German positions began at 5 P.M., apparently only in a few cases was this a surprise.[3]

However, given the inequality in ammunition, training, and other elements, keeping the date a perfect secret would have changed little in the outcome. The rebels were alleged to have some 40,000 soldiers (at least 10 percent of them women) but in fact had only 20,000 and only minimal weapons and ammunition. In the few hours they had for mobilization, not all the soldiers could reach their gathering places, and the

74

small number of weapons were probably distributed only to some of them. Most units received the mobilization order of July 31 only on the morning of August 1. In the city center, with its dense settlement and in the ordinarily smaller gathering places, the AK did manage to mobilize between 60 and 80 percent of the soldiers. These were the worst armed: in the Old City, the largest unit of 901 men had only 103 grenades, 48 pistols, 8 automatic pistols, 9 rifles, 2 light and 1 heavy machine gun, and about 1,000 Molotov cocktails.[4] The farther from the center, the worse was the mobilization—especially disastrous since the units outside the city center were usually better armed.

The rebels confronted 13,000 to 20,000 German troops, some of them police and some of them regular army. The important positions—offices, barracks, airports, bridges—had been prepared for years for a possible uprising. At the same time, the German soldiers and police fought from the protection of fortifications, walls, armor plate, barbed wire, and sandbags; the rebels had to attack and could only dream of support by artillery, tanks, or planes.

The results of the first day of fighting reflected that situation. Attacks in the historic nucleus of the city, on the university buildings, police headquarters, and the palace of the Council of Ministers (all along Krakowskie Przedmieście) collapsed in the bombardment by the police units. Of the 120 soldiers who tried to occupy the air force barracks south of the city center, barely more than a dozen survived. In the hopeless attack on the central Warsaw airport Okęcie, the AK regiment "Gartuch-Gromada" lost 120 soldiers, and the assault on the Bielany airport in the north also failed.[5] Half the officers of the "Baszta" regiment fell in fights for a few positions in Mokotów, whose northern part section was part of the "police quarter"; in the attack on the Kierbedź Bridge in the city center, the 103rd AK Company lost forty-two men, including the company commander. Attacks on the other bridges also failed, so that ultimately none of the strategically important targets was captured. "In truth, at 'W' Hour, we were already packed together in the housing block that formed our exit base," one of the participants in the attack on the Poniatowski Bridge recalled decades later.[6] The rebels scored successes in only a few parts of the city center: on the very first day, there was a successful attack on the tallest skyscraper, the Prudential Insurance Company building, where the white and red flag was hoisted sixty-eight meters (238 feet) high. The labor office, the appellate court, and the former Czechoslovakian embassy were also occupied. In Stawki, north of the city center, a large warehouse with German uniforms[7] and foodstuffs was also captured—this loot turned out to be especially important since all five of the secret food warehouses, holding approximately 90,000 food rations, were now outside the range of the rebels. Three of these locations were in Praga, where the Uprising succeeded even less than in the western parts of the city.[8] Here and there, Germans were captured: Major Max Dirske, the highest-ranking German officer taken prisoner during the entire Uprising, spent the next sixty-three days in a prison camp in the city center. In one of the schools occupied by the SS, the rebels freed a group of fifty to one hundred Hungarian Jews.[9] Approximately half of left-bank Warsaw could be occupied—entire residential blocks, streets, and trolleys—but not a single one of the first-rate strategic targets.

The end result of the first day looked bad for both sides. Stahel later complained that from the very beginning, the "German occupation [turned out to be] helpless for street fighting with regard to tactics, leadership, and human behavior."[10] Despite all preparations and considerations, the Germans had to retreat from weaker bases and merge with others; a few others fought in isolation and without hope of relief. The so-called police quarter in Mokotów and the so-called government quarter south of the Old City were cut off from one another; some of the besieged "section guards" lacked all communication. The most urgent task of the German leadership now consisted of reinforcing the Warsaw garrison headquarters, which would enable the occupying power to launch an offensive and reproduce east–west communication through the city. The Poles had missed all their most important targets and suffered extremely high losses—approximately 10 percent of the mobilized soldiers in a single day! Along with Mokotów, where several units evaded the bloody clashes in the forests south of the city, the mood seems to have been especially bad in Żoliborz—the commander, Lieutenant Colonel Mieczysław Niedzielski ("Żywiciel"), recorded losses here of up to 30 percent of the manpower, a total depletion of munitions and of hope; German tanks and armored cars still controlled the main roads. At night, the rebels left this part of the city, went to the suburbs, and returned two days later; after the first battle, the German garrison was apparently so confused that it did not know how to take advantage of this gift from the enemy on August 2 and perhaps did not even notice it. After the first day of fighting, the commander in Warsaw, Colonel Chruściel, lamented the bad flow of information ("Couriers—the only means of communication—apparently fell on the way") and the failure of the first attack: "The most important objectives—the Academic House, the Sejm [Parliament], Szucha Avenue [headquarters of the Security Police], the city headquarters—were not taken." With respect to both sides, little was to change in the coming days and weeks. That the German flow of communication through telephone and teleprinter was not stopped by the rebels can hardly be overestimated, while the AK leadership, on the other hand, always had to struggle with great difficulties in transmitting its orders to the units in Warsaw—and especially to the partisan units outside the city. That was the main reason why a coordinated partisan campaign against the assembly of German reinforcements at Warsaw failed to materialize in the following days.[11]

Nevertheless, the morale of the AK and the civilian population in many places seems to have been optimistic. There was constant talk that the whole city had already been liberated, the Red Army had invaded, and the Germans were withdrawing. Women brought food for the soldiers, men built barricades and bases, the white and red flag was hoisted on many buildings. "It takes your breath away that we're finally free," noted one of the contemporary witnesses in his diary. Władysław Bartoszewski, then a twenty-two-year-old officer in the AK information office, reported two days later on the mood in the liberated part of the city center: "The attitude of the population toward the fighters is so warm and helpful that the boundary between fighters and participants has been erased."[12]

The rebels continued their offensive. On August 2 a new attack on the northern airport of Bielany failed. The rebels did capture the council hall; the main post office; a prison; and the government stocks and securities institution (thus the whole Old City was liberated); the tobacco-monopoly factory, with great stocks of foodstuffs and cigarettes; another prison; and the electricity works, where the German guard squad was driven into the cellar and then forced—with water hoses—to surrender. Even two "Panther" tanks were captured that day. But despite the reinforcement of tanks, the Germans could not manage to relieve the unit of seven officers and 157 soldiers besieged in the telephone company skyscraper (Polska Akcyjna Spółka Telefoniczna, PAST) in the city center. In his daily report, Stahel wrote of "bloody losses" involved in every offensive procedure against the rebels. He estimated his own losses after the first two days of fighting at five hundred men.[13] The high command of the Ninth Army made increasing efforts to communicate with the Thirty-ninth Tank Corps east of Warsaw; the railroad line from west to east still functioned, but street communication in the city center was cut off by the rebels. German soldiers, civilian authorities, and police insisted on the immediate reinforcement of the Warsaw garrison; the commander of the Security Police and the SD demanded the sternest reprisals and the use of Stukas (Ju-87). On the other side, the AK leadership demanded Allied transport planes, especially with arms drops for the rebels, and continued the attack.

On August 3 a few buildings in the so-called government quarter, including the main office of the German city authorities, fell into the hands of the AK. A tank column, probably from the elite "Herman Göring" division, drove several hundred civilians as a living shield against the onslaught of the rebels and, within two and a half hours, moved from the western edge of the city to the Poniatowski Bridge, where the surviving civilians, who had had to dismantle the barricades on the way, were released. In the afternoon, the East Prussian Fourth Armored Infantry regiment tried to fight free in the same way, this time from east to west, that is, from the Poniatowski Bridge. The attack, in which civilians were again used as living shields, came to an end in the city center in the evening. The east–west contact was also cut off, since the sea of rebels had closed again right after the breakthrough of the tanks of the "Göring" division. A harder blow for the Uprising that day was the end of the fighting in Praga. East of the Vistula, most of the AK went back underground; a few soldiers crossed the Vistula and joined the rebels in the city center. General Stahel was surrounded in the Brühl Palace and estimated his losses at that time at some five hundred to six hundred men.[14]

The people of Warsaw still hoped for a quick and victorious end to the fighting. The government delegate Jankowski called on the leader of the Jewish Fighting Organization (Żydowska Organizacja Bojowa, ŻOB), Yizhak Zuckerman, and the Communist PPR, to join the fight against the occupier. Jankowski spread the vision of a "democratic Poland, a Poland of social justice, a Poland of working people," Zuckerman declared that the AK fight was also the cause of the surviving Jews, and the Communists called for national solidarity. At the same time, the antiaircraft defense began organizing the administration of the liberated part of the contested city as the most important civilian service.[15]

Yet, by August 4, things began to change. The calls for help of Frank, Fischer, Stahel, and the supreme commander of the Ninth Army produced reinforcement of the Warsaw garrison. Along with individual parts of Wehrmacht and police troops, two big units were ordered to Warsaw, which, later, had a lasting impact on the course of the fighting. The first was the so-called Dirlewanger Regiment, which consisted of German criminals—poachers, professional criminals, SS members on probation. In its previous operations in the rear of the eastern front, it had already left behind a broad trail of blood. Now this notorious regiment was supposed to pacify Warsaw; its prevailing principle, "to shoot all inhabitants," went far beyond the guidelines for fighting partisans in the occupied territories of the Soviet Union.[16] The second special unit was the Storm Brigade SS RONA (Russkaia osvoboditel'naia narodnaia armiia) under Bronisław Kamiński, which consisted of former Red Army soldiers, and after several "actions" in Belarus, it had a terrible reputation even among the Germans.[17] Before the Uprising broke out, the plan was that a group of between twenty- and thirty-thousand RONA members and their families would settle down in the southern part of the GG as "defense farmers," but even before August 1 the idea was abandoned.[18] For Warsaw, the Kamiński brigade had apparently received a special license to "plunder," which the Germans themselves soon regretted. In addition, the notorious RONA placed only part of the "foreign national" troops in the operation against Warsaw, which at the time came to almost 50 percent of the attackers under German command and orders. Along with other reinforcements of southern and western Warsaw, the Kamiński and Dirlewanger units were initially assembled for the attack under the higher command of the SS and police leader of Wartheland, Gruppenführer Heinz Reinefarth.

Since August 3 the Wehrmacht used assault planes against the rebels. On August 4 and 5, units ordered to Warsaw by Himmler appeared, so that the number of German troops in and around Warsaw was double what it was on August 1.[19] The supreme command was assumed by SS Obergruppenführer Erich von dem Bach, active since 1943 as "head of the anti-guerilla forces"; he immediately described the Warsaw mission in his journal as "a suicide mission." It is doubtful whether he meant only the military aspect of his assignment—from the start, the fight for Warsaw was more than a mere war exercise, even on the German side. Back in 1940, the development planners in the GG assumed the "need" to "scale down" the city, which was to be reduced to 100,000 inhabitants as part of the future German settlement area. In the course of the occupation, the conviction of Warsaw's special significance as a center of the resistance movement became part of this strategic development approach, which was closely connected with the delusion of removing the Poles from their old national territory:[20] "We have in this country one point from which all disaster comes: it is Warsaw," noted Hans Frank in December 1943. "If we didn't have Warsaw in the GG, we wouldn't have four-fifths of the difficulties we have to struggle with. Warsaw is and remains a hotbed of unrest, the point from which all unrest in this land is brought."[21] Reichsführer SS Heinrich Himmler thought the same: "When I heard the news of the Uprising in Warsaw, I went immediately to the Führer," he told an interested audience of military area higher officers and commanding officers in September 1944. "I said: 'My Führer, the time is not right. Historically, it is a blessing that the Poles do that. We'll get over it in five or six weeks. But then Warsaw, the capital, the head, the intelligence of this sixteen to seventeen million people of Poland, is extinguished, this nation that has blocked our way to the east for seven hundred years and has been in our way ever since the first battle in Tannenberg. Then the Polish problem historically for our children and for all those who come after us, even for us, will no longer be a big problem.'"

Von dem Bach later stated that he learned of Himmler's or Hitler's order only after his arrival, which he summarized in 1946 at an interrogation by a Polish prosecutor:

1. All rebels were to be shot after capture, regardless of whether their actions during combat accorded with the Hague agreement or not.
2. The nonfighting part of the population would be massacred indiscriminately.
3. The entire city would be razed, meaning all houses, streets, and everything in the city should be destroyed.

Aside from von dem Bach's personal responsibility, it does not really matter when he learned of this order. What is important is that such an order undoubtedly existed and was carried out by several units.[22] In any case, the assumption of command by the "head of anti-guerilla forces" meant that, after a few days, the order came to be ignored—for reasons that are still not understood.

Already, by August 4, the Germans had tried to establish east–west communication from the Poniatowski Bridge through Jerozolimskie Avenue. On August 5 German troops launched a counterattack, this time focusing west and southwest of the city center. Despite a numerical superiority with regard to the Kedyw[23] group in Wola and despite support of heavy weapons, they advanced only a few hundred meters on that day. Thus the military consequences of the first German counterattack were insignificant. The real result of the battles of August 5 were the mountains of corpses left behind by the "Reinefahrt fighting group" in Ochota and, above all, in Wola.

On the very first days, German troops in Warsaw had murdered masses of AK soldiers and civilians: On August 1 at least 135 persons; on August 2, some 600 people in the Gestapo prison on Aleja Szucha alone; and several hundred in the entire city between August 1 and 3. In many cases, civilians were driven out as living shields by the attacking soldiers or tanks. But the order cited above about shooting all those arrested and destroying the city brought a new quality that surpassed even the usual occupation horrors and crimes. All day on August 5, this order was implemented in Wola mainly by the Dirlewanger Brigade—from children to old people, civilians were killed in mass executions without any excuse, nor did the murderers spare hospitals. In Ochota, the less systematic mass murder was accompanied by rapes and robberies of the RONA members. Nevertheless, Reinefahrt was not completely satisfied. In a phone call with the supreme commander of the Ninth Army, Reinefahrt reported that his troops had advanced only slowly, had achieved enemy losses—including people executed—"of over 10,000 shot," but there was still the question: "What should I do with the civilians? I have less ammunition than prisoners."[24]

Reinefahrt might have been happier if he had known that the actual number of victims was essentially higher. According to Polish estimates, which also included the victims from the following day, 30,000 to 40,000 civilians died in Wola; along Wolska Street and the surrounding area alone, forty-one sites of mass execution were later reconstructed. For comparison: the military opponent of the Germans in the west, the fighting group Kedyw, calculated its own losses on August 5 at twenty dead and forty wounded. That evening, von dem Bach, who had just appeared, called off the mass shootings of women and children. On the following days, "only" men could be shot—an instruction or toleration that was quite often disregarded; yet after the war, it might have saved von dem Bach's head: aside from all other crimes in the fight against the partisans, in his biggest campaign "in the east," he had reduced the bloodbath by at least one dimension.[25]

The massacre in Wola and Ochota on August 5 had far-reaching results for the Uprising. Tens of thousands of inhabitants of the southern and western quarters streamed into the parts of the city controlled by the AK. On the one hand, this mass movement increased the problem of provisions in the liberated part of the city. On the other hand, it gave the Uprising a new dimension. After it turned out that the Germans were killing civilians as well as captured AK soldiers, the Uprising became a fight for the lives of the civilian population; the AK troops became the protectors of women, children, and old people against a merciless band of soldiers. In the following weeks, the effect of solidarity between troops and civilians was exposed to countless endurance tests, as was the social peace between individual groups of civilians in the disputed city, where life became more unbearable from one day to the next. Yet, basically the existential dependence of the civilian population helped the leadership of the Uprising achieve an authority it probably never would have attained as a purely military undertaking.[26] The propaganda company of the SS "Viking" Tank Division reported, "after testing an evacuation trek," that the inhabitants of Warsaw had at first "very bitterly turned away from" the badly prepared uprising; but "after they had to watch the Germans mercilessly destroying the life and property of the inhabitants and razing all Warsaw, whether guilty or innocent, the mood changed completely." As a result, General Stahel, who was apparently horrified at this side effect of German terror, ordered "that, among the civilians coming out of Warsaw, counterpropaganda must immediately be deployed that opens people's eyes to the fact that it was not the

Germans who brought misfortune onto the city of Warsaw, but the rebels themselves."[27] Yet it was too late for that. Despite the strategic defeat of the attack, despite the lack of Soviet help, despite the complete breakdown of the Uprising in right-bank Praga, the fight now had to go on— the operation no longer consisted of just a military or political success but rather of the lives of the hundreds of thousands of civilians in the liberated part of the city.

One more dimension of August 5 should be mentioned here. In 1964, the German military historian Hanns von Krannhals, who has dealt extensively with this subject, commented: "The mass murder in Wola was not an air attack but an eye-for-an-eye of those who issued the orders, transmitted them, tolerated them, and executed them, and who are responsible for the cruelty to men, women, and children in that quarter of the city that did not fight. Its meaninglessness in the framework of the fighting only increases the weight of the guilt for those directly responsible. The tablets, small wooden crosses, and memorial stones on both sides of Wolska Street in Warsaw are the Calvary of a Passion, from which there is no acquittal before history."[28]

The Victoria Hotel at 26 Jasna Street in the center of town, conquered on August 1, served as the headquarters of Colonel Antoni Chruściel ("Monter"), the AK's factual commander during the Uprising.

Civilians often assisted with the construction of barricades. Shown is the barricade at the corner of Piusa XI. and Marszałkowska Street on August 2, 1944.

The Polish flag on top of the "House of the Tourists" at the corner of
Jerozolimskie Avenue and Starynkiewicz Square. The insurrectionists
conquered the house on August 3; it was abandoned again on August 13.

The PAST building at 37/39 Zielna Street was attacked by the insurrectionists several times. It was conquered on August 20.

Deployment of the "Piat" (anti-tank weapons) at the Kopernika Street barricade. The "Piats" came from the Allies and were in greatest demand among the insurrectionists.

Volunteers enrolling for service in the AK take their oath in public, in front of officers, one chaplain, and civilians.

Civilians leaving Warsaw through the Plac za Żelazną Bramą toward Pruszków camp.

7

Refusal from Moscow

THE POLISH PRIME MINISTER began his trip from London to Moscow on July 27. On the same day, Churchill implored Stalin to seek a compromise with Mikołajczyk "in the spirit [. . .] of sincere friendship and our twenty years' alliance." Continuing the conflict about Poland "would lead to a constant friction and might even hamper the great business which we have to do the wide world over."[1] He could not have been clearer; on the other hand, it could hardly have escaped Stalin that Roosevelt's letter of recommendation a day later sounded essentially more laconic. For some time, the British and Americans had been seriously uneasy about the Soviet-Polish conflict. Much more than serving as go-betweens, which in practice turned into "helpless hesitation," they either could not or would not offer to endanger the cohesion of the coalition.[2]

In Moscow, Mikołajczyk had to wait. On July 31 Molotov received him. Mikołajczyk appeared convinced of the impending eruption of the Uprising; Molotov was just as sure that the Red Army would soon take Warsaw. Mikołajczyk naturally did not know that a few hours after his discussion with the Soviet foreign minister, Stalin extended Directive no. 220145 of July 14—mentioned in chapter 5—which ordered the disarming of the AK in old eastern Poland, to all the land occupied by the Red Army.[3]

Not until August 3 did the prime minister get the news of the Uprising. In the evening, he was received by Stalin, who gave the impression that he knew nothing of the fighting in Warsaw. The substance of the two-and-a-half-hour discussion was a harsh disagreement about the future of Poland; the Uprising—considered by the Poles as a bargaining chip—turned out to be disadvantageous for Mikołajczyk's position since it made him seem like a supplicant. Stalin wanted one thing: recognition of the Lublin PKWN committee by the government-in-exile in London. He repeatedly disavowed the AK: he knew precisely that it was anti-Russian and consisted only of "small partisan groups," had no heavy weapons ("What kind of army is this without artillery, tanks, an air force?"), and avoided fighting the Germans. "Maybe they also want to fight, but they really can't," was Stalin's greatest concession in this discussion. "Good material for soldiers, but to make an army of them, you need weapons, and that they don't have." Nothing was agreed about the Uprising.[4]

To this day, the documents that would enable a reconstruction of the Soviet decision-making process in the first days of August are not known. Since the morning of August 1, the Second Soviet Tank Army was fighting east of Warsaw in a defensive position. Stalin did not touch on this subject on August 3—only on August 5 did he give Churchill detailed data on the strength of the German tank groups and hint at the failure of the Soviet offensive on the capital. Meanwhile, the tank battle east of the Vistula had already ended with the defeat of the Second Army, which allegedly lost more than 50 percent of its tanks on the first days of August and was no longer able to continue the attack. It does not seem likely that a secret order had been given by Stalin on August 1 or 2 to call off the attack—as has often been assumed since then:[5] The Soviet plan of a lightning capture of Warsaw had failed in any case. On August 5 Stalin asked the commanders of the First and Second Belarusian Fronts for an assessment of the situation. The commander of the First Front, Marshall Konstanty Rokossovskii, indicated difficulties of supply but pleaded for a resumption of the attack on August 10, calling in two new large units (the Seventieth and Forty-seventh Armies). The idea was rejected—was it by Stalin? Rokossovskii had to draw up a new plan in cooperation with the deputy supreme commander of the Red Army, Marshall Georgy Zhukov. This new plan anticipated attacks north and south of Warsaw. After fortifying the two bridgeheads, according to Rokossovskii and Zhukov, the attack on Warsaw could go ahead on August 25. This outline was presented to Stalin on August 8. His decision is not known, but it is relatively irrelevant for the uprising. The moment the Red Army gave up a rapid attack on Warsaw—and this was precisely the basic assumption of the plan of August 8—the preliminary decision about the fate of the rebels had really been made.[6] The unanimous judgment of the AK in the first week of August was that, without outside help, the Uprising would collapse within days.

The government-in-exile tried to raise this help. Ever since the news of the Uprising reached London on the afternoon of August 2, Polish politicians, diplomats, and soldiers had moved heaven and earth to induce the Allies to provide immediate support. Just as before August 1, the British and Americans had countless reservations—how and why should help be organized from Italy or England when the eastern ally was so close to the battles? Nevertheless, they did react immediately. By August 4, the first planes flew relief missions to Warsaw. In his speech in the House of Commons on August 2, Churchill—not yet informed about the outbreak of the Uprising—developed the vision of a union of Polish forces in east and west the moment the Red Army liberated Warsaw. On August 4 he instructed Stalin about the air relief for Warsaw; the following day, the British military mission in Moscow informed the Soviets of their inability to supply the Uprising from the air and asked them for information concerning the possible ability of the Red Army to provide help. The day after that, Stalin answered the British prime minister that the news from Warsaw was "very exaggerated" and "untrustworthy" and repeated his arguments from the discussion with Mikołajczyk two days earlier: The AK was weak, had no heavy weapons, and had no chance of capturing Warsaw. Once again, Soviet help for the uprising was out of the question.[7]

Thus, by August 5, a precarious situation had emerged that, presumably, none of the sides involved in the Uprising the previous day had calculated. First, the Germans had been able to hold the front east of Warsaw. Second, the Soviets thus had to swallow a failure of their plans for the immediate capture of Warsaw. Now they faced the perspective of temporarily helping the "sort-of allies" who had emerged from the underground and whose strategy obviously stood in the way of establishing a Communist Polish government, and also of rescuing a rebellious Warsaw where the Communist takeover was conceivable only under the military pressure of the Red Army. Third, after five days, the AK was fighting under conditions that had not been in any plan for the Uprising: there was no adequate preparation for or hope of a successful end; the battle already lasted longer than anticipated, and at the same time, their force was inferior in every respect to the not-quite-defeated enemy. Fourth, the calculation of the government-in-exile had not worked out either: instead of entering negotiations as the superior power in the liberated capital, they now had to go to Moscow as supplicants. The key was possibly here, between August 5 and 13: if Mikołajczyk could satisfy his interlocutors in the PKWN—indirectly the Soviets—with concessions, the Soviets might favor some form of relief for the Uprising by the Red Army. In this situation, the prime minister decided on direct negotiations with the Communists, whom he had excluded as interlocutors even before he left London.

The talks took place on August 6 and 7. They revolved around the usual subjects: eastern borders, the constitution, and formation of government. On the last point, the Communists demanded fourteen departments and offered the London government-in-exile four (including the chairmanship of the ministerial council for Mikołajczyk himself). With regard to the Uprising, the "Moscow Poles" appeared strangely uninformed: Wanda Wasilewska asserted that there had been no battles in Warsaw until August 4, and that the liberation of the city was a matter of two weeks at most. Mikołajczyk promised to present the ideas of the PKWN about future cooperation to the London government-in-exile.

In the parting speech on August 9, Stalin appeared essentially friendlier than in the first meeting. He asked precisely what kind of help was necessary for the Uprising, said that weapons drops were "a simple matter," offered cooperation in accepting a coded radio contact between the Red Army and AK, and even assured Mikołajczyk twice that the Soviets would provide all conceivable support. In the concluding part of the conversation, Stalin emphasized the need for Polish-Soviet friendship: "The Polish nation should not follow the Soviet Union, but rather go hand in hand with her. The Polish nation has its own ways. But these can run parallel to the ways of the Soviet Union and [consist] specifically in the common fight against the Germans, in the common defense."[8] No wonder Mikołajczyk left Moscow believing that the Polish-Soviet crisis had finally been overcome and that, above all, help had been guaranteed for the Uprising.

Stalin's note (dated that day) to Churchill and Roosevelt could have given exactly the same impression. Unfortunately, Mikołajczyk had not decided to fulfill the wishes of the PKWN immediately, Stalin wrote regretfully, but it was now clear that the prime minister was no enemy of compromise, that both sides wanted cooperation, and the first stage of relations between the PKWN and Mikołajczyk had been reached. Perhaps further development would be positive—a hope Churchill described as his, too, the very next day. The British prime minister immediately expressed his thanks for the alleged Soviet support for the Uprising (which Roosevelt did not do in his answer to the note of August 9), but three days later he came back to the same subject: Could Stalin not grant "further help" to the uprising, "as the distance from Italy is so great"?[9]

Despite the relative openness of the Russian archives in the 1990s, we still do not know what took place in Moscow between August 9 and 12. In the collection of sources with the promising title of "Before the Eyes of the Kremlin," there is a gaping hole between July 29 and August 21, 1944. In the selection, "Stalin and the Warsaw Uprising," we find no Soviet documents from the period August 8 through September 16.[10] And so we find ourselves in that state of knowledge where the more or less logical reasoning of the historian must replace information from sources.

In the summer of 1944, in Central Europe, the Red Army could hardly achieve anything—Operation "Bagration" was stuck at about the line of the Vistula. German resistance on the shortest distance to Berlin was considerable, the envisaged attack on Toruń and Łódź was untenable to a large extent. On the other hand, the great offensive in southeastern Europe, which was to begin on August 20, was prepared by the Soviets. This meant that strategic reinforcements and reserves went toward Romania; but it did not mean that a local attack on Warsaw—frontally from the east or out of the southern bridgehead of Baranów—was impossible; Rokossovskii and Zhukov had presented the relevant plans on August 8. Therefore, with regard to help for the Warsaw Uprising, political reasons may have been crucial for the decision-making process in Moscow. Stalin's behavior in the concluding talk with Mikołajczyk and his August 9 letters to the Allies suggested that he would provide help and at the same time hope for whatever kind of compromise that might work between the Polish prime minister and the PKWN. In light of impending events, the assumption seems thoroughly plausible that Stalin was playing for time and that all his good will was pure deception. Yet, this interpretation does not answer the question of why, on August 9, Stalin found this deception so important but did *not* three days later.

On August 9 two items appeared in *Isvestiia:* one, undated, was about a talk Stalin held with leading members of the PKWN; the other concerned the conversation with Mikołajczyk on August 3. Neither contained a word about the Uprising. On August 10 *Pravda* printed a TASS dispatch from London, which summarized a commentary of the Communist British *Daily Worker:* in "leading circles in London," one could get "no confirmation of recent communiqués about battles in Warsaw." "In the opinion of certain circles, stories of the fighting in Warsaw are a bluff," designed to put pressure on Moscow.[11] On August 13 the Soviet press published a TASS communiqué: it was not true that the rebels (or "Polish circles in London") were in contact with the Soviets or with those who had coordinated the moment of the Uprising—therefore, responsibility for events in Warsaw "falls exclusively on Polish emigrant circles in London." Among the Allies, such discussion was not usually done in public but might still be allowed as a correction—in fact, the communiqué was just as accurate as the simultaneous denial of contacts with the Vatican[12]—although the appeals to the Uprising, broadcast by the Soviets and the PKWN on July 29 and 30, were smoothly hushed up. Naturally, the symbolic significance of the communiqué was more important: there was no Soviet responsibility for the Uprising—it was up to the AK alone to cope with the situation.

Stalin provided complete clarity in his note to Churchill on August

16. He was convinced that the "Warsaw campaign" was "a foolish adventure" that "involved meaningless victims among the population." The Soviet high command now saw itself compelled to "cut itself off from the Warsaw adventure," and could "bear no direct or indirect responsibility for the Warsaw campaign."[13] This assessment sealed the fate of the Uprising. Only the Soviets could rescue Warsaw, but they had decided, between August 9 and 12 at the latest, that such an action was not in their interest—even though the AK was fighting the Germans, even though Warsaw was one of the most important traffic junctions of Central Europe. So, for reasons that can only be explained politically, the Soviets had decided to refuse help. This calculation was later to cost the Soviet Union something. For the rebels, the Warsaw population, and the city, the Moscow decision was not a question of cost—they were now about to lose everything.

Meanwhile, in London, the Poles tried every means to move Great Britain to put forth a greater effort. The British, who had never promised the support hoped for by the Poles, conveyed the requests to the Soviets and consulted internally about their own latitude of negotiation. Without knowing about the beginning of the Uprising, the board of the Chiefs of Staff informed the government-in-exile on August 2 that not a single one of the Polish wishes could be filled, neither could the Polish fighter planes be transferred to Warsaw (neither side knew that there were and would be no airports available anyway), nor would the Polish paratrooper brigade be dropped over Warsaw. The British also considered supply flights for Warsaw as too risky. In these and subsequent talks, the British constantly made it clear to their Polish interlocutors that they considered Warsaw within the Soviet area of operations.

At Polish urging, the commander of the air force in Italy, Marshall John Slessor, who was extremely skeptical from the first about the chances of flights to Warsaw, launched an experiment with fourteen planes (seven Polish and seven British) on the night of August 4–5. The result was exactly as he had feared—only four planes reached the drop, and five planes (all with British crews) were lost. The great distance, German interceptors against unprotected bombers loaded to the hilt, the short summer nights, and finally the difficulty of dropping precisely over the target at minimal height (300 meters / 984 feet)—all these made the extremely dangerous action a potential disaster, as Slessor reported to the Chiefs of Staff.

After Polish protests against suspending the flights, it was decided that Polish RAF crews could continue the drops. On August 8 and 9, seven planes flew out. No more flights took place until August 12 because of bad weather. By August 10 the British rescinded their decision not to let their own crews take part in the enterprise, and on August 12 they began talks with the Americans about using the American air fleet. Until the Americans decided, British, Poles, South Africans, Australians, and Canadians flew; of ninety-three planes in the period from August 12 to 17, seventeen planes did not return, three crashed on landing. From mid-August to the end of the month, no drop succeeded over Warsaw (a few reached the AK in the surrounding area). Altogether, of the 170 flights during August, twenty-nine planes and twenty-six crews were lost. On August 28 the Polish squadron in Italy had only three more planes in working order.[14] After the discouraging experiments of the second half of August and the catastrophe of September 1–2—when four out of seven Polish planes were lost—all flights to Warsaw were discontinued.[15]

It was no accident that, precisely on September 1, the fifth anniversary of the outbreak of the war, in Order no. 19, the Polish supreme commander, General Kazimierz Sosnkowski, accused the British allies of a lack of good will at the very least: "It has been five years since the day when Poland, encouraged by the British government and provided with its guarantee, entered into an isolated battle against the German power." Today, "the people of Warsaw are left to their own devices, abandoned on the front of the common fight against the Germans—a tragic and horrible riddle that we Poles cannot decipher on the background of the technical possibilities of the Allies at the beginning of the sixth year of the war. [. . .] If the population of the capital had to die under the rubble of their houses for lack of help, if they are to be delivered to the slaughter through passivity, indifference, or some other calculation—the conscience of the world will be burdened with a horrible, historically unprecedented sin."[16] Sosnkowski was by no means the only one who recalled the date of the outbreak of the war on that September 1. The governors of several American states declared September 1 a day of homage to Poland. In New York, Thomas Dewey ordered the city decorated with Polish flags (Poland—First to Fight); bishops and congressmen delivered fiery speeches. But Sosnkowski addressed the real problem: Poland, oldest member of the anti-Hitler coalition, had thus definitely lost World War II, while all other states of the Alliance could meanwhile be certain of victory.

Sosnkowski was the eternal procrastinator. He had said so many clever things before August 1, but as supreme commander he had not managed to give a single order to the AK that would have prevented the outbreak of the Uprising. Soon after, under British pressure, he had to go because some of the formulations of his Order no. 19 resembled anti-British propaganda from Berlin ("England—Your Work," said the caption of pictures of the ruins of Polish and Dutch cities in Nazi posters of 1940). Yet the problem remained: If the coalition was not put to a real test

by the Uprising, it was considerably strained. One of the Polish demands of London was the publication of a declaration of the combatant
status of the AK—a demand that, given German crimes against the
rebels, was not likely to be refused. The British, who feared this step as
a potential snub of Moscow (since August 2 the Red Army had the order
to disarm AK units), waited several weeks until, on August 29, they
issued such a declaration. In the British journalistic landscape, most
papers—from the conservative *Times* under the Russophile E. H. Carr
to the Communist papers—were against the Uprising; they gladly and
indiscriminately accepted Moscow's arguments of "irresponsible ad-
venturers" and "anti-Soviet provocation." Finally, it remained for the
outsiders of that time, Arthur Koestler and George Orwell, to write
against the mainstream. Both published polemics in the well-known
British liberal *Tribune* against the point of view friendly to the Soviet
Union. Koestler wrote of "one of the major infamies of this war," Orwell
reminded that "dishonesty and cowardice always have to be paid for."
The press guidance by Whitehall worked,[17] but despite that and despite
the preponderance of voices in Whitehall genuinely sympathetic to the
Soviet Union, it seemed to have reached its limit when Moscow clearly
refused the Americans a single contribution for the air support of the
Uprising.

Basically, the Allied staffs probably knew precisely from the beginning that only the massive use of the U.S. fleet during the day could help
the Uprising with a big batch of weapons, ammunition, and supplies.
The catastrophic loss of the night supply flights in August confirmed
this assumption. Yet, the solution of the problem was in Moscow: without Soviet permission to land, the massive use of American long-range
bombers threatened to lead to a debacle. That is, the American Air Force
had known for a long time that even the extremely strong B-17, the most
modern and biggest bomber of its time, suffered high losses without
fighter coverage in battle against German fighter planes. Because the
latest American fighter planes had a smaller range than the bombers, the
Americans sought Soviet landing places in campaigns east or south of
Germany so that after the bombing raid, they would not have to fly back
the whole distance but only a short section behind German lines.

By August 16 the Americans had presented the Soviets with a plan for
Operation Warsaw to use the landing places in the Ukraine that had been
used for months for similar campaigns. Operation Frantic had been in-
troduced on June 2, with an attack on a locomotive factory in Hungarian
Debecen. The Flying Fortress B-17s of the Eighth and Fifteenth Air
Squadrons then attacked several targets in southeastern Europe under
cover of Mustang P-51s, and landed at three Soviet airfields between
Kiev and Kharkov (permission for which the Americans had been

granted only in February 1944, after tedious negotiations). The distance between England, targets in east central or southeastern Europe, and the Ukraine filled the crucial prerequisite that the heavy bombers had to fly under cover of fighter planes all the time and had to cross German occupied territory only once. After refurbishment in the Ukrainian air-force bases, they attacked enemy industrial centers on the way back—primarily munitions factories and oil refineries in Hungary, Romania, and Poland. Losses were generally low. One exception was the result of Operation Frantic 2 on June 21, with targets in Germany and Poland: of the 163 B-17s, eighteen returned, three were lost, but fifty-three were destroyed in the Ukrainian airfields the next day by a surprise attack of the German air force. The Soviet air defense had failed completely.

Hesitantly, under pressure of the Polish leadership, the American military proposed Operation Warsaw as Frantic 6.[18] The issue was so important that it needed to be presented to Stalin in person. Ambassador Averell W. Harriman and General John R. Deane, chief of the American military mission in Moscow, went off to the Kremlin—and got a flat refusal. Years later, George Kennan, the Moscow Embassy counselor at that time, recalled: "I was personally not present at this fateful meeting with Stalin and Molotov; but I can recall the appearance of the ambassador and General Deane as they returned in the wee hours of the night, shattered by the experience. There was no doubt in any of our minds as to the implications of the position the Soviet leaders had taken. This was a gauntlet thrown down in a spirit of malicious glee, before the Western powers. What it was meant to imply was: 'We intend to have Poland, lock, stock, and barrel. We don't care a fig for those Polish underground fighters who have not accepted Communist authority. To us, they are no better than the Germans; and if they and the Germans slaughter each other off, so much the better. It is a matter of indifference to us what you Americans think of all this. You are going to have no part in determining the affairs of Poland from here on out, and it is time you realized this.'"[19]

Kennan personally was willing to draw the conclusions. In September 1944 he composed an impressive memorandum ("Russia after Seven Years") that anticipated the thinking of his *Long Telegram* of February 1946 in many respects. Essentially, it was a warning about Russia, whose participation in the anti-Hitler coalition had produced no change in its totalitarian character—quite against the ideal of the optimists in Washington and London. But the Kennan memo of September 1944 landed in the files of the State Department without having any effect: the time was not yet ripe in Washington for a change of thinking; the Warsaw slap was accepted in the name of the higher goals of the coalition. Thus, the next decision against the Warsaw Uprising was made.

8

German Counteroffensive and Battle for the Old City

I N THE NORTHERN PART of Wola is a block of four cemeteries: two big ones in the northern part (the Roman Catholic and Jewish ones), and two smaller ones in the south (the Evangelical and the Calvinist). After the heavy fighting on August 5, this was where one of the strongest Warsaw AK units, the combat group of Lieutenant Colonel Jan Mazurkiewicz ("Radosław") with more than one thousand soldiers, had withdrawn. This group consisted to a large extent of Kedyw units, the elite troops of the AK, who had been directly subordinate to headquarters until August 1 and had been used in attacks on especially dangerous or hated representatives of the occupation forces. The Radosław combat group had fought on the front lines since the beginning of the Uprising, was relatively well trained and equipped, and—at least before the massacre in Wola on August 5—its morale was good. Now for a week, they were to bear the main burden in defending against the German offensive.

On August 6 the German attack was concentrated on the two smaller cemeteries in the south. In a ten-hour battle, the attackers succeeded in occupying the Evangelical and Calvinist cemeteries, and AK headquarters was withdrawn from the nearby Kamler Factory in the Old City. Even during these battles, though, Radosław concentrated his reserves on the Jewish cemetery. This unexpected attack from the north surprised the Germans; within an hour they had to forfeit the Evangelical and Calvinist cemeteries, and the situation returned to the starting point. Despite air force support, the German combat group did not succeed in occupying the cemeteries on the next day either. In the next few days, there were violent battles, which took place in the cemeteries and the former area of the Ghetto, and both sides suffered great losses. Radosław held the cemeteries until August 10. In the fighting on the morning of August 11, the Miotła battalion once again succeeded in pushing the Germans out of the Stawki warehouse; but in these five hours, Miotła lost half of its manpower. The last of the two captured "Panther" tanks, which the rebels had been able to use, were also damaged. On the same day, German attacks from the south began on the Old City, which was under artillery fire and constantly bombarded from the air.

Despite the threatening encirclement, Mazurkiewicz had waited until the end for relief from a strong partisan unit from the Kampinos Forest north of Warsaw. But the partisans—sixteen hundred soldiers—decided not to attack the German troops at the cemetery; on August 11, when they finally moved from the northwest to the area of the Catholic Powązki Cemetery, they discovered that the rebels had already given up this position, and they turned around. In the following weeks, a few hundred chose the simpler way to northern Żoliborz.[1] This was the first in a series of breakdowns in coordinating events of the Uprising with attacks from the countryside around Warsaw. Not one single action ever came off. The German nightmare of a fight on two fronts did not materialize, apparently because the flow of communication between Warsaw headquarters and the partisans (usually through couriers, since there was no direct radio contact) never functioned properly. It seems that the lessons of Vilnius could also be applied to Warsaw.

The Radosław combat group was pushed out to the northeast by the Germans in fierce battles; in the last week, it had lost some 50 percent of its soldiers. To the south, the Reinefahrt combat group led by the Dirlewanger battalions had an essentially easier game. By the afternoon of August 6, the group had fought its way through from the southwest to the Brühl Palace and thus relieved Stahel, the trapped city commander. Part of the improvised AK unit that was set to defend this section fled, other frightened soldiers were released; only the newly arriving units put an end to the spreading panic. On August 7 the Reinefahrt combat group, which opened a connection from the Wolska to the Saxon Garden in the government quarter despite a strong counterattack from the AK, managed to hold it. Not only was the Radosław combat group endangered from the south as a result, but with Dirlewanger's success, which was accompanied by mass executions and other excesses of soldierly rabble-rousers, the area of the Uprising was split into three zones: the northern part of the Old City and Żoliborz (with the German wedge in the government quarter and the Krakowskie Przedmieście in between); south of that area the city center, where the German pressure had previously been essentially minimal; and even farther south the Mokotów section. Between August 5 and 11 Kamiński's RONA brigade forced the AK units in Ochota (southwest of the city center) to retreat; here the

"Goliath" minitanks, loaded with explosives and steered by remote control, were first used and apparently had a devastating effect on the defenders' morale.

Colonel Chruściel, as virtual commander in the area of Warsaw, established these three sections—north, center, and south. As commander of the first section, he appointed the forty-nine-year-old professional officer Lieutenant Colonel Karol Ziemski ("Wachnowski").[2] Along with units in the Old City, Żoliborz, the Kampinos Forest, and the Radosław group, the North Group had more than nine thousand soldiers. Ever since the beginning, Ziemski's contact with the Monter command and with Żoliborz was constantly cut off so that Wachnowski in fact guided the defense of the Old City on his own. Ever since August 7, the battles from the west approached the Old City center; there were air raids, several fire fights, and smaller attacks on the government quarter. The main burden of the fighting, however, was still borne by Radosław, whose combat group slowly withdrew to the Old City. In the meantime, barricades were built, improvised hospitals set up, and two drops from Allied planes on the night of August 12–13 brought weapons and ammunition. On the following night, the planes dropped all the supplies over the larger downtown area, which was not veiled in smoke and fire.

At the end of the first week of the Uprising, the Old City offered an almost peaceful picture—compared to the hell of Ochota and Wola: the shops were open, at first only bread was rationed, there were Polish flags, office signs, and nearly twenty newspapers. The 75,000 to 100,000 civilians—many of the refugees from Wola had found shelter in the few square kilometers—were clearly hopeful. But in the following days, life gradually shifted from the street to the cellar and, with the loss of electricity and water, the conditions of supplies and sanitation grew dramatically worse. The civilian administration of the Old City does not come off well in anyone's memory. Not only was everything lacking, something even the best administration could hardly have changed, but the defenseless people apparently got no care, consideration, or empathy—everything was given to the soldiers. According to a few reports, in the second half of August, the civilian population longed for the Red Army and considered the AK, especially its leadership, responsible for the catastrophe. In the final phase, the tension between civilians and soldiers threatened to turn into uncontrollable outbursts of hatred, especially since, to the end, the commander of the Old City, Colonel Ziemski, forbade defecting to the German side.

After August 5 the Germans also reorganized and reinforced their units. On that day, the staff of the Ninth Army often complained of intolerable conditions in Warsaw: supplies for the troops on the right side of the Vistula had to be transported along a sweeping curve running north of Warsaw through Modlin; the available means were inadequate to quash the Uprising. Therefore, the next big attack targeted the Old City and aimed to restore the communication lines across the railroad and Kierbedź Bridges, both of which lay undestroyed just outside the Old City. On August 13 the newly formed "von dem Bach Corps" numbered almost twenty-six thousand soldiers, twenty-six tanks, thirty-eight attack guns, several artillery units, one of them supplied with the biggest mortar of World War II (600mm, nicknamed "Karl"), and it received air support. From the west, the Reinefahrt combat group moved against the Old City with some eight thousand men; in the south, they were supported by five thousand soldiers under Stahel.[3] Outside the city, this superiority would have meant an immediate defeat of the rebels. In the Old City, with only a few square kilometers and more densely populated than any other quarter of Warsaw, the defeat was merely postponed. The Poles retreated from the barricades into buildings, from ground floors to cellars or back courtyards, to the next street or the nearby church. Battles disintegrated into countless small fights for individual targets that were often captured and lost again, always with serious losses among both combatants and civilians. No technical means was decisive: nine "Tiger" tanks did shoot up countless houses and barricades in the Old City but could hardly advance along the burning rows of houses without costly infantry protection. Large caliber mortars spread fear and death; decades later, many people still had the sound of these "cows" in their ears. But the mortars served more for terrorizing the civilian population than for real fighting.

Right before the beginning of the attack on the Old City, the IC of Ninth Army—the officer responsible for intelligence—warned of the clever tactics of the rebels. While they "systematically held the streets under fire" on the first days, "as soon as the Germans appeared, the enemy now let the attacking raiding party, flame throwers, and even tanks proceed to a certain place in order to annihilate them with well-aimed sniper fire. Soldiers and the wounded who returned from the action reported that the fatal losses had been caused almost only by shots in the head. [. . .] The firing ports [of the snipers] are half the size of bricks and most of them cannot be seen. Even at night, no jet of flame is to be seen and only a very weak bang is to be heard. The sniper probably pulls his weapon so far back from the port that the bang and jet of flame are contained in the room. The snipers shoot mostly from elevated positions, behind chimneys and attics, roofs and upper floors. Firing from cellars and lower floors was hardly observed. As before, the bandits will rarely be caught. If they fall into the hands of our soldiers, they immediately get killed and so no prisoners are available for interrogation."[4]

The big attack began on August 13 at 10 o'clock in the morning.[5]

From the start, the fight for the old city center was violent and bitter. The Poles suffered the greatest losses on the first day, not because of real fighting but rather due to chance. The Germans used a new technical innovation during the attack: a tank-like vehicle that carried a container laden with up to 500 kilograms of explosives and was used, among other things, to destroy barricades. On August 13 insurgents set one such vehicle on fire in front of the barricade; the driver fled before he could set the automated timer. After a few hours the insurgents took possession of the tank (apparently they did not know about its special construction) and drove it behind the barricade into the Old City. For unknown reasons, not until then did the explosives detonate amidst the cheering crowds.

Members of the high command apparently were not spared the depressing impression of the first day of fighting either. Bór-Komorowski, who had made a de facto transfer of his complete authority to Chruściel, the commander of Warsaw, had his order printed the next days in the rebel press (!), ordering the AK units outside Warsaw to a concentrated deployment and attack on the city. Bór-Komorowski's impotence, the failure of all plans for uprising, and the helplessness of the AK leadership could hardly have been documented more starkly.

Day after day the Germans attacked. Between the actions of infantry and tanks were mortar and artillery fire as well as air raids. Within a few days the Old City lost about a third of its structures; casualties among civilians were in the thousands. On August 17 fewer than five thousand AK soldiers defended an area of only 1,200 meters wide by 600–1,100 meters long (about three-fourths of a mile wide by about one-half mile long).[6] On the night of August 16–17, the attempted relief from Kampinos Forest failed. On August 18, von dem Bach offered the AK leadership a surrender; Chruściel refused after consultation with Bór-Komorowski.

With every day, the Old City became more of a hell where thousands of people sought safety, food, and their loved ones in vain. Of the 75,000–100,000 civilians who were originally confined in the Old City center, at least ten thousand were still in the area, which had already been occupied by the Germans, but a good 40,000 were still able to stay in the rebel area. The rebels fought in a frenzy, repelling several attacks every day, but gradually had to give up the ruins of the shot-up and bombed buildings. On the night of August 20–21, a relief attack from Żoliborz on the Gdańsk railroad station, less than one kilometer north of the Old City, failed. It was to have restored communication between the rebels in both parts of the city. The action was carried out mainly by AK units from the area around Warsaw, who had come through the Kampinos Forest to Żoliborz. The partisans, unfamiliar with the local area, felt uncertain in the city at night. They had no experience in street fighting and an apparently poor leadership made the action a complete fiasco. Seven hundred fifty well-armed AK soldiers were caught almost immediately in the barrage of the Schmidt combat group, and after a brief clash involving heavy losses, they retreated to their starting positions. Some 15 percent of the attackers were killed or wounded.

On August 21 the rebels numbered about two thousand wounded and dead (30 percent of the manpower of August 8), the territory defended by them had dwindled to one square kilometer. Munitions and grenades were lacking everywhere. Up to this point, all attempts by individual groups of civilians to force a surrender had been ignored by the military, but now it seemed as if only a spectacular success could avert the impending fall of the Old City. The chief of staff of the high command, General Pełczyński, personally took command of the second action against the Gdańsk railroad station. It was carried out on the night of August 21–22 by almost one thousand soldiers from Żoliborz and the Old City. But the Germans could not be surprised, and coordinating the attacking troops north and south of the railroad station turned out to be much too difficult. The battle lasted longer than on the previous night, but the losses were even greater: some four hundred dead, wounded, missing, and captured. We will never know if—with better preparation or under better leadership—the attack might have had any chance of success. In any case, once again it turned out that, in defense, the rebels were a hard nut to crack even for regular front line troops with tank and artillery support. But if they had gone on the attack in open terrain, without a similar support—which they could not get—they would have become simple cannon fodder, as on August 1.

The defeat of the second attack on the Gdansk railroad station has often been considered one of the crucial episodes of the entire Uprising. The extremely high losses and the psychological effects on both AK soldiers and civilians were the most important consequences. Another was that the Old City could be saved only by a miracle: without the restoration of communication with Żoliborz, it had to fall victim to the superior opponent in the foreseeable future. In the center and in Mokotów, the situation had previously looked anything but dramatic, since the Old City united almost all the active forces of the enemy. After the fall of the historical city center, this changed quickly.[7] On August 22 the AK high command decided to leave the Old City for the downtown area through the sewers, but they did not carry out this decision until the night of August 25–26. At the same time, a reinforced "silent" withdrawal of an unknown number of soldiers and civilians on the same path was registered in the city center. From today's perspective, it is truly amazing why all defenders and civilians did not join the secret exodus: in the Old City, dysentery spread (among other reasons, because the water in the few wells still in operation was increasingly polluted) and the sick and the wounded could hardly be helped. Anesthesia had run out by August 20, doctors were operating without narcotics, and since August 22, there was no more bread—even for the soldiers.

The German attack lasted with undiminished force, but the 9 (Army Supreme Command 9) kept complaining about the shortcomings of the fighting forces, made up primarily of police units and "foreign" reinforcements. In the "instructions" of August 21, the staff officers pointed out several errors that had resulted in the fact that "despite the support of several of the most modern weapons, our own successes after three weeks of fighting [are] only insignificant." "The many heavy support weapons—guns, mortars, attack guns, explosives, etc.—were used sporadically and did not have corresponding success. The effect of the heavy weapons is not exploited by an immediate advance," "our own troops mainly use the streets for action" and avoid both houses and allegedly "impassible" ruins of houses, where the rebels were often lurking, "the tanks are drawn into missions like knocking down barricades, etc., for which they are no match." The "instruction" challenged the attackers not only to develop a "more appropriate cunning" vis-à-vis the "maliciously underhanded enemy," but also to cope with their own problems through a ruthless deployment of the civilian population: "All able-bodied civilians are to be enlisted mercilessly, even under enemy bombardment for clearing work, etc. The mass of the civilian population directly or indirectly helped the bandits." General Stahel's detailed report two days later omitted the subject of the annihilation of the civilian population but otherwise went in the same vein: in the attack, one should "always slog away, not fiddle around," fight for houses and not push through the streets. It was a "fight against hundreds of small fortresses, a fight in three dimensions (from roof to cellar)," the attackers would be better advised if—like the rebels—"they avoided streets, used communications within the blocks of houses."[8]

Throughout the next week, the Old City was attacked from the air and from all directions. The Germans were reinforced with fifteen hundred men by the RONA brigade, but the defenders of the Old City by only a few units that came through the sewers from Żoliborz on August 25. Later, the possibilities of movement and communication were reduced to the sewers (toward the downtown center) and to the last radio transmitter (three of which had been destroyed in the meantime). After the reinforcements from Żoliborz had been integrated into the troops, the able-bodied fighting force consisted of some three thousand completely exhausted, increasing undernourished soldiers. Food consisted of a thin soup with groats, sometimes potatoes or noodles, and remaining stocks of dried turnips and potato flour. On August 25, a group of AK and an even bigger group of soldiers of the Communist AL and their families (some 100 people) went to the sewers without permission and illegally reached Żoliborz. In the night of August 27–28 another 300 soldiers of the AL took this route. Under these circumstances, illegal was naturally a relative term: those captured by the rebel police force argued that they had to give their totally exhausted soldiers a rest or that they wanted to get weapons and ammunition in Żoliborz, and the civilians pleaded for nothing more than a chance to survive. All or almost all of them had permits to enter the sewers.[9]

On August 26 the Germans set foot on the Kierbedź Bridge, and the rebels in the Old City could do nothing against it. On that and the next day, the mood among soldiers and civilians seem to have reached its nadir: in the landscape of ruins, there was a widespread fear of a repeat of the bloodbath of Wola. Starting at 8 A.M. the same day, Stukas flew nine missions against the Old City. Twenty houses were completely destroyed. One of the bombs hit a house on Freta Street, where the staff of the Communist AL was discussing the situation—only two officers survived. The leadership of the AK north section in the nearby Dominican church was luckier. Hit by six bombs, the nave collapsed; there were dead, wounded, and some buried alive, but the staff members survived. The attacks from all sides on August 26 brought the Germans an important victory: for the first time, with support from tanks and "Goliaths," they succeeded in penetrating the building of the government securities institution, which had been under fire for a week. This immense building, completed in 1929 of modern concrete technology on the northern edge of the Old City, was the pillar of the northern defense section. On the morning of August 26, just as a new attack began, one of the AK units left its position on its own, in order to escape the Old City through the sewers. The flight and the ensuing panic were checked, but until evening, the rebels with their last reserves (the lightly wounded now stayed in the battle line) were able to win back only a part of the Old City. Every inch was fought for. In the ruins of the cathedral in the southern section of the front, rebels and Germans fought with flame-throwers and grenades; here too, the defenders could no longer force the attackers to retreat.

Despite this success, a crisis was felt on the German side. That evening, von dem Bach reported to the commander of the Ninth Army that he could hardly advance with the exhausted and decimated troops now available (losses thus far of ninety-one officers and 3,770 noncommissioned officers and men; 150 a day in the fight for the Old City alone). He feared that the Uprising would get relief from the interior at any moment. Fresh soldiers might filter into the city through the allegedly "widespread sewer system and passageways" and help the Uprising or at least the theoretically sealed-off Old City to survive. Von dem Bach concluded that he needed "a fighting unit of division strength that was well-coordinated (not patched up), both in leadership and troops" in order to end the fighting. General Nicolaus von Vormann, the commander of the Ninth Army, added nothing to the report and sent it on to the Middle Army-Group.[10]

"Horrible stink," an officer of the AK staff noted on August 26; "graves on every lawn and they increase from one hour to the next." In the Old City, there were now seven thousand wounded (including an estimated 70 percent of civilians), who virtually could no longer be helped. Hunger and thirst were now joined by stark fear. Civilians, but also representatives of the authorities, soldiers, and officers, kept making louder demands for the evacuation of the Old City, especially since the rumor had meanwhile circulated that the high command had left the burning rubble through the sewers on August 26 and had moved into the downtown area.[11] The conflicts between the rebel military police, which had a particularly strict regiment in the Old City, and the others confined there, reached their first climax. Nevertheless, Wachnowski consistently carried out the order to defend the quarter "to the last." First, he completely forbade evacuation through the sewers; on August 27 he relaxed the ban to allow persons with proper permits into the sewer entrances. Wachnowski was now under increasing pressure from the civilians—only a few thought that the fight in and for the ruins of the Old City still made sense.

On the morning of August 28 a new attack forced the remnants of the rebels out of the ruins of the securities building. Wounded and prisoners were shot immediately by the Germans as so often happened in the Old City battles. The ruins of the cathedral were also definitely lost. Now the German units in the south (the cathedral) and north (the securities building) were only seven hundred meters apart. Between them were still some 2,000 AK soldiers and an estimated 35,000 civilians, who prayed in cellars and ruins for their survival or tried in vain to get to the sewers; the military police shot into the air, there were tussles, curses, and threats. In the violent fights of the next two days, the distance between the attacking German troops became even shorter, and the situation of the last remnants of the rebels clearly became hopeless.

At 6 P.M. on August 30 the Wachnowski commanders received the order to be on alert for an armed breakthrough that night. The plan was for a simultaneous offensive of the AK from the city center, which was to facilitate the breakthrough by an attack toward the Old City. In fact, the Center units did attack as planned, for it was not known that the Old City sections had to postpone the beginning of the attack—sometimes for hours. The short time was not enough to regroup the dead-tired units; at least not for the thousands of civilians who were in the way of this operation and who waited in the streets of the Old City for an end to the fighting or for a chance to leave the ruins. Quite against the intentions of the planners, a series of individual fights broke out at night in the ruins occupied by the Germans between the Old City and the downtown area. What was left of the elite Radosław unit, which waited in vain until 3:30 A.M. for the agreed-on signal, were the last to attack and suffered great losses in this assault. In one of the surprising fire fights within the ruins, three officers of the Brody battalion fell, along with the entire group of flame throwers. Many who had miraculously survived the fight for the cemeteries and the hell of the Old City met their death in the battles at dawn. At 4:30 A.M., as it began to grow light, Radosław broke off the hopeless attack—only two assault groups of his unit had managed to break through.

Fortunately for the rebels, the Germans had not noticed that, between midnight and morning, the AK positions in the Old City were virtually unoccupied. Now the rebels returned to the defense positions, albeit hesitantly and thoroughly discouraged. In the battle at night, their losses were some one hundred fifty dead and wounded, and discipline had noticeably deteriorated. The next day, August 31, the situation was even worse: the German ground troops did attack hesitantly—they had also suffered big losses in the last days and in the battle at night—but the constant bombardments produced catastrophic consequences on what little territory of the Old City remained: in one single house, three hundred soldiers were allegedly buried alive. Once again, there was turmoil at the entrances to the sewers as a few units tried to force their right of way with weapons. Finally, Monter gave the green light to give up the Old City as well. Late in the evening of August 31, he allowed the retreat of the armed troops through the sewers to the city center. The wounded who could not be transported and the remaining civilian population were supposed to wait for the occupation of the quarter by the enemy. Wachnowski and his staff drew up a plan of retreat that provided for the transport of at least some of the wounded to the Center.

On September 1, 1944, exactly five years after the German assault on Poland, German troops commanded by Reinefahrt launched the last attack on the Old City. In all probability Reinefahrt understood that he had given up the chance of a nearly uncontested victory twenty-four hours earlier, but his troops were as decimated as the AK. After the RONA brigade had withdrawn because they were unable to fight—its commander Kamiński had meanwhile been shot by his German bosses because of several accusations—there were hardly more than five thousand soldiers available. After the week-long massacre between the royal castle and the securities building, in which nearly half of the attacking troops had been killed or wounded, the morale of the German units could no longer have been very high. The big attack on September 1 proceeded accordingly. Despite massive air force support, by 4 P.M. none of the German actions had succeeded. The rebels shot their last rounds of ammunition, consumed their last reserves—and miraculously held the positions they had kept that morning, by and large. In the afternoon, the fighting died down.

At 8 P.M. the evacuation of the Old City began. Two sewers were available: the main sewer, two meters (six and a half feet) high, was just two kilometers (a little more than a mile) long at the section between the Old City and the city center. The sewage was knee deep. The parallel supplementary sewer was somewhat shorter but was considered much harder to get through because it was impossible to stand upright, and the stink was even worse. If nothing got in the way, a unit could pass through the sewer in three or four hours and come out at a drain in the northern part of Nowy-Świat Street (at the corner of Warecka). Those to be evacuated were divided at the entrance into marching columns of about fifty people each. They were led by city sanitation workers and couriers, who were familiar with the sewers. Some eight hundred soldiers chose the way north to Żoliborz. Fifteen hundred able-bodied rebels and another three thousand persons, including the wounded who could be transported, went south and arrived in the city center the next morning.

After an artillery barrage that lasted several hours, the Germans occupied the ruins of the Old City the next day. Only a massive crowd of civilians made it clear to them that the AK had given up the quarter. The next mass murder began: hundreds of wounded were shot and burned (including 430 people in a single hospital on Długa Street). Some of the wounded survived because German prisoners in the same hospital opposed the massacre. Before the evacuation, the rebels had collected some one hundred German prisoners in the cellar of the Old Archive and had left them behind. Now the German communiqué about the occupation of the Old City announced the liberation of these prisoners as well as the "capture" of some 35,000 civilians who had been taken to concentration camps or shipped off to the Reich for forced labor. Not mentioned were the 25,000–30,000 civilians and 5,000 AK soldiers for whom the Old City ruins had become a grave.

9

In the Shadow of the Old City
Center, Mokotów, and Żoliborz in August

B Y AUGUST 4, the downtown area or city center was largely in the hands of the rebels. The Germans occupied the eastern part of Jerozolimskie Avenue (the most important east–west thorough-fare) up to the National Museum, and therefore they split the Center into two parts (south and north); the Poles, however, controlled the western part of Jerozolimskie Avenue, thus stopping the east–west traffic of the enemy. Within the city center, there were isolated islands of German resistance. The most important was the telephone company (PAST) sky-scraper and the telephone central exchange on Pius Street. On August 5, the day of the massacres in Wola and Ochota, the Germans tried at sev-eral points to break through the emerging defense line of the AK in the Center. Several times they drove civilians, mainly women, in front of the attacking tanks and infantry. None of the attacks succeeded, Jerozolim-skie Avenue remained blocked, and nests of resistance of police and Wehrmacht within the Center were still isolated.

In the following days when the German attack was concentrated on Ochota, the path to the government quarter, and the cemeteries in Wola, the Center experienced a period of relative calm. The production of weapons (mainly hand grenades), provisioning the civilian population, and the organization of a fire department ensued; on August 8, the rebel radio transmitter Blyskawica ("Lightning") began operation, and the Scouts established an Uprising post office that functioned at least within the Center. Chruściel limited military activities to defending and liquidat-ing individual nests of resistance in the Center, urged the construction of an efficient communication system, and wanted to launch offensive

107

actions only after a radical improvement of the supply of munitions. A few fights on Jerozolimskie Avenue, along the bank of the Vistula (where, among other things, the municipal electric company was located, which was in the hands of the AK), and in the western outskirts of the Center brought few changes. The intensity of these fights, in which both sides had a lot of room to maneuver and thus enough possibilities to escape, hardly seemed comparable to the grim determination of the battle of the Old City that started at the same time.

On August 10 the AK started a few local attacks, including some on Jerozolimskie Avenue. It was somewhat easier now for the couriers, because now the mail was pulled with a cord over the dangerous streets under German bombardment. After the withdrawal of the last rebel troops from Ochota on August 11, however, the RONA brigade attacked from the southwest. On the night of August 13–14, the AK units were caught in a German barrage in an attack toward the Old City, and on August 13, the first attempt to occupy the university campus also failed. Between August 12 and 14 the rebels received considerable support from Allied air drops: forty-seven containers with machine guns, MPs, and antitank guns, some of which were captured in skirmishes with the enemy. Moreover, two functioning German armored cars were also captured.

Yet, by and large—compared to the situation in the Old City— things remained relatively calm in the Center. For incomprehensible reasons, the rebels did not take advantage of this situation to come to the aid of the Old City; even after August 13 there would still have been chances to do that. Instead, Colonel Chruściel prepared for a decisive attack on the police quarter in northern Mokotów: According to the extremely optimistic assessments of Monter, a concentrated deployment of the forces of the fighting group "south" in Mokotów (which was to be reinforced by units from outside Warsaw) was sufficient to capture the fortified quarter south of the Center. However, coordinating the troops turned out to be difficult, particularly concentrating and transporting the units out of the forests south of Warsaw. Ultimately, the big attack did not take place.

On August 14 the Germans turned off the city water supply. Wells were built. Lines in courtyards quickly became commonplace in the city. On August 15 tanks attacked in the western part of the Center, apparently to make the suspected rescue of the Old City impossible. The attack ended after several hours with a complete fiasco; seven tanks were supposedly destroyed or damaged, over one hundred Germans fell, and a few dozen were captured. The use of heavy mortars, which began on August 15, initially had no effect on the stalemate in the battle for the Center. Two days later, on August 17, however, the Germans scored an important success: in the west, they succeeded in driving the AK out of the Haberbusch brewery and a food warehouse. The rebels lost huge supplies of grain, flour, groats, and sugar. On August 19 the fighting group Rohr achieved its biggest success to date: after several hours of fighting, supported by tanks and "Goliaths," it occupied the spacious complex of the Technical University in the southwestern part of the Center. AK losses were minimal; the rebels gave up the important buildings because they could not control the fire that had broken out inside the college when a "Goliath" exploded.

On the other hand, compared with von dem Bach's troops, the AK generally was not technically inferior. The attack on the second most important German island in the Center, the eight-story PAST building, began on the day the Technical University was lost. Here the Poles had all the advantages normally found on the German side in the Warsaw Uprising: they were in the majority, and they could assemble their troops calmly and determine the timing of the attack. (Of the 164 German soldiers and officers, eighteen had previously fallen, including five suicides.) Since August 13 the PAST building had been completely shut up, and attempts at relief no longer got through. If we can believe a journal of one of the defenders published later in the rebel press, hunger had prevailed in the PAST building since August 14, and the mood of the defenders was hardly certain of victory.[1] The carefully prepared attack began on August 20 at three in the morning with the explosion of several mines. Then the building was systematically set on fire. By 5 P.M. the last of the defenders surrendered. The rebels took 115 prisoners, six Germans were wounded, twenty-five fell in battle. Polish losses amounted to five dead and ten severely wounded. In psychological terms, the capture of the PAST building was perhaps *the* success of the Uprising; the occupation of the prominent skyscraper with a nominally large German staff and the red and white flag over the building was often cited in the future as proof of the military success of the AK in the "battle for Warsaw."

The fight for the Technical University continued on August 20 and 21. The Polish counterattack was successful at first, since the still burning ruins had not yet been occupied by the Germans. Ultimately, however, the remnants of the building remained in the hands of the Rohr Combat Group. On August 22, at 4:15 A.M., the AK attacked the second nest of German resistance in the Center, the telephone exchange on Pius Street. Despite the use of mines, grenades, and flamethrowers, the fight lasted almost twenty-four hours. Of 112 defenders, twenty-one fell, seventy-six were taken prisoner, and the rest fought through to the German lines. As soon as this fighting was over, at dawn on August 23, the AK attacked the police headquarters in Krakowskie Przedmieście

Street. At noon German resistance collapsed: thirty were dead and eighty were taken prisoner. The rebels also suffered significant losses. In the same battle, the rebels occupied the Holy Cross Church not far from the university, which was also on fire. But with that, the chain of AK successes in the Center was broken: the attack on the nearby university complex in the Krakowskie Przedmieście—from whose garden the Germans kept part of the Vistula quarter under a barrage—failed, and both sides suffered severe losses. The AK had concentrated four hundred soldiers here (only a fourth of them armed); despite support by two armored cars, they had no chance at the well-fortified university campus against the crushing superior force of the police contingent.[2] Again, rebel coordination failed. Some of the units waited in vain for the signal to attack, while others already had to withdraw under German fire.

The successes of August 20–23 did not lead to a decisive change in the situation. In the following days, both sides limited themselves to local operations in the Center. Colonel Chruściel had over half of all soldiers (an estimated 23,000 of 47,000 in the whole city, most of them still unarmed) in the city center; yet for a long time he was not aware of how critical the situation in the Old City had become in the meantime. German artillery barrages and air raids, which increased at the end of August, could not excuse the passivity of the well-supplied and experienced units of the Center. On the night of August 30–31, when they finally started toward the Old City for the relief attack, it was too late. The unsuccessful attack was called off at four in the morning, after 100 dead and 150 wounded were left behind in German fire.[3] It was the biggest defeat of the AK in this part of the city since August 1. However, it was to be much more important for the future that the relatively comfortable situation of the Center in August had not earlier prompted an attempt to relieve the Old City. After the forty-five hundred rebels from the Old City had arrived on the night of September 1–2, a new day was soon to begin here, too.

The situation in Mokotów developed differently. After the serious defeats of the AK in the first days, about seventeen hundred rebels—with new volunteers and members of dispersed units joining their ranks every day—occupied the core of the quarter (Górny Mokotów) south of the police quarter. East, toward the Vistula (Dolny Mokotów), the sparsely built area was partly in the hands of the AK and partly in the hands of the German police. The road south to the Kabaty Forest remained open to a large extent. Here, too, buildings gradually became sparse, and the road passed through gardens, fields, isolated settlements, houses, and villages. This offered nearly ideal conditions for the replenishment and reinforcement of the rebels by partisan units, which could freely penetrate the Kabaty Forest and force their way from there to Mokotów—but south of Warsaw, against all the Uprising plans, hardly any units were prepared. Thus they could hardly take advantage of the additional stroke of good luck that south of Warsaw were units of the Hungarian Fifth Infantry division, who had officially refused to fight against the Uprising and unofficially generally shut both eyes to the AK.[4] The planned assault of the AK units from the district of Radom-Kielce (more than five thousand soldiers), who were still some eighty kilometers south of Warsaw on August 25, failed to materialize. Given the strength of the German troops between them and Warsaw, the partisans decided to pull back.

In the weeks after August 5, what took place in Mokotów were mainly mass shootings of civilians by the police as well as several isolated skirmishes. As in the Center, neither side dared launch a big offensive: the Germans deployed their main forces against the Old City and kept only some two thousand men in and around Mokotów for defense. After the debacle of early August, the rebels did not risk any attack on the fortified buildings. The AK, whose core was formed by the well-supplied and relatively battle-experienced Baszta regiment under Colonel Stanisław Kamiński ("Daniel"), reorganized; the units were dressed in overalls from captured Luftwaffe supplies, and food was no problem in such a spacious area with so many fruit and vegetable gardens.

Between August 18 and 22 the rebels captured several quarters in Dolny Mokotów as well as south of Mokotów, altogether some nine square kilometers. The attack on the palace and the park in Wilanów at the southern end of the city failed, but nevertheless several hundred AK partisans came out of the Kabaty Forest to Mokotów. On August 22 Lieutenant Colonel Józef Rokicki, a fifty-year-old professional officer, took command of the "South" section. After assimilating the reinforcements from the Kabaty Forest and volunteers, he now had three thousand soldiers available (about 10 percent of whom were women), who were scattered over a wide area in the south, consisting largely of gardens, fields, and meadows. On the nights of August 26–27 and 27–28, the rebels risked a major attack along the flat terrain between the Vistula and Mokotów going toward the Center. However, they could not break the German resistance in the barracks around Łazienki Park. Contact with the Center was still broken.

On August 29 the German offensive against Mokotów began. The Rohr fighting group attacked several sectors but concentrated the offensive on the southern pillar of the defense of Mokotów, the settlement of Sadyba, some 1.5 kilometers from Dolny Mokotów. The fighting lasted a few days and ended after severe losses of the AK with a precipitate retreat from Sadyba, which led to a massacre. Between Sadyba and the rebel-occupied Dolny Mokotów lay those same fields and meadows; Sadyba was left defenseless to the bombardment of the pursuers: "It was a nightmare," one of the couriers remembered. "No cover in the area. We ran, we crawled, and kicked bodies out of the way. Everything was full of corpses, and the Germans sawed up the ground with bullets and rockets. Then we came to the [AK positions on] Chełmska Street. They [the rebels on Chełmska Street] didn't want to believe us: 'You're the ones from Sadyba?'"[5] On that day alone, the rebels in Sadyba lost some two hundred soldiers. After the occupation of the settlement, the wounded, prisoners, and civilians were shot en masse; the road to Górny and Dolny Mokotów was now open for the Rohr combat group.

The situation in Żoliborz in August developed like that in Mokotów. The Germans left the rebels alone to a large extent. The rebels profited from the open communication with Kampinos Forest in the north, whence big and small partisan units kept infiltrating; the Twelfth Hungarian Infantry Division, which guarded this sector, was as friendly to the Poles as the Fifth Division in the south. Nevertheless, the AK in Żoliborz barely used their relatively favorable situation to come to the aid of the Old City. After the failure of the attack on the Gdańsk railroad station on August 21 and 22, this opportunity was definitely missed. In the next week, several units withdrew from the Old City to Żoliborz through the sewers, including a big group of the Communist AL with three hundred men, most of them during the big evacuation of September 1 and 2. On August 30 the Hungarians were relieved by the RONA brigade, and thus contact with the Kampinos Forest became much harder—literally cut off. The AK now entrenched in Żoliborz waited passively for the enemy attack and, until mid-September, remained on the periphery of the Uprising.

At the end of August the status of the rebels also changed under international law. Under the massive pressure of the government-in-exile, London and Washington decided on August 29, that is, not until four weeks after the outbreak of the Uprising, to recognize the AK as part of the regular Polish armed forces. The British and American declaration warned the Germans against further shootings and abuses of Polish soldiers.[6]

The normative impact of the Allied statements is hard to estimate. Up until the end of September captured rebels were shot, but the likelihood of surviving seemed to be much higher even in the second half of August than on the first days. On September 7, von dem Bach and the AOK 9 received orders from the Führer's headquarters to treat members of the AK as combatants in surrender negotiation, namely, as members of regular troops. The German negotiators followed this order both during the failed negotiations in September as well as in formulating the surrender document of October 2, which guaranteed the "soldiers of the Home Army all the rights of the Geneva Convention of July 27, 1929, concerning the treatment of prisoners-of-war."[7]

On the other side, captured members of the Wehrmacht were transferred to prison camps; attempts at lynching them, which occasionally happened, were prevented by AK escorts. Members of the SS, the police, and the "Eastern Troops," on the other hand, were usually shot after a short trial; several Volksdeutschen must have suffered a similar fate. The number of captured Wehrmacht soldiers and interned civilians (Reichsdeutsche and Volksdeutsche, Ukrainians, suspect Poles) may have amounted to two thousand persons altogether.[8] The German prisoners suffered the biggest losses in the "Hollywood" Cinema in the city center on September 16, when the building collapsed after an air raid. Of the 211 imprisoned Germans, 104 died there, along with some of the guards, the camp commander, and his deputy. In the city center alone, over 300 prisoners were turned over to the German troops after the surrender.

10

September

Struggle for Surrender

A FTER THE FALL of the Old City, the surviving rebels saw another world: "The first, strong impression: the houses are standing. At first glance, you don't see damages and local losses. The street's still a street. . . . The second impression: the people aren't crawling around, but are simply walking erect. They don't feel that something can fall on their head any minute. The third impression: the passers-by are dressed normally and are clean. They comb their hair and bathe. . . . People aren't living in cellars, but quite simply in flats. . . . The difference is produced from two facts: first, the intensity of the danger per space and time unit here is incomparably less; second, there is not this horrible crowding. . . . There [in the Old City], in many cellars, it wasn't only that people couldn't lie down, but that they couldn't even sit and stand in the crowd. . . . The final emotional exhaustion in the Old City came from both the excessive danger and the excessive density. It also resulted from the ever clearer feeling of being in an untenable position. The peace and power of the human groups was even more conspicuous in the Center, especially in the area of passages through internal courtyards and cellars. Clear signposts, light in the corners, polite explanations [. . .]."[1]

On September 2 Bór-Komorowski radioed London that, despite the defeat in the Old City, he had decided "to defend Warsaw to the limit of possibility. We have food until September 7, bread until September 5, nearly exhausted ammunition. [. . .] The spirit of the soldiers is good, the population is suffering from a lack of food, water, housing, clothing, and bad health. [. . .] The possibility of holding out does not depend only on our stamina, but rather on help from you or from the speed of the Soviet success on our sector."[2]

Since September 2 the Center had been under a reinforced artillery barrage, of 380mm and 600mm mortars. The air force also joined the bombardment. In the afternoon, strong units of the AK attacked the university campus with two armored cars. The attack failed, and the rebels' last two armored cars were nearly lost because the retreating AK troops had run out of ammunition. On September 4 the Germans launched an attack on the area between the university and the bank of the Vistula (Powiśle). The Center was now under a strong artillery barrage, and several local skirmishes made it impossible for the AK to come to the aid of the troops on the Vistula. In the center of the downtown area, a series of large fires broke out for the first time; one of the buildings that fell victim to the flames was the highest building in Warsaw, the sixteen-story Prudential Building.

Von dem Bach was now in a hurry. The Poles were fighting "like heroes," he confided to his diary. The likelihood of the Soviet attack on Praga was growing and the German attack was proceeding only slowly.[3] Therefore, the next operation was concentrated on the west bank of the Vistula. The strong push to Powiśle (the Germans attacked along the Vistula from north and south) soon yielded results: on September 6 the rebels withdrew from this area and thus from the electric company as well. They had suffered great losses and had hardly any ammunition left. Thousands of civilians streamed into the Center with the AK. They arrived in a burning part of the city that looked nothing like the relatively civilized image of a week before. The next day, the leadership of the underground government radioed to the government-in-exile in London: "Catastrophic deterioration of our territorial assets, lack of food, water and light, extreme exhaustion of the population and no immediate efficient aid put the question of giving up further fighting for Warsaw on the agenda. Awaiting immediate answer."[4] Von dem Bach proposed a truce so that at least some of the civilians could leave the city. The Red Cross managed to make General Rohr agree to a two-hour truce in the western sector of the front line, while the civilians were allowed to leave the rebel area. On September 8, between noon and 2 P.M., some six thousand civilians took advantage of this opportunity.

Meanwhile, the artillery barrage and the attacks of air and ground forces went on. With every day, the grimness of the fighting and the conditions of life in the Center became more like the inferno of the Old City. The decimated AK units suffered increasingly under a shortage of munitions; everyone, both soldiers and civilians, suffered from lack of food. By September 6 Bór and the government delegate had warned the government-in-exile that, in view of the rapidly increasing pressure of the Germans and the great losses among the civilians, the likelihood of a surrender within a few days had increased sharply: "Of course, after the fall of Warsaw, power in the whole country will fall into the hands of the Communists. Their [the Allies] immediate aid by bombings and supply could improve the mood and delay the crisis somewhat."[5] London answered on September 8 that the chances of a massive operation of the allied air forces were zero at the moment, the Third Reich would not surrender in the near future, and that the leadership in Warsaw was authorized to make decisions, which the government-in-exile would cover with regard to foreign countries in any case.[6] Thus, the Warsaw AK leadership and the government delegate received a de facto authority for surrender negotiations.

On September 9 Jankowski radioed to London: "After almost six weeks of sporadic fighting, Warsaw has fallen. From the Gdańsk railroad station to Jerozolimskie Avenue—a landscape of ruins and rubble. Without hope for aid, we have to give up. The situation in the Center has grown worse. The stamina of the soldiers is at the limits of human possibilities. Hopeless situation. We keep losing ground, are pressed into increasingly smaller islands." Without immediate aid from the air— bombardments and drops—Warsaw had to surrender. London was supposed to inform by evening if the big Allied expedition to Warsaw would take place the next day.[7] On the same day, Bór-Komorowski prepared a letter to Rohr announcing the willingness of the Uprising to surrender.

The letter remained in the drawer. On September 9 the rebels saw Soviet fighter planes over the city for the first time. The Soviet air force, which, for five weeks, had had the opportunity to force the dozen obsolete Ju-87s out of the sky over Warsaw and thus wreck the greatest German advantage—the constant control of the air—scared off the Stukas simply by appearing. From now on, the Stukas risked operations only when there were no Soviet fighter planes around. The next night, Bór-Komorowski received a statement from Monter. The commander of the Warsaw AK troop was definitely against a surrender: the situation in the Center was not hopeless, surrender on the other hand was possible only in the most extreme case, since "no one trusts the Germans. People want to die with weapons in their hand, in battle, not after being disarmed. The general conviction prevails that, after laying down their arms, the rebels will be exterminated." They had to contact the commander of the Polish troops on the side of the Red Army, General Żymierski, and "promise him loyal cooperation. [. . .] Everyone who helps us deserves gratitude, the rest will somehow ensue. [. . .] We prefer cooperation with Żymierski to surrendering. In the history of the Polish army, these are only fragments."[8]

Presumably, Monter's hope was not exclusively his that day. Increased artillery fire was heard from Praga; in spite of everything, the military situation in the Center did not yet look as dramatic as in the Old

City ten days earlier; Mokotów and Żoliborz remained intact to a large extent. At this point, the staff of the AK also hesitated: Rohr had really accepted the original Polish conditions of surrender (rights of combatants for the troops, acknowledgment of the civilian authorities) and had announced the continued evacuation of civilians from the city after the surrender. London now promised a massive bombing raid in the next hours. At the same time, the appearance of Soviet airplanes over Warsaw and their success against the German air force created a new atmosphere—despite German victories in individual street and house fights on September 10. And on that very day, when Bór-Komoroski was delaying the negotiations with the demand for additional German guarantees,[9] the Soviet-Polish attack on Praga began. It had an immediate impact on the course of the battles in the Center: on September 11 the German attack lost its impetus; the next day the rebels even launched a counterattack here and there. The surrender negotiations, now intentionally delayed by the Polish negotiators, still dragged out on both days. The last letter from Bór, which reached the Germans at noon on September 11, once again indicated the rebels' lack of trust of the guarantees from the other side for the combat status of the AK, and made the enemy responsible for terminating discussions. Therefore, the negotiations came to a halt.

At the beginning of September, the German defense line around Warsaw was still twelve to eighteen kilometers (seven-and-a-half to eleven miles) east of the Vistula. Within a few days, the attack of the Soviet Forty-seventh Army, supported by the Eighth Tank Corps and the First Polish Infantry Division, burst through the three German defense rings. Despite a hard counterdefense, the Wehrmacht had to start withdrawing from the eastern part of Warsaw on the night of September 13–14. The First Polish Division had lost almost eighteen hundred soldiers in the attack; Soviet losses amounted to some six thousand. On September 14 the attackers stood on the east bank of the Vistula, separated by only a few hundred meters of water from the burning downtown area. North of Praga, the attack of the Seventieth Soviet Army developed more slowly but was insignificant in any event: the local offensives of the Forty-seventh and the Seventieth Armies served to straighten the front. Meanwhile, south of Warsaw, the Germans had withdrawn to the west bank everywhere, except for the big bridgehead east and northeast of Warsaw. Apparently, Soviet headquarters was not thinking of a major flank attack. But with the local success in driving the Germans out of Praga, the question of Moscow's relation to the Uprising assumed a new and urgent current dimension. Since September 14 Soviet and Polish units had watched the catastrophe on the west bank not only figuratively but literally. It is easy to imagine that, after the weeks of passivity of the Red Army outside Warsaw, the morale of the Polish troops on the side of the Russian soldiers was not friendly to the Soviets.[10]

Moscow, which probably knew of the surrender negotiations between Komorowski and Rohr, and had lost a lot of foreign political trust in the last six weeks by refusing to allow Allied bombers to land, changed its position on September 9. The operation of Soviet planes—which had made many drops for the rebels since September 13—over Warsaw that day was the first indicator; the attack on Praga the second one. In the meantime, back on September 10, Stalin gave in on another question that had caused the most bad blood among the British and Americans: he released Soviet landing spaces for American support flights to Warsaw. Yet, Operation Frantic was not set into place until September 18. The Polish Communist troops' salvation operation for the Uprising, which would have been impossible without Moscow's agreement, was already under way at this time.

Only now—after the liberation of Praga—did the AK succeed in establishing direct radio contact between the rebels and the Red Army. The rebels had tried several times since August 1 to open this vital line of communication. At first, they fell for the hoax of a certain Captain Konstanty Kalugin, who passed himself off as a Soviet reconnaissance officer and sent a dispatch with a demand for drops on Warsaw to Stalin personally (!) over the AK radio contact. In mid-August, an AL attempt to establish direct contact through couriers who crossed the Vistula failed.[11] On September 11 Komorowski tried with a dispatch sent through London to Moscow, then transmitted to the commander of the First Belarusian Front, Rokossowskii. The commander of the AK offered the Soviet marshal wholehearted support in the case of an announced Soviet attack, and asked for artillery and air support. On September 10 and 11, couriers of the AL and another organization subordinate to the AK dared to go through the front line. A few of these operations succeeded, so that from September 14 on, the Red Army and the First Polish Army had a relatively current picture of the Uprising. In the next two weeks, radio contact between both banks of the Vistula functioned but only after a fashion;[12] compared with previous weeks, when no possibilities of communication existed at all between the AK and the Red Army, this was a certain progress. Measured by the needs of the rebel troops, it was insufficient.

Even during the battles for Praga, the Polish units on the side of the Red Army were regrouped. The decimated First Division was relieved by other units of the First Army under General Zygmunt Berling, who had hastily retreated from the southern bridgehead in Magnuszew. On September 14 some of these troops were already in Praga, others were in the eastern suburbs of Warsaw. Supposedly without consulting with his Soviet superiors, Berling ordered the attack over the Vistula for the night of September 15–16.[13] After the long march of the last days, his troops were exhausted. They had virtually no front-line experience; the Second and Third Divisions had none at all; and, aside from Praga, the just withdrawn First Division had fought in the line only in the battle in Lenino back in November 1943. All three divisions did have experienced Soviet officers in their ranks, but the manpower came predominantly from the recruiting campaign of the last months and had fought—if at all—only in September 1939 or as partisans. The main task was assigned to the Third Division under Soviet General Stanisław Galicki, which was now to come to the aid of Radosław in Czerniaków. Along the axis of the central Poniatowski Bridge (destroyed on September 13), the First Polish Cavalry Brigade was supposed to cross the Vistula; the units of the Second Infantry Division were supposed to cross the river farther north, toward Żoliborz. Several artillery batteries were to provide suitable fire cover.

In Czerniaków, meanwhile, the situation had escalated dramatically. That part of the city was cut off from its southern neighbor, Mokotów. After the fall of Sadyba on August 29, there was a phase of relative calm in Mokotów. On September 15, however, the Rohr combat group attacked in full force. After heavy fighting the combat group forced the AK in the southern part of Mokotów to withdraw that day. The unit that defended this part of the city numbered 189 soldiers after the withdrawal; since September 10, 178 had fallen or were badly wounded (including sixteen officers). However, the way for a German attack on Czerniaków along the Vistula was now open from the south; if it succeeded, the rebels in the center would be cut off from the riverbank. North of Czerniaków, Powiśle had been attacked by the Reinefahrt combat group from the north (from the Poniatowski Bridge) and the west (from the Parliament Building) since September 11. On September 12 German troops drove the AK out of the streets east of the center; thus Powiśle was separated from the downtown area. The attack continued on September 13, and on that day, as mentioned above, the Germans blew up the Poniatowski and railroad bridges, later in the evening the Kierbedź bridge, and then concentrated their fire on the few battle-ready AK troops in Powiśle, who held the southern center area open for the Soviet and Polish troops from Praga. On September 15 Radosław, whose command was in Powiśle, assembled his last five hundred soldiers in the streets of Czerniaków directly on the Vistula; the front zone was now only about a half-kilometer long and no farther than this from the Vistula. The same day, an initial patrol of the First Army arrived at the positions of the AK. Of fifteen soldiers sent, only five arrived in the company of a wounded officer. In the attempt to make contact with the reconnoitering troop under German fire, five rebels fell, including the legendary "Morro"—twenty-one-year-old first lieutenant Andrzej Romocki, who was later commemorated as a symbolic figure for the "lost generation" of war and uprising in the most famous novel of the Uprising.[14]

On the night of September 15–16, the Radosław combat group defended its front along the bank of the Vistula. The first wave of the Third Division reached the battle positions relatively intact. The second was decimated by violent German fire; the Soviet smoke mortars had covered the few hundred meters of water where the boats were to cross the river so that the Germans knew precisely where the operation was taking place. Altogether, only 420 well-armed soldiers of the Third Division were counted in Czerniaków on the morning of September 16. The undertaking was to be repeated the next night with more means and troops; the transport of tanks and antitank weapons on the west bank was also planned. The deputy Soviet supreme commander, Marshall Georgy Zhukov, was to have approved the plan and, in case of a successful first phase of attack by the Poles, was to have considered support from Soviet ground troops.[15]

In the course of September 16, the Poles waited in vain for the promised big pontoons to transport their heavy weapons. The next night, the Third Division conveyed some 450 soldiers of the Ninth Infantry Regiment with the means that were in increasingly short supply. The losses in this operation amounted to some 10 percent; only light 45mm guns, grenade throwers, and antitank weapons could be brought to Czerniaków. During the day, the Radosław group and the units of the Ninth Regiment under chief of staff Major Stanisław Łatyszonek repelled heavy attacks by the Germans, who were trying to liquidate the bridgehead with everything they had before it got too bad. The Poles were now supported by heavy artillery fire from Praga, and they now had air superiority. Nevertheless, they suffered serious losses in the first two days, particularly the Ninth Infantry Regiment. Not only did the soldiers lack front-line experience, but they were totally unprepared for the specific conditions of a battle in the ruins of a big city. The battles looked increasingly like the final days of the Old City; the lightly wounded were no longer withdrawn from the line; every house became a battlefield. Civilians, especially men, were shot en masse by the advancing German troops.

On the night of September 17–18, only small conveying operations succeeded. The next night, and on September 19 (this time the operation was not interrupted and continued during the day with heavy losses), success seemed greater: in total, almost nine hundred men with six 45mm rifles, mortars, and flamethrowers came to the rebel area. But the heavy artillery was stuck on the sandbanks; they didn't even try to convey the tanks. Some of the soldiers of the Third Division landed north of Czerniaków at the top of the Poniatowski Bridge and were soon surrounded by the German counterattack: twelve hundred meters from the rebel positions in the center, who knew nothing about the landing of the units of the Third Division, six hundred meters from the combat group in Czerniaków, which now could only be in a defensive position, and so the two battalions of the Third Division were annihilated within two days. Units of the Second Division, which had landed in the north at the altitude of Żoliborz, were wrecked in the coming days in the German defense, waited in vain for the relief attack of the rebels, and in view of the hopeless situation, crossed the Vistula toward Praga on the night of September 22–23.[16]

Yet, before the badly prepared Vistula crossing turned out to be a military fiasco, Warsaw experienced a day of great hope. On September 18, when the defeat on the riverbank was still yet to happen, the long-desired American air force appeared over the city. After Moscow had withdrawn its objection to landing American bombers at Soviet airports, it still took a week until the residents of Warsaw saw the powerful squadron of more than a hundred B-17 bombers. The American demonstration of might seems to have left an overwhelming impression among both civilians and soldiers: all reports of this day talk of general enthusiasm, with laughing and applauding people. Aside from this psychological aspect, the American shuttle-bombing principle was worthwhile, even in view of their own losses: of the 110 bombers that took off, three turned around and only four planes and eleven airmen were lost. More problematic was the extent of the aid for the AK. Of the 1,284 dropped containers, only 228 got into the hands of the rebels; most fell into the parts of the city occupied by the Germans.[17] Along with Soviet artillery fire, the deployment of Soviet planes over Warsaw, and the land operation of the First Army on the nights of September 15–19, Operation Frantic 7 created the long awaited psychological prerequisite to continue the Uprising. On September 19, General Nicolaus von Vormann, commander of the Ninth Army, gave an alarming report: "[. . .] the fighting strength of the forces deployed in Warsaw, after a loss of 9,000 dead and wounded since August 1, 1944, is now exhausted. The soldiers capable of street fighting are bled dry" and most of the available troops in Warsaw were suitable "only for protecting the city quarters and outlying districts still in the hands of the enemy. [. . .] They cannot be made into a combat group that can also be deployed if necessary to defend the Vistula [. . .]."[18]

The trepidation of the AOK 9 would have been thoroughly justified if the Soviets had in fact started the major crossing of the Vistula. Since the beginning of the Uprising, the Ninth Army had lost almost thirty-seven thousand men (a fourth of them in Warsaw), had gotten replacements of only ten thousand men, and could not have withstood a concentrated attack of the Red Army. But because Moscow was not thinking of rescuing the Uprising, the weakness of the Ninth Army did not matter. Neither the limited Soviet activities, nor the Polish-Communist operations, nor the American enterprise changed the essential hopelessness of the rebels' situation. On September 18 the situation of the AK was certainly better than on September 9, but holding out for a long time—not to mention a military victory—was out of the question. Żoliborz, which had been left in peace to a large extent in August, had been fighting since September 10. Since September 14 the thousand or so rebels, who still controlled part of the west bank of the Vistula, found themselves under the increased pressure of the Twenty-fifth Tank Division and a unit of the "Vlassov Army." On the very first day of the attack, there was a withdrawal of the AK units, who were to defend a two-kilometer-long front without heavy weapons against a superior enemy; now new mass murders of civilians and the wounded were recorded. The Soviets dropped weapons and ammunition and deployed their antiaircraft against the German Stukas, which were again hitting the rebels. On September 15 and 16, the AK in Żoliborz defended itself more successfully than on the first day, even though the attackers deployed several tanks: once again, the crushing material predominance of the Germans did not matter. After three days the rebels had 120 dead and 200 wounded, the Germans 110 dead and 240 wounded. On September 17 the Twenty-fifth Tank Division stopped its attack[19] and soon withdrew from Warsaw. The next day, von dem Bach proposed a truce to the AK troops in Żoliborz to evacuate the civilian population. The local AK staff replied with the offer that the Germans lay down their weapons: "I can assure you," read the memo of September 18, "that all soldiers of the Wehrmacht will be treated according to the international Geneva Convention and will not be murdered, as the Germans do." As an appendix to the memo, photos of bodies of women and children murdered in Żoliborz on September 14 went to von dem Bach.

In the early morning hours of September 19, a battalion of the Sixth Infantry Regiment of the First Polish Army crossed the Vistula and landed, as mentioned above, on the west bank, in Żoliborz. The rebels were barely one kilometer away but knew nothing of the deployment. In the next hours, the soldiers of the Sixth Regiment fought in isolation for their lives. They did get support from the east bank, but only on September 20 did the commander of the AK in Żoliborz, Colonel Mieczysław Niedzielski ("Żywiciel"), learn that a few hundred meters from his positions, the units of the First Army were bled dry. The attack of the AK on September 21 was not a success because the battalion of the Sixth

Regiment knew nothing of the deployment attempt. On September 22 the Germans launched a counterattack and decimated the soldiers of the First Army, who were entrenched on the bank of the Vistula. In the four days between September 19 and 22, 248 of them fell. Thirteen healthy soldiers and 137 wounded were rescued on the night of the September 22–23 on the east bank. The AK in Żoliborz was now hopelessly closed in again.

Meanwhile, things looked even worse in Czerniaków. After heavy German attacks on September 18, only a third of the soldiers of the First Battalion of the Ninth Regiment, whose commander had fallen, were fit for battle. On the 19th, the rebels and the Ninth Regiment suffered more heavy losses, but did not give up most of their positions. Soviet and Polish artillery fire along with Soviet air raids brought the German attack to a standstill in the afternoon. However, given the crushing superiority, in the late evening Radosław decided to retreat through the sewers to Mokotów. On the 20th, the 200 soldiers arrived there; half of them, like Radosław himself, were wounded. Another 160 AK soldiers and the remains of the Ninth Regiment still held the last houses in Czerniaków. In that day's report, the German Ninth Army numbered 300 prisoners from the Third Polish Division; the next day after more bitter fighting, 130 prisoners, and 470 on September 22. Both the AK and the remnants of the Ninth Regiment were at the end of their strength, and the resistance in Czerniaków collapsed. On the morning of September 22, a one-hour truce proposed by the Germans was accepted. Civilians rescued some of the wounded from the inferno of three thousand square meters.

At exactly 9 A.M., after the expiration of the truce, the fighting started again. The rebels waited all day for a signal from the other bank of the Vistula so they could begin crossing the river, under cover of the smoke and artillery, as agreed. The operation began in the evening and became a total disaster. Some of the pontoons sent from Praga were destroyed on the way by German artillery barrages, and some on the way back. Panic broke out. A group of four under Captain Ryszard Bielous "Jerzy" managed a cinematic breakthrough to the center, where they arrived in the morning. Others tried to swim to Praga, and several of them drowned or were shot. A group of eight managed a two-day hike over the Poniatowski Bridge whose skeleton now lay in the Vistula. Most met their fate in the ruins. On September 23 at 6 A.M., a clergyman waving a white cloth went to the German positions. In the ruins the Germans found thirty-five corpses and took eighty-five soldiers of the Ninth Regiment and fifty-seven AK soldiers prisoner. An unknown number of AK soldiers and civilians, including many women, were shot.

After the surrender of the last house in Solec on September 23, the death throes of the Uprising began. The Germans now controlled the

whole west bank; the worn-out units of the First Army in Praga had neither the means nor the opportunity to come to the aid of the Uprising.
Even on September 23, the German Ninth Army still assumed the opposite and feared a new attack from the east; but in reality, the isolated
centers of uprising in Mokotów, the entire downtown area, and Żoliborz
could now be liquidated one by one without any obstacles. The AK had
lost any ability to maneuver; given their own weakness, offensive action
was now out of the question. The commander in Żoliborz (now the
Eighth Infantry Division), Colonel Mieczysław Niedzielski "Żywiciel,"
had only radio contact with Monter, and had lost all contact with the
units that were theoretically subordinate to him in the nearby Kampinos
forest. The commander in Mokotów (Tenth Infantry Division), Lieutenant Colonel Rokicki, had telephone contact with the downtown area
and could send couriers through the sewers. The AK was now better
supplied, but on September 20 there was hardly any hope of success
anywhere.

After a reinforcement by the remnants of the units from Czerniaków,
who had come through the sewers, the rebels in Mokotów numbered
about 2,750 soldiers. The German attack began on September 24. The
hardest fighting developed in the south; with heavy losses on both sides,
the Germans advanced relatively fast. Two days later, given the "catastrophic morale of the troops"—and against Monter's express order—
Rokicki decided to start the withdrawal through the sewers to the downtown center. On this day, the remnants of the Tenth Division showed
clear signs of a willingness to surrender; as in Radosław's troop, too,
which, after almost two months of fighting in Wola, the Old City, and
Solec, barely included any of the soldiers who had joined on August 1.
The mood among the civilian population could not have been worse:
within a two-hour truce at noon, about nine thousand civilians left
the burning quarter; in Mokotów the AK still defended an area of only
a few square kilometers. At 8 P.M. the evacuation began through the
sewers toward downtown. In the early evening, some eight hundred
wounded, soldiers, civilian authorities, and the division staff left
Mokotów. "While traversing the second kilometer of the sewer system
[. . .] one saw ghosts of people in the most varied poses, standing and
kneeling, sitting, half-lying, crawling in sewer mud. Some were no
longer alive, in others a human spirit throbbed, but the whole made an
eerie impression, looked like a madhouse."[20]

The march through the stinking, wet, dark sewer has been commemorated in Andrzej Wajda's legendary film *Kanał* (1957). Contemporaries—civilians and fighters—felt that the scenes representing nights
in the sewer between Mokotów and the downtown vicinity were a cred-
ible reconstruction;[21] people fainted and drowned, wounded people fell

off the stretchers. A few groups strayed into the secondary sewers and tried to find their way back to the main one, there were human traffic jams at the crossings, the imposed silence was broken, which, in the early morning hours, attracted the attention of the Germans in the streets above. They poured carbide and kerosene into the sewer entrances and ignited it. Thus far, only literature and film have succeeded in describing this inferno; the historian can hardly add anything. Late at night, there was another traffic jam and people could hardly move. Not until five in the morning did it ease up; the last 150, mainly wounded soldiers, still made it out.

After his arrival in the center, the commander Rokicki was arrested and interrogated. Apparently he was able to prove that the situation in Mokotów was hopeless, for the charge of desertion was dropped. Rokicki was supposed to return to Mokotów, but on September 27 this order became irrelevant. That morning, chaos broke out among the last defenders of Mokotów. Some of the units refused to return to the fighting and tried to go down to the sewers: "After forty-eight hours of covering the withdrawal of the staff, the unit received the order to return to position. The first lieutenant refused the order. Insubordination. Revolt. They're going to fight through to Bałuckiego Street. At the secondary manhole, the crowd of soldiers grew. A mess. We wait. 10 o'clock: Germans attack. Shoot at the crowd at the manhole. . . . A mess. Some throw off their uniforms and hide in apartments, others try to get into the sewer. Groups stand in battle formation. Shoot. The German attack becomes stronger, they're already across Racławicka Street. On a balcony, a white flag rises, even though shooting comes from this house. Someone shouts 'Madman, don't let the civilians go to the dogs, shoot a bullet into your own head!' Another 'Don't surrender. Fight to the end!' Another white flag in the window. Self-justice. The Germans are now in the Szustra Palace. For a long time, Captain Janusz has held out on Dolna Street. It ends up with some shooting others."[22]

At ten in the morning the resistance in the southern zone collapsed, at noon Mokotów surrendered: the Germans took two thousand soldiers and five thousand civilians prisoner. Unlike Czerniaków four days earlier, in only one place was there a mass murder of captured AK soldiers. Civilians and the wounded were brought first to the racetrack and later to the camp in Pruszków.

The German attack on Żoliborz also started on September 24 but was initially broken off. The Eighth AK Division numbered 2,500 soldiers, 1,500 of whom were armed. The Germans assembled a few battalions of the Nineteenth Tank Division with battle experience (over 2,600 soldiers), which were reinforced with 5,000 men from various other units. On the morning of September 29, they attacked in several places after heavy artillery barrages with tank support. The bitter fighting lasted through the next day. The Eighth Division received the news from the First Polish Army in Praga that, at 11 A.M., pontoons would be provided so the rebels could cross to the right bank of the Vistula under artillery and air cover. As a result, the rebels tried to break through to the bank of the Vistula, but during the attack on the German positions, news came that the time for the crossing had been postponed until 7 P.M. At 5 P.M., the Germans called off their fire and a Polish delegation was allowed to go through to the center to conduct the surrender of Żoliborz; the Eighth AK Division surrendered at 6 P.M. Ten minutes later, the news came from Praga that the breakthrough of the rebels to the bank of the Vistula was expected at 7:30—an operation the Germans knew about for obscure reasons. By midnight, the Eighth Division had given up their weapons; a few dozen soldiers (including a few Jews who had fought in their own unit) made their way to Praga or behind the German positions under cover of night. Sixty officers and 1,300 soldiers, 130 women, and 400 wounded were taken prisoner in Żoliborz.

Even more dramatic was the fate of those AK units in the Kampinos forest, on which so many hopes were placed in the early weeks of August. The front between Żoliborz and Kampinos was occupied by Hungarian troops, who kept demonstrating their sympathy for the Uprising and behaving neutrally whenever possible; but until August 22, despite comparatively favorable conditions, this troop managed to provide neither relief nor direct aid for the Uprising. All of the following month, with small exceptions, the troop spent fighting RONA and German troops—quite successfully, but without any influence on events in the city. For the time being, it numbered almost 2,400 well-armed soldiers. On September 27 the Germans began operation "Shooting Star" against the AK in Kampinos. The small forest area offered little cover, and the rebels were very soon pushed to the south into a more or less open terrain. In the decisive battle on September 29 southwest of Warsaw, the Polish commander fell, 150 of his men were killed, 120 wounded, and 150 taken prisoner. Most probably managed to flee to the surrounding villages, and only a few hundred fought through the German blockade southward as united groups.

In late September, the center was threatened less by fighting than by starvation. Supplies had held out longer than was estimated at the beginning of the month, but after September 20, the lack of food became an acute and insoluble problem—at least for the civilian population. On the 27th, von dem Bach tried once again to enter negotiations with Komorowski. The Polish commander hesitated but sent two negotiators who were to arrange the modalities of a truce and the evacuation of the civilians from the ruins of Warsaw. On the 28th, the highest-ranking AK officers prepared the German surrender and evacuation offer with the delegate. In the discussion, which is described in the next chapter, only Chruściel energetically advocated continued fighting and opposed moving civilians because that would ruin the morale of the troops. The delegate urged evacuation and surrender because further losses would drain the "biological substance of the nation." Bór-Komorowski chose the middle road: immediate negotiations for a truce and departure of the civilian population, and additional conditions for surrender, which were to delay this final act.

The truce was set for October 1 and 2, between 5:30 A.M. and 6:30 A.M. On Sunday, October 1, people could hold their heads up again, suddenly there was food again—now, apparently the last supplies really were brought out—and here and there, goods were sold or exchanged.

At the same time, in Ożarów, a suburb west of Warsaw, von dem Bach was negotiating the terms of surrender. Von dem Bach had no interest in continuing the fighting. He did have to clarify a few points of negotiation with Hitler's adjutant, SS Gruppenführer Hermann Fegelein; the Poles did haggle "over every word [. . .] they wanted to come off as honorably as possible." Yet, after twelve hours, the result was that, at least on paper, the AK was offered decent conditions. The Germans acknowledged the rights of combatants not only of the AK but also of the Communist units fighting in the Uprising; the civilian authorities were granted impunity for their activities during the Uprising. Only on the long-planned "evacuation" of Warsaw—which created the prerequisite for the destruction of the rest of the city—did the German negotiators hold firm, but with the euphemistic codicil: "The evacuation of the civilian population from Warsaw ordered by the German leadership is to be carried out at a time and in such a way that the population is spared avoidable hardships."[23]

Von dem Bach tempted the Polish negotiators not just with concessions with regard to the announcement of the surrender; even during the Uprising, he had staged gestures that were to prove his respect for Poland and its national symbols.[24] Now, during the surrender negotiations, he emphasized the Polish roots of his family, often praised the courage of the rebels, and presented the need for possible German-Polish cooperation against the Soviets. The AK leadership was not taken in by these enticements. Komorowski, who had just been ostentatiously appointed supreme commander of the entire Polish armed forces by the government-in-exile, turned down an invitation to von dem Bach's villa; later, he consistently avoided German attempts to recruit him in a joint anti-Communist front.

After the surrender was signed on the evening of October 2, the great exodus from Warsaw began on October 3. Those members of the

Warsaw AK corps who could walk left Warsaw in closed ranks on October 4 and 5, and were taken captive. In the center, the Germans counted almost 12,000 prisoners; along with those who were taken prisoner in the other parts of the city, over 15,000 rebels, including more than 900 officers, were taken prisoner in the last days of the revolt. The almost 5,000 wounded were evacuated from the hospitals a few days later.

The symbolic imprisonment of the Polish supreme commander by a German officer was recorded in several photos. The Germans still cherished the hope of integrating the AK into the anti-Soviet front—an illusion that was soon to be shattered. Some of the hard core of the Warsaw organization of the AK had indeed escaped imprisonment and in the next months began to rebuild the conspiratorial network under the leadership of General Okulicki. It was natural for that network to mutate into an anti-Soviet underground in the foreseeable future; but cooperation with the Third Reich was consistently avoided by the underground.

11

The Civilian Population

T HE PEOPLE OF WARSAW keep recurring in the preceding chapters: as victims, spectators, a living backdrop, refugees, and as one of several reference points for military decisions. This chapter attempts to focus on the group of several hundred thousand people as subject and object. The difficulties of such an attempt are enormous. Let us begin with the fact that there were very different groups and classes within the city whose mood and situation were determined by place of residence and personal suffering, but also by prosperity or poverty, and not the least by belonging to a social milieu. The owner of a villa with a vegetable garden in Żoliborz, where there were no big battles until mid-September, viewed a completely different uprising than the one experienced by a refugee from Wola, who had lost family members right at the beginning and had since marched through Warsaw as a nomad, dependent on insufficient social help, persecuted by bombardments and artillery barrages, often packed into cellars with strangers for weeks. On the other hand, the fate of the refugees and those who were bombed out was completely different, depending on whether they had friends or family in the part of the city where they fled to, and depending on the fate of those possible helpers and their actual willingness to help. During the Uprising, the number of homeless and needy grew in proportion to the destruction of the city and the intensity of the fighting. In the end, in all probability, only a small percentage still lived in their own homes, where for weeks there had generally been no electricity or water.

Right after the problem of the existential inequality of conditions of life, we come up against the problem of sources. The battles are documented in countless reports by both sides; the living conditions of the population is only in the Polish sources. These sources are varied—from diaries and memoirs that reconstruct hundreds of individual fates, through the Uprising press and reports of attitudes, especially of the Biuro Informacji i Propagandy (BIP; Office for Information and Propaganda) of the AK, to documents of the military police, the civilian administration, and the social welfare institutions. The latter especially show the material circumstances of life; the reports of the BIP reflect mainly the political mood; while the military police was naturally concerned with conflict, crime, and maintaining discipline. All in all, there is a wealth of sources, but the quantity varies from one part of the city to another (the largest stock is from the downtown center; the smallest from Wola and Ochota, where the Uprising lasted five and eleven days respectively), and in places they can be compared only with difficulty—among other things because of the different interests of the authors. Joanna K. M. Hanson, the author of the most important treatment of our subject, emphasizes in several places of her book the incompleteness of our knowledge, which is complemented by individual reports, but in all probability will long remain fragmentary.[1]

Let us begin with the numbers. We do not know how many Warsaw residents lived in the quarters where the Uprising was to take place on August 1, but the number may have been far less than one million and far more than 500,000. As a result, the most convincing estimate is that, at the end of July, there were some 200,000 people in Praga and some 720,000 in left-bank Warsaw.[2] The most densely populated area was the downtown area with Powiśle (18 square kilometers with about 550,000 people before the war; after the annihilation of the Jews, this number may have been at least a third less), the most thinly populated areas were Mokotów and Żoliborz. The movements of these masses of people in the weeks during the Uprising are known only according to trends; more precise data are usually lacking. After August 5 some 100,000 persons fled from Wola and Ochota, mostly to the Old City and the downtown center; 50,000 to 60,000 left the Old City through the German lines by the end of the fighting there on September 2. At the end of August at least 5,000 people left the Old City for Żoliborz and its center; in the first days of September a few thousand people went from Powiśle to the western area. On September 4 the AK estimated the number of civilians at 260,000; of those, 20,000 to 30,000 left the area of the Uprising between September 8 and 10, and went behind the German positions. On the last days of the Uprising more than 150,000 people may have been housed in the center. After the surrender, the Ninth Army counted 216,000 Warsaw residents who had to leave the city; other data and estimates are 260,000 to 280,000. About 200,000 people had fallen in battle and died, including 15,000 soldiers.

The living conditions for the initial 700,000 Warsaw residents were quite different. They depended, however, not only on the assumptions mentioned above, but to a large extent, on the efficiency of the Uprising administration that began operations in every part of the city—with varying degrees of success. Many complaints were conveyed from Mokotów that the administration had virtually no influence on the life of the population there; from the Old City, that it had failed despite many attempts, under the extremely difficult conditions. In the center, where the civilian administration had the best possibilities of development, the AK initially organized an antiaircraft defense, the building of fortifications, lines of communications, and the like. After more than a week, an administration for the district of Warsaw subordinate to the government delegate came to light, whose first headquarters was in the municipal building. It was based on the former city administration, the Rada Główna Opiekuńcza (High Committee for Social Welfare, RGO; a social welfare institution working legally under the German occupation), and the Polish Red Cross. At the lowest level, in the individual houses and residential areas, the antiaircraft defense initially played an important role: it had been organized in 1939 and reactivated in 1941, before the German assault on the Soviet Union.[3] The civilian administration was supported by several police services that had emerged in the "underground state," yet in part also harked back to the officials of the "Polish police" of the GG (who, on the other hand, had often served in the government police before 1939). Moreover, the image of Warsaw in the Uprising is inconceivable without the scouts, who helped the administration in communication, recording and post offices, welfare and fire departments. Local initiatives at the residential level were integrated within these structures, which were at times exposed to brand new tasks and working conditions during the war. These volunteers and specialists of the initiatives maintained, for example, water and electricity supplies for as long as possible. Food, transportation, accommodations, and nursing were some of the most important branches of the administration, which sometimes acted under different names in different parts of the city.

The level of social organization under the extreme conditions of Warsaw during the Uprising was also uneven and thus dependent on objective facts as well as on individual energy and creativity. On the one hand, the expectations with which defenseless people reacted to the endangering of their lives emerged everywhere: "The administration," "those on top" would take care of security, at least for a socially compatible assessment of the dangers and burdens. On the other hand, it is hardly conceivable that people who had amassed food supplies would now enthusiastically hand these over to the administration. All attempts to make private property—even in the form of intact housing—available to the community, that is, the administration, seemed to come up against stalling and resistance. When there was doubt about a happy outcome of the Uprising, misery increased, social solidarity within the civilian population declined, and tension between civilians and soldiers intensified. Requisitioning by the troops and the various police forces certainly did not enhance the popularity of the Uprising leadership. The announcement of a work conscription for men issued on August 18 in the center triggered little enthusiasm and could hardly be implemented in the following weeks.

Communication between administration and civilians took place through several channels. One means was orders and bans conveyed orally through house and block committees to the residents. Another consisted of duplicating announcements that were posted on walls. There was even a gazette that may have reached the fewest persons affected; and finally, local radio stations, which addressed the population over radio receivers—at least those that had not been handed in, defying the orders of the occupation forces—loudspeakers, and loudspeaker patrols. The press also published instructions and recommendations. During the Uprising, some 130 titles covering all political trends appeared, from the central organ of the BIP, *Biuletyn Informacyjny,* with a circulation of 25,000–28,000 copies, through the socialist *Robotnik* (circulation 5,000–10,000) and the *Rzeczposolita* (circulation 5,000–10,000) to the local stenciled papers, of which only a few copies are extant. The distribution of these papers, which were usually read by more than a few people—often read aloud in a group—varied quite a bit, and was best in the downtown area. How much the civilians believed the Uprising press and followed the instructions of the administration is another story.

On the other hand, for locating people, the mail service was important. The scouts, whose older cohorts continued in the underground between 1940 and 1944, had organized it in the first weeks from the city center. At first, a letter reached the addressee in the city center on the same day. Mail was also delivered to Żoliborz, Mokotów, and the Old City. In August, the Uprising mail service shipped over 116,000 letters, 3,000 to 6,000 a day; in September letters were forwarded only within the center; in the last weeks, this system also collapsed.

The mood of the witnesses and victims of the fighting was very capricious. The attitude of the population can be said to have been shaped directly and persistently by the course of events of the Uprising; undoubtedly, the mood was best from August 1 to August 5. After the massacre in Wola and the German counterattack, it quickly reverted to an amalgam of mixed feelings: people hoped for the Russians, more in August than in September; they hoped for Allied support; and they feared a German mass shooting and expulsion. Trust in the military strength of the AK differed from quarter to quarter and from day to day, depending on the course of fighting in that area. At least according to the reports of the BIP, an increase of pro-Soviet, sometimes also pro-Communist sympathies seemed to be quite widespread and was often linked with the harshest criticism of their own leadership. In the week after September 9, when Soviet planes appeared over Warsaw, the Red Army moved to the east bank of the Vistula, and units of the First Army landed on the west bank, many residents of the city seemed to believe in the impending deliverance from the nightmare of the past weeks. If the Russians had in fact successfully carried out the major attack, Warsaw would probably have been the first Polish city to greet them with overwhelming celebration, at least by the civilian population. At the end of August, the twenty-two-year-old Józef Szczepański "Ziutek," a noncommissioned officer in the almost completely annihilated elite unit Parasol and author of two popular Uprising songs, wrote a poem in the Old City, which is still considered the best summary of the ambivalent feeling of the fighters and civilians of Warsaw toward the Red Army—titled "The Red Plague."[4]

Widespread opinions about their own leadership were also extremely ambivalent. The crisis of trust began to escalate in late August in the Old City, when several civilians wanted to persuade the military leadership to surrender and preferred defecting to the German side to staying in the bombed ruins. The crisis continued in the center, where the sight of the evacuees from the Old City was obviously shocking and was intensified by the German attack at the same time. The AK's willingness to surrender just before the Soviet attack on Praga seems to be closely linked with this outbreak of despair, accusation, and discouragement among the more than 250,000 civilians. After the shot of optimism injected first by the Russians and then by the big American airdrop on September 18, the mood soon reverted to the old ways; yet, until the end of the Uprising, it seems to have been only sporadically as bad as in late August in the Old City and early September in the center.

As of mid-August, the Uprising was constantly plagued by illnesses—dysentery and typhus. On August 14 the Germans occupied the urban waterworks on Filtrowa Street, cutting off the central water supply. Aside from small local establishments, the inhabitants of Warsaw were now dependent mainly on several dozen homemade wells (forty-two were dug in August alone), which soon became the central life-giving supply. As the water supply decreased, the danger of disease increased. But despite many alarms, at no time did the feared mass epidemic break out; the source of disease apparently could still be kept under control. How this was possible we do not know, for there was virtually no medical care either for soldiers or for civilians. Despite great efforts, doctors and nurses could barely help the wounded, given the lack of drugs and beds, and later, electricity, gas, and water. The report of the Franciscan Stefania Śmietanka, who worked as a trained nurse in the operation block, is from the hospital at Marszałkowska 79:

> There was a corner where the bodies were discarded, sometimes a lot of them. I often slept behind these bodies. The patients lay two in a bed, on the floor, on covers, on a mattress, or on a blanket. [. . .] The wounded were in various conditions. If it was a shot in the stomach, it wasn't operated on, because we didn't have the right conditions for that. Head wounds were generally not treated either. We did leg and arm amputations and applied plaster casts. Memories of operations are unforgettable. What was the sterilization of surgical instruments like? We had two clay pots (flowerpots), a lot of ammonia (disinfectant), some water. I poured water into the pot, some ammonia, and then put in the instruments. After a while, I took out the instruments. And those were disinfected instruments. Then, we washed our hands and operated. After the operation, the blood-smeared instruments were put in the same pot. I had a second pot with ammonia where I did the instruments. There were no infections.[5]

Tens of thousands were wounded during the Uprising, everyone—or almost everyone—suffered from hunger. In the first days, this could not be predicted, because the AK had captured several large warehouses that included clothing, cigarettes, and food. Nevertheless, from the beginning there was rationing, and in the first two days, German food coupons were still valid. The shops soon closed, barter replaced money; in other cases, prices for food reached astronomical heights. From mid-August on, considerable problems emerged, particularly in the Old City. In Mokotów, with its many garden plots, the food supply was relatively good up until the end. In Żoliborz, which was also considered a "green" quarter, it was worse, especially in September. In the Old City and the downtown area, however, hunger and lack of water were considered one of the main reasons for giving up the quarter or surrendering. In the center, where most of the civilians lived, the supplies of community soup kitchens ran out by mid-September, but coffee and sugar remained. On September 18 the public soup kitchen ceased operations; the kitchens in the smaller houses and residential blocks kept at it, as did the kitchen of the Rada Główna Opiekuńcza, which tried to go on cooking with the remnants. The so-called "spit soup" (*pluj-zupa*) of acorns and barley remnants was famous. A week before the surrender, on September 26, the last supplies of halfway edible raw materials were estimated at "three days of hunger rations." However, one should not forget the episode in the first days of October when suddenly, in view of the impending surrender, food reappeared on the streets and was even offered in exchange for money. Apparently many people had hoarded foodstuffs, so that the state of supplies had appeared even more catastrophic as seen from the perspective of the civil administration—whose views were imperative to the AK-leadership. This does not mean that ten of thousands—mainly the homeless who were dependent on the administration—did not suffer from hunger. It only shows once again that, contrary to appearance, extreme conditions of life were not extreme for everyone; and up to the end, some Warsaw inhabitants suffered much less from hunger than most of their fellow citizens.

In the first days of the Uprising, the mood of such horrific scenarios was still miles away. The civilians rejoiced at a bit of freedom after almost five years of occupation, helped the soldiers, offered food and blankets, organized volunteer guards and auxiliary services, and took down German street signs and replaced them with Polish ones. The festive mood assumed that very few civilians were aware that the first attack of the AK had led to a strategic defeat; nor did the civilians know that the Red Army had gone into a defensive position several dozen kilometers from Warsaw. As a result, the first order of the civilian administration concerned internal order: lynching, which had apparently been done already, was forbidden. Germans and Volksdeutsche were to be turned over to security officials; the property of German authorities was protected in writing against plunder.

After August 5 and the mass flight from Wola and Ochota, the authorities faced a brand-new dimension of problems. The refugees, especially, could hardly be lodged in the densely constructed Old City, whose previously available food situation was now suddenly strained. Nevertheless, after a few days, the quarter still looked the same: shops and pubs were open, national flags hung in the windows, there were intact playgrounds, nearly twenty newspapers were on sale. A widespread system of cellar passages, sometimes well built, provided with signs and lighting, enabled communication in streets and quarters under fire. A few days later, however, the idyll was only a distant memory—people wandered in the cellars, and the first signs of hunger and apathy could be seen. The shops closed, barter and soup kitchens now replaced selling. Noodles and ersatz coffee were consumed, along with thin soup, beans, canned goods, rusks, and sugar from the captured warehouses. Soon, the most precious commodity was water, which came mostly from the new wells dug during the Uprising. The hospitals were overfilled and must have presented a Dantesque image with the progressive lack of water, medicines, and bandages. The atmosphere grew correspondingly worse. There was massive criticism of the AK leadership and the allegedly privileged soldiers. Civilians refused to cooperate in clearing and fire-fighting, and had to be forced into it by the military police. Many sources report a massive outbreak of piety in the Old City. The escape to prayer, however, had accompanied the Uprising from the very beginning. On August 6, the first Sunday in the liberated parts of the cities, "clergy held celebration services. In private homes, in air-raid shelters and cellars," reported one newspaper, "believers gathered together and prayed fervently. The wonderful, dignified words of religious hymns ring in the streets."[6] If the Catholic masses in the first days gave the impression of an apparent return to the normality of the pre-occupation time, in later weeks, they became more of an anchor and a mental escape from hell. In the Old City, during the second half of August, people prayed en masse and for hours in courtyards and cellars, an image that was later to be repeated in the downtown center.

In the last weeks, signs of exhaustion, hunger, thirst, disease, stench, and poverty increased along with indications of rebellion and despair. Civilians tried to force the Uprising leadership or even individual parts of troops to surrender, or they tried to reach the entrances of the sewers to get to the center. White flags were sporadically raised on the ruins of houses; a few groups went over to the German positions. The inferno in the last forty-eight hours of the Old City, when there were violent disputes between civilians and soldiers, is described in other places and other chapters. It should be added here that relations between military police and civilians were often strained, sometimes because the police had the difficult task of mercilessly implementing leadership, but in several cases also because they abused their position for extortion and looting. In the center, six military police were shot by firing squad a week before the end of the Uprising, and in the second week of September there was a mass murder of fourteen or fifteen Jews by four soldiers who had previously been considered plagues of the civilian population.[7] On the other hand, immoral behavior among civilians was also observed; there was theft, alcoholism, ruthlessness against the weak, and the like. Without the police, maintaining social discipline would certainly have been more difficult.

In the eastern part of the downtown area along the Vistula, the chronology of events was similar, except that it culminated in a brief period of a few days due to the longer reprieve. In mid-August, the number of refugees here was only 4,000 out of 26,000 inhabitants; only in the next week did the number of homeless rise to 13,000 (including 2,700 children). There was electricity in Powiśle until the fall of the electric company on September 3 (in the center, temporary power stations that tried to supply the munitions workshops and a few hospitals later worked). Stores and other small services were open, there were several local newspapers, and in the last days, ten public soup kitchens distributed 8,000 meals a day. Two dozen new wells and pumps provided water. All that collapsed with the first German attack. By September 2 many civilians fled to the center; the next day, the AK called on the residents of Powiśle to stay in their houses. Most observed the appeal.

In the downtown district, the appearance of a halfway normal world held out longest. (The impression made by this area on the arriving refugees is described at the beginning of chapter 10.) Nevertheless, it should have been noticed that the appearance was deceiving: even in the center, most of the apartments were overcrowded. Of the 260,000 inhabitants (including Powiśle) at the end of the first month of the Uprising, 125,000 of them were refugees. Welfare tried to guarantee public soup kitchens, and at least 134 of them were operating. There was a shortage of meat, lard, vegetables, and fruit, but at least at the beginning, oats, bread, beans, sugar, and dried fruit were available. Even in August, many of the refugees and those whose homes were bombed were living in cellars. The water supply did not seem to be a big problem in August, and twenty-three new wells were dug here too. Nevertheless, there were massive cases of lice, a high rate of infant mortality, as well as dysentery and the onset of typhus. In the first four weeks, medical care seemed to be relatively stable—which does not mean that it corresponded to normal conditions—but later the hospitals and improvised clinics quickly filled up. On September 3 the electricity was turned off; at about the same time, the last, bombed-out bakeries ceased production. The arrival of the exhausted, sick, starving, and frustrated soldiers and civilians from the Old City also seemed to have had a great impact on the general mood; the administration immediately identified them as sowing disorder and unrest.

German propaganda, which had tried for weeks to make giving up the city palatable to the civilians, now celebrated its first success. For a month, transition camp #121 in Pruszków (southwest of Warsaw) had been waiting for the big influx of refugees. Men who had fought were to be put in concentration camps; noncombatants, women, and children were to be sent to Germany for "normal" forced labor. By the terms of the surrender negotiations between Rohr and Komorowski, a truce was agreed for the afternoons of September 8 and 9, which the civilians could take advantage of for voluntary departure from the city.[8] Between September 8 and 10, probably 20,000–30,000 people left the center to go to the German side, within the terms of the agreement of the AK and General Rohr. Thus, at the climax of the morale crisis, despite all warnings and the fear of being shot, an estimated 10 percent of the surrounded Warsaw residents decided to trust in German promises of proper treatment and not in the hope of a victory of the Uprising. The reaction of the majority who remained in the city seems to have vacillated between apathy and rejection.[9] During this time, some 50,000 people chose a third way and left the hell of Warsaw in the Uprising behind, slipping past the German lines into freedom.[10]

After the brief period of hope between September 10 and 18, the life of the population in the last two weeks of the Uprising shifted to the cellars. Disease, lice, hunger, and lack of water were now ubiquitous. Cats, dogs, and pigeons were eaten. Countless people waiting in lines at wells fell victim to bombs and artillery barrages. The aggression of the civilians toward uniformed forces increased, as did looting and assaults; but at the same time, there was also an increase in the general apathy with which most Warsaw residents awaited the impending fate. Similar things were reported from Mokotów and Żoliborz. In the southern part of the city, living conditions until mid-September were better than elsewhere, even though the civilian administration had contributed little to that. In the next ten days, welfare collapsed here too. On September 26 civilians began raising white flags, and during the afternoon truce, 9,000 people took the opportunity to leave the area of the Uprising. An unknown number of Warsaw residents saved themselves the next night by going through the sewers to the downtown area with the soldiers; the remaining 5,000 were led by the Germans to the racetrack the next day, and later taken to the transition camp in Pruszków. In Żoliborz, a part of the city with relatively big settlements of socialist residential cooperatives, the self-administration took over the tasks of the government delegates to a large extent. In the last days of the Uprising, there was a considerable lack of water here, too; there was looting and robbery, hunger and hopelessness among the homeless. People waited for the end in parks that were like big camps. A cholera epidemic broke out in Żeromski Park.

During the negotiations on September 28, von dem Bach proposed to the Polish negotiator, Colonel Zygmunt Dobrowolski, to evacuate the civilians from the city even if the fighting continued. Dobrowolski reported the proposal to the AK leadership. During the discussion, the Warsaw commander General Chruściel opposed this proposal: his soldiers could still fight for another few days, but without the civilians in the rear, they could not see any more sense in that: "Today the soldier knows that, in the fight, he is also defending the civilian population of the capital. If the inhabitants are gone, the soldier can be expected to feel isolated and will no longer want to defend these heaps of rubble that represent Warsaw today."[11]

Jankowski, the government delegate, violently opposed the Warsaw commander; continuation of the Uprising was "madness," and at least the civilian population should be evacuated. Pełczyński and Komorowski agreed with this view: negotiations about the evacuation of the civilians were to be carried on; the German proposed an inspection of the transition camp in Pruszków; the hospitals and temporary prisoner-of-war camps were to be examined. On the very next day, von dem Bach approved the inspections. Komorowski cabled London news of the impending exodus of the Warsaw residents, which was presumably to begin on October 1. If the Russians attacked, the AK would resume fighting, and the evacuation would be stopped; if not, the rebels had to surrender. The Red Army did not move. Even though the inspection of the camp in Pruszków was not encouraging, the beginning of the evacuation set for October 1, between 5:30 A.M. and 6:30 P.M., was to continue the next day.

On Sunday, October 1, for the first time in two months, peace prevailed in the city—or more precisely, in what remained of it: the fighting had been stopped by agreement. People came out of the cellars, searched for their loved ones, wandered through the rubble apparently aimlessly; suddenly there was food to buy again. The first Warsaw residents—some 8,000, mainly women and children—set out for the long trek west. Fear of the Germans, and therefore the need to stay with the soldiers, was still strong, so that the majority stayed behind the front for the time being. By October 2, the day the surrender agreement was signed by Komorowski, 24,000 residents had already left the city. In the afternoon the stream of refugees clearly increased: frightened, uncertain, angry, distrustful people. "A long trail of many thousands of people, dragging bundles, knapsacks, and cases with them. Small children were pushed in prams, the weak were taken by hand. Our Polish exodus could probably be compared to the exit of Jews from Egypt," noted one of the evacuees. Three decades later, Miron Białoszewski particularly remembered the slowness: "People walked slowly. Because people used the whole width of the street. They walked and walked. Even though the street wasn't long. Everyone who left Warsaw at that time looked alike—and not like other people at all." Everything was packed into the rucksacks, bags, and suitcases, depending on how much the individual owned: from food to clothing, photos, tools, gold, and gold coins.[12]

In the surrender agreement, civilians were promised that they were not subject to collective family arrests, and that functionaries of the Uprising administration were to be immune from punishment. The people were apathetic; many openly cursed the AK and the London government-in-exile, most asked themselves why they had had to endure these last two months. The other question of what awaited them behind German lines must have been just as tormenting. But either way, the Warsaw residents had no choice: on October 3, twice as many people, that is, 48,000, left the city; in the next three days, almost 130,000. Warsaw now was nearly empty.

Epilogue

T HE FIGHTING IS OVER," wrote the main press organ of the AK, the *Biuletyn Informacyjny,* on October 4, in the commentary on the Uprising mentioned in the introduction. "The two months of one of the most noble and tragic pages of our history is closed. It is still too soon for an objective judgment of this period. The accounting of our gains and losses, credits and errors, victims and achieved values—we must entrust to history." Poland was not lost; belief in the recovery of independence was the most precious legacy of the Uprising.[1] On that same October 4, in right-bank Praga, the Party committee of the Communist PPR (which had been freed by the Soviets a few weeks earlier) held an assembly devoted to "the fight against reaction," that is, against the AK.[2] The surviving remnant of the resistance loyal to the government after the debacle of Warsaw tried to avoid the debate about the defeat. On the other side, on the day after it was over, the Warsaw drama became an argument of the Communists against the previously anti-German, now stronger anti-Soviet, underground.

After the exodus of the civilian population and the AK soldiers in the first week of October, what remained in the capital were a few hospitals (the last one closed on October 24), occupation troops, and a few hundred persons who stayed hidden in the ruins. Most of the civilians (probably some 350,000) were scattered in the GG or were conscripted for forced labor (about 90,000 people) or sent to concentration camps (60,000), in a clear violation of the terms of surrender. According to the agreement, the 18,000 members of the AK, men and women both, went to prisoner-of-war camps (so called Stalag for soldiers and Oflag for officers), and more than 1,700 female soldiers, who refused to work at forced labor, were taken to a punishment camp. Most of the 400–1,000 "Warsaw Robinsons," including a group of fifteen Jews who had fought in the Ghetto Uprising of 1943,[3] survived in the ruins under unimaginable conditions.[4] On November 20, 1944, a young German soldier, later known as Joe J. Heydecker, went through the city. Fifty years later, he remembered ruins, neglect, silence, stench, debris, and firewalls—and always graves, whole cemeteries in courtyards and streets, a "monotony of destruction, the infinity of its spatial expanse, the absence of every human dimension [. . .]. I think that there was no moment in the past and that there will hardly be any in the future when a man encountered the absolute standstill of time. No other ruins, no other field of ruins can evoke this state."[5] The appearance was deceiving, the ruins were not completely empty of humans, and time did not stand still. On the contrary, in Warsaw, between October 1944 and January 1945, an enterprise was going on that is part of the most disgraceful chapter of this history.

Right after the evacuation of the city, the Germans began preparations to implement the insane idea of Hitler and Himmler for the total destruction of Warsaw. During the Uprising, some 30 percent of the city was destroyed. There were already the first systematic campaigns of annihilation, independent of the fighting: thus, before mid-September, most of the royal castle was blown up. One week after the surrender, the AOK 9 learned that von dem Bach "had received the mission from Reichsführer SS to carry out the total destruction of Warsaw." Two days later the Warsaw governor reported to Generalgouverneur Frank: "Before departing, all raw materials, all textiles, and all furniture is to be cleared out of Warsaw." On October 12 Himmler repeated that the city was to be totally destroyed and the houses were to be razed. Only the railroad and its buildings were to be spared, but even the German troops were gradually to move into the cellars. As a result of a later instruction of the Reichsführer, objects of value like furs, clocks, or coins were to be sent for Himmler's personal disposal.[6]

The operation of "measures of dispersal, evacuation, immobilization, and destruction" was guided by the so-called evacuation staff, led by the Warsaw SS and police chief Paul Otto Geibel. In this campaign, the biggest libraries were destroyed (except for the university library, since the university campus was still used by the police). In October 1944 German sappers patiently set fire to the enormous amounts of paper that had been stored in the cellar of the collection camp in Okólnik. This is where some of Warsaw's most valuable books had been stored during the war. These books had been damaged but not destroyed by the artillery barrage during the Uprising. All of these papers and books were reduced to ashes. The last library still standing, the public library on Koszykowa Street with its half-million volumes, was destroyed on January 16, 1945, the day before the invasion of the Red and Polish Armies.[7] That evening, German troops withdrew from Warsaw.

The National Archive for New Documents and the Municipal Archive were blown up, along with the Saxon and Brühl Palace (the latter, built in the mid-eighteenth century by order of the Saxon minister Heinrich Brühl, had survived the Uprising in amazingly good condition), as well as many other prestigious buildings and monuments. In late December, the clearly infuriated deputy commander of the Forty-sixth Tank Corps of the Wehrmacht, Major General Kinzel, wrote directly to Himmler (!) to put Geibel and his explosives under his command: "SS-Brigadeführer Geibel is currently blowing up objects that are especially important politically, and completely unimportant tactically."[8]

Several palaces and the national museum were mined but not exploded. According to the estimates of the art historian Władysław Tomkiewicz, losses in the three-and-a-half months until mid-January amounted to some 30 percent of prewar collections and thus were roughly comparable to the losses of the two months of the Uprising.[9] At this same time, a great number of art objects and anything else of value were dismantled and transported to the Reich. Stanisław Lorentz, the director of the national museum, and his staff were officially enlisted to participate in the robbery as experts. They secretly hid some of the cultural properties in Warsaw and the surrounding area, but even that was not much help. Indeed, in the next decades, it was to turn out that these fragments of stolen cultural monuments played an important role, especially in the reconstruction of the royal castle.

In the fifty years that followed, the debate about the position of the Warsaw Uprising in the Polish national tradition became a mirror image of the political history of Poland. At first the Communists respected the deep emotions connected with the anniversary. In the early years, the focus of the official celebrations was the "common fight" of the simple soldiers of the AK and the "leftist," namely, Communist, resistance against the German occupiers. But even in 1945, the leadership of the AK—and thus the entire "bourgeois" resistance—was accused of passivity with regard to the Germans; before the Uprising, only the AL had fought. Another charge was formulated in February 1945, only four months after the surrender: Bór-Komorowski, the "bloody traitor," had deliberately ignored the opportunity to evacuate his troops to the right bank of the Vistula. The Soviets and the First Polish Army would have provided the means of transportation, but the anti-Soviet "representative of the London clique" had preferred "to turn over thousands of soldiers to German capture than to allow them to go over to their brothers fighting along with the Red Army."[10] In the Communist takeover phase from 1945 to 1948, official propaganda emphasized this distinction between the "traitors" in the leadership of the underground state and the innocent, heroic "people of Warsaw," or the "simple soldiers" of the AK. On August 1, there were requiem masses, which were announced even in the journal of the Polish Communist party, and representatives of the highest national authorities participated in the memorials.

During Stalinization after 1948, the principles of the national policy of remembrance changed. The "London camp" was now reduced to a "reactionary clique," which had pursued the road to collaboration with the Third Reich through anti-Sovietism. Only "the left" had managed a genuine resistance. By August 1, 1949, mention of the simple soldiers of the AK had disappeared from the anniversary article of the central journal of the Polish United Workers' Party (PZPR). The only positive heroes were now the "people of Warsaw." The alleged plot of the highest AK circles against "Poland's most loyal allies—the Soviet soldiers" was now described as a conspiracy staged by the "bourgeois" resistance in conjunction with German information. In 1950, for the first time, the anniversary of the Uprising was not mentioned at all. In 1951, however, an abstract of a political sham trial appeared in which a high-ranking AK officer confirmed all charges against the "reactionary" AK. In the next two years, silence prevailed on August 1. In 1954, for the tenth anniversary, almost a year and a half after Stalin's death, government propaganda returned to the model of 1949: the intentions of the leadership of the Uprising were represented as a joint plan of the AK and German counterintelligence or the Gestapo. On the other hand, the "patriotic people of Warsaw" returned as positive heroes

One substantive expression of the systematic struggle for every remembrance of the Uprising was that no memorial was erected to the fighters and victims of 1944. However, the fifth anniversary of the 1943 Warsaw Ghetto Uprising was commemorated with a monument by Nathan Rapoport and it soon became world famous.[11] In 1948, when the memorial was officially opened, the persecution of the AK members was in full swing. After being liberated from German captivity, most of the higher- and highest-ranking officers had gone into exile, particularly to London. The "people's force" now took revenge on those who had remained or returned, including quite often simple members of the "reactionary" resistance movement. Between 1947 and 1954, at least seventy-four persons were arrested just from the group of those responsible for security in the Warsaw Uprising (members of counterespionage forces, police officers, and noncommissioned officers, judges, and prosecutors). Several of them were tortured during investigation, seven were sentenced to death and shot, and four more starved in detention or prison. In the first postwar decade, belonging to the AK became a mark of Cain that could end, in the worst case, with a political trial, but it thwarted any chance for education or professional advancement.

Thus, in the first half of the 1950s, the hostile silencing of the Uprising and its victims dominated public opinion. August 1 was completely overlooked as a memorial day by the official national celebration of the Polish People's Republic, which was celebrated from July 22 through the end of that month. Even in 1955, when de-Stalinization had already begun in Poland, the press was full of reports of the International Youth Festival that began on July 31;[12] the anniversary of the Uprising was silenced almost completely. Yet that changed the next year, when the especially intense de-Stalinization in Poland restored the Uprising along with a few other national icons to the semiofficial cultural memory. Since the Uprising could not yet receive a memorial dedicated to it,[13] one part of the 1956 celebration was held with a certain piquancy on Stalin Boulevard (formerly—and subsequently—Aleje Ujazdowskie), where the AK had carried out a successful attack on the SS and police chief of Warsaw on February 1, 1944 (i.e., six months before the Uprising). Another part of that 1956 celebration concentrated on the unveiling of a tablet commemorating an attack of the Communist Gwardia Ludowa, which had also taken place long before August 1, 1944.[14] From then until the end of socialist Poland, August 1 was to remain a day of remembrance of 1944 but with different emphases and a correspondingly different protocol. In the commentaries on the anniversary, the difference was established between the heroism of the soldiers—even from the "bourgeois" camp—and the civilian population on the one hand, and the allegedly criminally selfish—but no longer traitorous—policy of the leadership of the "London camp" on the other. By 1956 Polish national radio broadcast a program on "W" hour (typically, only late at night). For the twentieth anniversary in 1964, the corresponding celebrations were in Warsaw's biggest auditorium, Congress Hall in the Palace of Culture, and were broadcast on radio and television, as was the twenty-fifth anniversary in 1969.

Also around 1969 several fictional and documentary films dealing with the Uprising appeared on television on July 31 and August 1. In 1964 there were some three hundred small memorial tablets in the city commemorating the events and losses of the summer of 1944; in 1969 more than a dozen books on the Uprising appeared—mainly the memoirs of the combatants. The explanation for this somewhat scattered and limited yet prominent Uprising boom was simple: in the 1960s, the Party attempted to win over to the system the masses of former fighters—along with the memory of the Uprising itself—by means of an integrative policy of history (which still ignored the political decision-makers of the former opponent). Former soldiers and officers of the AK were accepted into the national combatants' unit and occasionally received first class, if only honorific, functions. In 1964, in his speech for the twentieth anniversary on August 1, the Central Committee Secretary in charge of ideological issues, Zenon Kliszko, himself an officer in the Communist AL in 1944 and author of a recently published book on the Uprising, spoke of the "antidemocratic policy of the London camp," of the "lunacy and political diversion" of the AK leadership. He also emphasized that, in the summer of 1944, the "people of Warsaw" showed "heroism and patriotism"; the "common sacrifice" of all Warsaw residents led to the current insight "that the page of the former distinctions is closed. We, who fought at the barricades under the banners of various groups— against Poland's deadly enemy—are no longer separate."[15] In 1968, at the climax of the nationalist propaganda of the Communist Party, the memory was raised to a higher level. "The cynical political game [of the 'London' politicians] is superceded by the national remembrance of the armed act," said a commentary of August 1. "The Warsaw Uprising has become the people's uprising."[16]

In the 1970s, the government-organized remembrances developed even more in the direction of a total national solidarity. On August 1, 1974, the greatest potential for love of freedom of Polish society exploded. The Party journal *Trybuna Ludu* explained away the ongoing and difficult legacy: unfortunately, the countless dead, the human energy, and love of homeland had fallen victim to the "selfish class calculation" of the "reactionaries." "The Uprising could not be a success," opined the party journal, since it was "against the most vital interests of the nation." Only the Party had drawn the right conclusions from this inability of the old, reactionary political class.[17] Anyone who read carefully between the lines of such sentences could hardly misunderstand. The old elites had been unable to compromise with Moscow, and only the Communists accepted by Moscow could protect today's society adequately from a new version of the debacle, meaning, from the rage of the Soviet Union. Parallel to this geopolitical admonition, there was also a conciliatory variant of the memory: the heroic "soldiers of all political trends who were united by their love of Poland and hatred of the Hitlerian perpetrators of genocide" should "be honored by our everyday work. By doing so, old Warsaw will be rebuilt and reconstructed so that it is ever richer and more beautiful, and life in the city will be happier and more comfortable."[18]

Yet this idyllic image, in which the dutifully clipped "reaction" played an increasingly smaller role, was soon overcast by an emerging counterpublic opinion that, in the second half of the 1970s in underground publications, demonstrations, and discussions, demanded the whole truth about the Uprising—especially about the Soviet share in the catastrophe. Pope John Paul II alluded to this in June 1979 in his sermon at the Warsaw Victory Square—which soon became the most famous event of his first trip to Poland as leader of the Catholic Church. During the Uprising celebration on August 1, 1981, while Solidarność (Solidarity, the Polish independent trade union federation formed in 1980 and led by Lech Wałęsa) was still legal despite all previous ambitions of the Party, the tradition of the Uprising had clearly been taken over by the anti-Communist opposition. After years of silence the suppressed, but best-known, truth about the position of the Red Army in the summer of 1944 turned out to be an argument against the legitimacy of People's Poland. This was not to change again until 1989; August 1 remained a difficult date for the Party, even if it finally agreed in 1984 to erect a memorial to the Uprising. Even though the groundbreaking ceremony was attended by the Party leader Wojciech Jaruzelski (a young officer in Berling's army in 1944),[19] and even though this same Jaruzelski attended the dedication celebrations in 1989 (with the Primate of Poland) and certain semiofficial representatives of the state were quoted in interviews that even the Polish Communists were surprised in 1944 by the Soviet position toward the Uprising, this no longer changed anything. The Party had definitely lost the battle for August 1, 1944.

In the Third Polish Republic, commemoration of the Uprising has degenerated into a holiday ritual with dwindling political significance. The memory of the Warsaw Uprising had been a thorn in the flesh of the old Party, the entire government, and its censorship. After they collapsed, the Soviets no longer had any defenders. The focus is now on the victims—Warsaw, its civilian population, and the young soldiers of the AK. The German criminals are mentioned less. The central political message is the treason of Moscow, which is understood, along with the murder of Polish officers in Katyn, as one of the most important steps in Stalin's strategy to destroy the leaders of anti-Communist Poland. The decision of the underground leadership to include Warsaw in planning for the Uprising, despite all obvious risks, has gradually become a wise, even self-evident decision. It is only Moscow's allegedly unexpected reaction that condemned the plan to failure.[20]

More complicated is the relationship of the "silent majority" to the Warsaw Uprising. A public opinion poll of May 1994 shows that the Uprising ranks relatively high—number eight on the list of the most important events in the history of Poland—and is considered an important event by 86 percent of those surveyed. Only a third of those polled believe that triggering the attack served primarily for the quick liberation from German occupation; exactly half, on the other hand, consider it a means against a Communist takeover. Again, half think the Uprising had to happen, a third that it should not have happened. Only 22 percent of those polled judge themselves as unemotional about the events in

Warsaw in the summer of 1944; over two-thirds consider it too significant to be exclusively rational about it. All in all, people in Polish society
in the 1990s seem to be relatively united in a fundamentally positive assessment of the Uprising, but that does not mean they share the same
opinion about the political aspects of August 1.[21] The Warsaw Uprising
as a subject of passionate debates, as it was before 1989, is hard to imagine in these days.

Only once, in 1994, did the anniversary celebrations of the outbreak
of the Uprising get big headlines. The American vice president, the
British prime minister, and the German president came to the fiftieth anniversary of August 1; the Russian president refused. The presence of
the Allies, whose pilots had flown the hopeless missions from Italy to
Warsaw, evoked hardly any emotions. The week-long public discussions
focused on the question of the participation of Russia and Germany.
Moscow's rejection was generally felt as an expression of refusal to bear
the burden of the Polish-Russian past. On the other hand, a few combat
groups opposed the participation of the German president—it was too
soon to forgive the enemy and destroyer of Warsaw. This attitude received additional fuel from a slip of the tongue from the German president, Roman Herzog, prior to the visit, when he confused the 1944 Uprising with the 1943 Warsaw Ghetto Uprising. Nevertheless, during the
ceremonies on August 1, Herzog found the right words: in a brief and
dignified speech, without legal or other reservations, he paid homage to
the tragedy of Warsaw and asked "forgiveness for what has been done
to you by Germans."

The host of the ceremonies, President Lech Wałęsa, also made the
best possible speech. Poland, Warsaw, and the rebels had fallen victim to
two totalitarian regimes in World War II. After the Uprising, Wałęsa admonished, "none of the great men of this world had [thought] of the issue for which Warsaw had died. No one proclaimed: 'I am a Warsavian'
[. . .] No one raised the question: Quo vadis, Europe? Truly moving in
the direction of freedom? In total harmony the sovereignty of Poland
was broken up. The same sovereignty in whose defense the Second
World War had broken out. In the name of peace, in the name of a better
future, in the name of a misunderstood unity, zones of power and influence were staked out."[22] Wałęsa was often to repeat this train of thought
in the context of Poland's efforts to be accepted into NATO: the warning
that an overly pragmatic understanding of Western interests meant
betraying Poland and would not serve the West in the long run. But
Wałęsa's 1994 speech also indicated a turning point in the history of the
impact of the Uprising in that, prior to 1989, the justification of an
anti-western—mainly anti-German—position was always derived officially from the "lessons of the past." Now the national leader of the new

Poland held out his hand to both enemies of 1944, both Russians and Germans. The address of August 1, 1994, spoke of building bridges and friendship with Russia, and of friendship and good neighborliness with Germany; the great celebration of the fiftieth anniversary also served to clear the air, to lift the burden from the future, and not to mobilize national resentment. Thus, after 1989, the legacy of the Uprising gradually became part of a common "memory culture of the Allies," to whom Poland had belonged in 1944 and to whom it belongs again today. It should link the Third Republic with the outside world and not separate her from it, not even from previous enemies.

Is there such a binding function of the history of the impact of the Uprising inside Poland, too? In the 1990s, for the first time, combatants of the rightist National Force (NSZ), whose fighting in the conflict had been kept silent until 1989, participated in the celebrations. Thus, representatives of both extreme wings of the resistance participated in the same event. The events no longer make big headlines; the national consensus about the historical magnitude of the Warsaw summer of 1944 is hardly disturbed even by professional historians. The idea that the commanders of the AK and the others responsible for the "crimes, [. . .] for excessive, careless, and unnecessary victims" really belonged in a court of law—a demand formulated right after the war by General Władysław Anders, the commander of the Polish troops on the Italian front of 1944—is now taken up only by outsiders in the media discussion.[23]

Thus, the final sentences of this book are prefaced by a Bulgarian writer living in Paris, a writer who is not connected with the subject, who, after treating the Warsaw Uprisings of 1943 and 1944, emphasized an amazing similarity in the type of argumentation of the Jewish and Polish leadership in the underground: in both cases, honor and honorable death were often discussed. The semiotician and essayist Tzvetan Todorov concludes that the Uprising in the Ghetto in fact had no chance of success; while in the summer of 1944, saving human dignity, "the feeling of despair in view of political hopelessness," to which those responsible were later to refer, represented only one among many concomitant circumstances. Nevertheless, the Uprising of 1944 was "in reality not inevitable; it was a result of a miscalculation in a situation that also allowed other solutions. It sacrificed the interests of the individual in the name of love of the abstract; its unleashing helped no one, neither then nor later, neither on the spot or elsewhere."[24]

It can never be proved, but Todorov may be mistaken about the last point. It is thoroughly conceivable that without the physical destruction of the elite troops of the AK, the Communist takeover would have been essentially bloodier in Poland than it was anyway. It is also conceivable that, without the memory of their own impotence in the summer of 1944, the Poles would have dared that uprising in 1956 that turned out so horribly for the Hungarians. And finally, it is within the realm of the possible that, without the defeat of the—hopefully last—big uprising, the Poles would have invented neither a legal anti-Communist trade union in the context of real existing socialism in 1980 nor the roundtable nine years later that introduced the peaceful dissolution of the regime and the way to freedom.

Notes

Introduction

1. Melchior Wańkowicz, *Ziele na kraterze*, New York 1955, pp. 368–72, 378–82.

2. Hanns von Krannhals, *Der Warschauer Aufstand 1944*, Frankfurt a/M 1962, pp. 87–92; quotation, p. 91.

3. Data are from Thomasz Szarota, *Warschau unter dem Hakenkreuz. Leben und Alltag im besetzten Warschau. 1.10.1939 bis 31.7.1944,* German trans., Claudia Makowski and Ryszard Makowski, Paderborn 1985. In a negative population growth (an increase of the death rate in all age groups and a declining birth rate), the only source of population increase was the settlement of Poles, who were banished or had fled from the areas incorporated into the Reich.

4. Not many of the contents of the most important Warsaw libraries—including the Parliamentary and National Library—were taken to the Reich. Another part, however, was temporarily housed in the Krasiński Palace, where it was damaged during the Uprising. After the Uprising, the special collections of the Warsaw libraries were systematically burned and destroyed by fire units. See Andrzej Mężyński, "Die Verluste der polnischen Bibliotheken während des Zweiten Weltkriegs im Lichte neuer Archivforschungen," in *Displaced Books. Bücherrückgabe aus zweierlei Sicht,* Hannover 1999; and epilogue.

5. See Eugeniusz Duraczyński, "Powstanie warszawskie—badań i sporów ciag dalszy," in *Dzieje Najnowsze* 27, vol. 1 (1995): 71–88; quotation, p. 71. See more detail in the concluding part.

6. Statement of Marcin Zaremba in *Archiwum Polski Podziemnej. Dokumenty i materiały 1939–1956,* Warsaw 1995, p. 10. Meeting of the Komisja Główna Rady Jedności Narodowej (Central Committee of the Council of National Unity) of November 7, 1944.

7. Kazimierz Wyka, "Dwiejesienie," in *Życie na niby,* Warsaw 1959, pp. 98–173.

8. For the history of the origin of the work first published in 1962, see Adam Borkiewicz, *Powstanie warszawskie 1944,* Warsaw 1969, introduction, pp. 13–16.

9. *Polskie Siły Zbrojne w II wojnie światowej*, Vol. 3, Armia Krajowa, London 1950.

10. It also won the "Silver Palm" in Cannes in 1957 and, interestingly, the Gold Medal of the World Festival of Youth and Students in Moscow the same year.

11. Adam Borkiewicz, *Powstanie warszawskie 1944: zarys działań natury wojskowej*; Jerzy Kirchmayer, *Powstanie warszawskie*, Warsaw 1959 (11th edition 1989).

12. *Powstanie warszawskie 1944 r. Bibliografia selektywna*, 3 Vols., Warsaw 1994.

13. For new works, see Duraczyński, "Powstanie" (as in note 5); *Der Warschauer Aufstand 1944*, ed. Bernd Martin and Stanisława Lewandowska, Warsaw 1999.

14. Thus, Hanns von Krannhals, *Der Warschauer Aufstand 1944*, Frankfurt a/M 1962, who corrects the military historical treatises of Borkiewicz and Kirchmayer in a few points; probably for reasons of censorship, both editions of his book (1964) were hardly reviewed in Poland, most reviews appeared in exile.

15. See, e.g., P. M. H. Bell, *British Public Opinion, Foreign Policy and the Soviet Union*, London etc. 1990, pp. 147–64.

16. For one of the few exceptions, see the historical reporting of Jean-François Steiner, *Varsovie '44*, Paris 1975.

1. Occupation and Resistance

1. Documents on German Foreign Policy 1918–1945, Series D (1937–1945), vol. 8, Washington 1954, pp. 164–66.

2. Jan T. Gross offers a concrete representation, *The Revolution from Abroad: The Soviet Conquest of Poland's Western Ukraine and Western Belorussia*, Princeton 1988. The collection *Europa nie prowincjonalna*, ed. Krzysztof Jasiewicz, Warsaw 2000, contains a good survey of the current state of research.

3. General accounts include Martin Broszat, *Nationalsozialistische Polenpolitik 1939–1945*, Stuttgart 1961; Czeslaw Madajczyk, *Die Okkupationspolitik Nazideutschlands in Polen 1939–1945*, trans. Berthold Puchert, Cologne 1988.

4. Quoted in *Das Diensttagebuch des deutschen Generalgouverneurs in Polen 1939–1945*, ed. Werner Präg and Wolfgang Jacobmeyer, Stuttgart 1975, p. 53.

5. Ibid., p. 104.

6. Wolfgang Jacobmeyer, "Die Polnische Widerstandsbewegung im Generalgouvernement und ihre Beurteilung durch deutsche Dienststellen," *VfZ* 25 (1977): 658–81; quotation, p. 667.

7. For details, see Jan T. Gross, *Polish Society under German Occupation: The Generalgouvernement 1939–1944*, Princeton 1979, pp. 280–81.

8. See the list in Tomasz Strzembosz, *Bohaterowie "Kamieni na szaniec" w świetle dokumentów. Wstęp, opracowanie i wybór tekstów*, Warsaw 1994.

9. This will be discussed in the paragraphs following. For the internal political aspects of the first underground organizations, see especially Jerzy Janusz Terej, *Na rozstajach dróg. Ze studiów nad obliczem i modelem Armii Krajowej*,

Wrocław 1978; Wolfgang Jacobmeyer, *Heimat und Exil. Die Anfänge der polnischen Untergrundbewegung im Zweiten Weltkrieg,* Hamburg 1973. The best documentation of the initial phase of the underground is in Andrzej K. Kunert, *Illustrowany przewodnik po Polsce Podziemnej 1939–1945,* Warsaw 1996.

10. See the publication mentioned in note 8, which documents the role of these factors for the emergence of a conspiratorial scout group.

11. Gross, *Polish Society,* pp. 215–26; Tomasz Strzembosz, "Refleksje o polskim podziemiu," *Zeszyty Studium Społecznej Nauki Kościoła* 14 (1988): 21–47, quotations, pp. 25–34, 37–40. And see Jacobmeyer, *Heimat und Exil,* pp. 23ff.

12. A few reports are reproduced in *Armia Krajowa w dokumentach 1939–1945,* vol. I: 1939–1941, London 1970.

13. For this question, which has recently come under a great deal of discussion, see Jan T. Gross, "'Jeder lauscht ständig, ob die Deutschen nicht schon kommen.' Die zentralpolnische Gesellschaft und der Völkermord," in Włodzimierz Borodziej and Klaus Ziemer (eds.), *Deutsch-Polnische Beziehungen 1939–1945–1949. Eine Einführung,* Osnabrück 2000, pp. 215–33; here p. 563.

14. Quoted in Andrzej Friszke, "Rząd na obczyźnie wobec państwa podziemnego w Kraju," in Zbieniew Błażynski (ed.), *Władze RP na obczyźnie podczas II wojny światowej,* London 1994, pp. 562–623; here pp. 224–32.

15. For a detailed account, see Christoph Kleßmann, *Die Selbstbehauptung einer Nation. NS-Kulturpolitik und polnische Widerstandsbewegung im Generalgouvernement 1939–1945,* Düsseldorf 1971.

16. Data in Friszke, "Rząd," pp. 571–72.

17. See "Rozmowy PPR z Delegaturag Rzasdu," in *Archiwum Ruchu Robotniczego,* vol. 9, Warsaw 1984, pp. 5–24.

2. The "Polish Question"

1. *Poland in the British Parliament 1939–1945,* compiled and edited by Wacław Jedrzejewicz, New York 1946, vol. 1, p. 188.

2. The protocol of the discussions of August 25, the draft treaty, and the text signed on the same day were all published in 1971 by Henryk Batowski. Reproduced in *Władze RP na obczyźnie podczas II wojny światowej,* London 1994, pp. 120–41.

3. The discussion of Polish-British and Polish-Soviet relations is based on the essays of Magdalena Hułas and Marek K. Kamiński, ibid., pp. 163–264, 636–88, as well as that of Detlev Brandes, *Großbritannien und seine osteuropäischen Alliierten 1939–1943,* Munich 1988.

4. For 1920, see Norman Davies, *White Eagle—Red Star: The Polish-Soviet War 1919–1920,* London 1972, pp. 178ff. Alan J. Forster, "Die britische Presse und Osteuropa in der Anfangsphase des Kalten Krieges," in Eva Schmidt-Hartmann (ed.), *Kommunismus und Osteuropa,* pp. 101–33; quotation, p. 126. For characteristic British reactions to the guarantee declaration of 1939, see Hermann Graml, *Europas Weg in den Krieg, Hitler und die Mächte 1939,* Munich 1990, p. 182.

5. For more detail, see Forster, esp. p. 130; Brandes, *Großbritannien,* p. 250.

6. For more detail, see Magdalena Hułas, "Memorandum Stafforda Crippsa z 22 października 1940 r. Polskie aspekty," *Dzieje Najnowsze* 25, no. 4 (1993): 81–93; Brandes, *Großbritannien*, pp. 145–46.

7. Some of the Soviet documents on this issue, which were either inaccessible or denied prior to the 1990s, are in *Katyn: Documents on Genocide*, Wojciech Materski (ed.), Warsaw 1993.

8. Polish-Soviet Relations, 1918–1943. Official Documents, Washington [no date], p. 108.

9. A few new documents on this question are in *Armia Polska w ZSRR*, Wojciech Materski (ed.), Warsaw 1992; *Konflikty polsko-sowieckie 1942–1944*, Wojciech Roszkowski (ed.), Warsaw 1993.

10. This argument reached an irreconcilable climax in the note of January 5, 1942, in which Moscow stated that the occupation of the "West Ukraine" and "West Belarus" had not been a real occupation, because it had served to annex this area to the Soviet Union—"as the result of the freely expressed will of the population of this area."

11. This is the thesis of Sarah Meikeljohn Terry, *Poland's Place in Europe: General Sikorski and the Origins of the Oder-Neisse-Line, 1939–1943*, Princeton 1983.

12. For details, see Terry, *Poland's Place*, pp. 127ff., 247ff.

13. See Churchill's remarks to Sikorski on April 26, 1942: "The current war is the continuation of the first, Russia demands only the return of part of that territory with which she entered the war in 1914"; Władysław Pobóg-Malinowski, *Najnowsza historia polityczna Polski*, vol. 2/2, London 1960, pp. 220–21.

14. For details, see Brandes, *Großbritannien*, chapter 3.7, 4.5.1.

15. These fears were also confirmed by the first frontline use of the Polish Communist First Division, which was formed after the break of diplomatic relations between Moscow and the government-in-exile and went to the front in October 1943. After the battle, the communist Wanda Wasilewska called Molotov and asked "how high the losses were. 'Normal, he answered; 30 percent.'" Wasilewska contacted Stalin and said "that in relation to the several million man Soviet army, that would be something else; but with regard to the small group of the Polish army, that means that in three days, we would no longer have a division." As a result, the First Division was withdrawn from the front for several months. *Archiwum Ruchu Robotniczego*, vol. 7, Warsaw 1982, p. 391.

16. O'Malley's note and the minutes of his colleagues and superiors in Louis FitzGibbon, *Unpitied and Unknown: Katyn—Bologoye—Dergachi*, London 1975, p. 58.

17. The first indications of British reservation about the Polish resistance in 1941 were given years ago by David Stafford, *Britain and European Resistance: A Survey of the Special Operations Executive, with Documents*, Toronto/Buffalo 1980, pp. 63–64. The SOE-NKVD agreement of September 30, 1941, was discovered and commented on by Magdalena Hułas, "Wojenna współpraca SOE I NKWD oraz miejsce w niej Polski w świetle dokumentów SOE," in Włodzimierz Borodziej and Paweł Wieczorkiewicz (eds.), *Polska między Niemcami a Rosją. Studia ofiarowane Marianowi Wojciechowskiemu w 70 rocznicę urodzin*, Warsaw 1997, pp. 60–72.

18. Brandes, *Großbritannien*, pp. 482–87; Kamiński, *Zarys*, pp. 730–31.

3. Planning the Uprising and First Attempt of Transition

1. For the establishment of the ZWZ and Instruction No. 1, see Jacobmeyer, *Heimat*, pp. 62–72.

2. For Rowecki's part in planning the uprising, see Tomasz Szarota, *Stefan Rowecki "Grot*," Warsaw 1983, chapter 6.

3. Quoted in Szarota, *Rowecki*, pp. 167–68.

4. According to Terej, *Na rozstajach*, p. 141, the number of soldiers within the organization dropped from 75,000 to 54,000, i.e., almost 30 percent.

5. The description of the plans of uprising is based on Terej, *Na rozstajach*, pp. 163–83; Marek Ney, *Krwawicz, Powstanie powszechne w koncepcjach i pracach Sztabu Naczelnego Wodza i Komendy Głównej AK*, Warsaw 1999; and Jan M. Ciechanowski, *The Warsaw Rising of 1944*, Cambridge 1974. The documents cited—unless otherwise noted—are reproduced in *Armia Krajowa w dokumentach*, vols. 2 and 3.

6. With appendixes, reproduced in *AK*, vol. 6, pp. 134–71.

7. For the relevant plans of the ZWZ, see Jacobmeyer, *Heimat*, pp. 159–60.

8. See the detailed report of March 27, 1941, in *AK*, vol. 6, pp. 178–83.

9. Order of January 22, 1943, in *AK*, vol. 6, pp. 285ff.

10. Szarota, *Rowecki*, pp. 203–8.

11. For details, see Tomasz Strzembosz, *Akcje zbrojne podziemnej Warszawy 1939–1944*, Warsaw 1983. On the other hand, assassination attempts against the higher SS and police leader in the GG, on Hans Frank, and the commander of the Warsaw Gestapo, failed.

12. This is developed most clearly by Terej, *Na rozstajach*, pp. 175–79.

13. The text of the agreement is in *Armia Krajowa*, vol. 3, pp. 157–79.

14. *AK*, vol. 6, pp. 385–86.

15. For the following, see Ryszard Torzecki, *Polacy i Ukraińcy. Sprawa ukraińska w czasie II wojny światowej na terenie II Rzeczypospolitej*, Warsaw 1993; Michał Fijałka, *27. Wołyńska dywizja piechoty AK*, Warsaw 1986; the essay on Volhynia in Krzysztof Komorowski, *Armia Krajowa. Rozwój organizacyjny*, Warsaw 1996; and Ciechanowski, *Rising*. Also see Chiari (ed.), *Die polnische Heimatarmee*, Munich 2003, pp. 255–99.

16. As a concrete example of the tortuously confused relations in spring 1944, see Grzegorz Motyka, "Ukraińska orientacja," in *Karta* 23 (1997): 54–73.

17. Moldenhauer cites the corresponding order by Stalin in "Der sowjetische NKVD und die Heimatarmee im 'Lubliner Polen' 1944/45," in Chiari (ed.), *Die polnische Heimatarmee*, pp. 275–99; quotation here p. 279.

18. On April 20 Stalin expressly ordered to break off all contact with the "underground units of General Sosnkowski"; Moldenhauer, "Der sowjetische NKVD," p. 281.

4. The Dress Rehearsal: Lwów, Lublin, Vilnius

1. For Vilnius, see especially Piotr Łossowski, *Litwa a sprawy polskie 1939–1940*, Warsaw 1985; *Społeczeństwo białoruskie, litewski i polskie na ziemiach*

pólnocno-wschodnich II Rzeczypospolitej w latach 1939–1941, ed. Małgorzata Giżejewska and Tomasz Strzembosz, Warsaw 1995.

2. The first climax of this quarrel is represented by the capture of a large Polish partisan unit by the Soviets in late August 1943. Most of the Poles were released or integrated into the Soviet unit, but eighty-five imprisoned AK partisans were shot. For more detail, see the publications by Chmielarz et. al., cited in note 3.

3. Recently this part of the history of the Polish resistance has also been relatively well researched. The once sensational work of Roman Korab-Żebryk, *Operacja wileńska AK*, Warsaw 1985, was followed recently by Stanisława Lewandowska, *Życie codzienne Wilna w latach II wojny światowej*, Warsaw 1997; Zygmunt Boradyn, Andrzej Chmielarz, and Henryk Piskunowicz (eds.), *Z dziejówrmii Krajowej na Nowogródczyźnie i Wileńszczyźnie (1941–1945)*, Studia, Warsaw 1997. The latter deals mainly with the organizational and military history of the AK, the former with the Polish-Soviet conflict.

4. Bernhard Chiari sheds new light on the course of events in his "Kriegslist oder Bündnis mit dem Feind? Deutsch-polnische Kontakte 1943–44," in *Die polnische Heimatarmee*, pp. 497–525.

5. The city gate in Vilnius, where the image of the Madonna (*Matka Boska Ostrobramska*) was kept. This was a Roman Catholic cult object known well beyond Vilnius.

6. The role of Führer Order no. 11 of March 8, 1944, which introduced the formation and absolute defense of "strongholds," is analyzed in the context of Vilnius by Korab-Żerbyk, *Operacja*, pp. 115–25; quotation, p. 116.

7. Quoted in Korab-Żebryk, *Operacja*, pp. 440. The most important documents of the AK to operations in Vilnius and Lemberg are published in *Armia Krajowa w dokumentach*, vol. 3.

8. Korab-Żebryk, *Operacja*, pp. 465ff., mentions that on these days the heads of the British and American military missions based in Moscow were visiting the headquarters of the Third Belarusian Front; naturally, the Vilnius AK was not a subject for either side.

9. Sierov's first report was passed on from Beriia to Stalin on July 16; *Teczka specjalna Stalina. Raporty NKWD z Polski 1944–1946*, Warsaw 1998, pp. 36–39.

10. Most of the officers returned from the Soviet internment camp in November 1947. Several fell in battle against the NKVD or were shot. "Wilk" escaped from the internment camp, was arrested by the NKVD, released in Poland, arrested again, and died in 1951 in the prison of the Polish Security Police. The Infantry Reserve Regiment no. 361 of the Red Army was made up of five thousand soldiers of the AK (with Soviet noncommissioned and commissioned officers), but the regiment refused to take the oath of the Red Army and was thus sentenced to forced labor.

11. For the Lublin AK, see Ireneusz Caban in *Armia Krajowa. Rozwój organizacyjny*, Warsaw 1996, pp. 75–97. The dispatches of July 25–31 in *AK*, vol. 3, pp. 575, 588, 591–92.

12. The description of the Lwów and the Burza campaign there is based on the publications of Bolesław Tomaszewski and Jerzy Węgierski, *Lwowska AK*, Warsaw 1987; and Jerzy Węgierski, *W Lwowskiej Armii Krajowej*, Warsaw 1989.

13. Filipkowski was arrested because he refused the integration to the Polish Communist troops; the same happened to several officers and some of the soldiers. But on the whole, fewer seemed to be affected by this fate in Lwów than in Vilnius or later in Lublin, since the AK units that had amassed outside the city withdrew and avoided disarmament or internment by dissolving on their own.

14. The data are rather vague and assume a few hundred dead in Vilnius and Lwów; the number of civilian victims may also have been relatively low.

5. On the Way to the Decision

1. The most important discussion of this subject, Jan M. Ciechanowski, *The Warsaw Rising of 1944*, Cambridge 1974, has been supplemented by more recent works by the same author, primarily *Na tropach tragedii*, Warsaw 1992.

2. Quoted in Krannhals, *Aufstand*, p. 348.

3. See Włodzimierz Borodziej, *Terror und Politik. Die Deutsche Polizei und die polnische Widerstandsbewegung im Generalgouvernement 1939–1944*, Mainz 1999, pp. 185–89; Grzegorz Mazur, *Biuro Informacji i Propagandy SZP-ZWZ-AK 1939–1945*, Warsaw 1987, pp. 96–119.

4. Wojciech Baliński, *Człowiek w cieniu, Tadeusz Pełczyński—zarys biografii*, Warsaw 1994.

5. For Okulicki's role in July 1944, see Andrzej Przemyski, *Ostatni komendant—General Leopold Okulicki*, Lublin 1990, pp. 133–34, 136–37.

6. One of the paradoxes of the state of research is that, to this day, there is no scholarly biography of Komorowski. His abilities and leadership may be underestimated—yet the extant literature forces acceptance of the image summarized in the following.

7. Quoted in Ciechanowski, *Rising*, pp. 215–16.

8. The manifesto is reprinted in *Manifest PKWN*, Warsaw 1976.

9. Komorowski explicitly demanded an "uncompensated expropriation" of the big estates; the "Manifesto" did the same but generally anticipated a "support of the former owners," as well as a higher support for estate owners "who could prove patriotic service in the fight against the Germans."

10. Quoted in the Polish edition of Ciechanowski *Powstanie*, p. 350.

11. Jean-François Steiner, *Varsovie 44. L'insurrection*, Paris 1975.

12. See Marek Ney-Krwawicz, *Komenda Główna Armii Krajowej 1939–1945*, Warsaw 1990, pp. 311ff. Headquarters, where 3,000 people worked, was subdivided into three parts. Only the first moved into the Kamler factory, but only some of the anticipated officers arrived there on August 1.

13. The biography of Iranek-Osmecki is from Andrzej K. Kunert, *Słownik biograficzny konspiracyjnej Warszawy*, vol. 2, Warsaw 1987, pp. 69–71.

14. The text of the dispatch is in Ciechanowski, *Rising*, pp. 221–22.

15. The discussions of the AK leadership as well as the informal meetings of individual officers, along with the meetings of the high command, were not recorded for security reasons. There are several reports, letters, and memoirs about the meetings described here between July 21 and July 31; the first are from

the war period (like Okulicki's notes of December 1944 and from prison in Moscow in April 1945), but most are from the 1950s to the 1970s, when the eyewitnesses and actors wrote their memoirs or answered relevant comments of colleagues or the questions of historians. This discussion mainly accepts those themes confirmed by several reports.

16. Many of the MPs and grenades came from the underground's own production, which had begun in 1940, and these weapons were not necessarily reliable. Grenades had been produced in the underground workshops since 1940 (total production between 1940 and 1944 was 350,000–400,000 pieces), automatic pistols (Sten guns) since 1943 (about 2,000 pieces), as well as 800 to 900 flamethrowers. During the Warsaw Uprising, the underground workshops achieved their highest output. See Kazimierz Satora, *Produkcja uzbrojenia w polskim ruchu oporu 1939–1944*, Warsaw 1985.

17. We do not know precisely what data Monter gave in the July 26 meeting. The numbers cited above are estimates from the postwar period; from the memoirs of the AK officers responsible for munitions, the actual situations could have been even more modest. On the other hand, many weapons may not have been recorded in the registers of the higher AK stages ("well" supplied units must have calculated that some of the stocks of weapons would be taken from them to arm the weaker troops). Nevertheless, the estimates give a more or less reliable impression of the inadequacy of the supply of weapons and ammunition—even if there had been twice as much, the Warsaw AK still would have been catastrophically badly armed.

18. Chruściel corrected himself in the discussion with the leaders of the AK section in Warsaw the next day. On the one hand, he was supposed to have said that rebels without weapons would be supplied "with axes, hoes, crowbars"— given the arms of the enemy, a suicidal perspective. On the other hand, he was supposed to have explained that it was not about an attack on "strong targets," but rather about the enemy "on the street [. . .] the occupation of the city, we are too weak to destroy the opponent"; quoted in Ciechanowski, *Powstanie*, p. 369.

19. After the breakthrough from Volhynia (see chapter 3), the Twenty-seventh Division was refurbished in the area of Lublin and had taken part in the Burza action there.

20. Dispatch of July 27, quoted in Ciechanowski, *Rising*, p. 227.

21. Jan Nowak, *Courier from Warsaw*, Detroit 1982, pp. 313, 315. In those days, Nowak lived in the downtown area and observed how the defeated German troops were led west through the side streets while the reinforcements ostentatiously marched west through the main streets.

22. See Włodzimierz Borodziej, "Die Sicherheitspolizei und der Warschauer Aufstand," in Martin and Lewandowska (eds.), *Warschauer Aufstand*, pp. 118–23.

23. "At the meeting of the Government of the Republic, it was unanimously decided that you can declare the uprising at the moment you determine. If possible, inform us in advance." Both quoted in Władysław Pobóg-Malinowski, *Najnowsza Historia Polityczna Polski*, vol. 2/2, reprint Warsaw 1981, p. 630.

24. For a detailed account, see Zbigniew S. Siemaszko, *Działalność Generała Tatara (1943–1949)*, London 1999, pp. 57–70; in most cases, it was dilatory con-

siderations of the supreme commander that were of no importance for the Warsaw AK because of their form.

25. Ciechanowski, *Powstanie*, pp. 376ff.

26. For the adventurous circumstances (and his fifth trip after the Uprising),
see his war memoirs, *Courier from Warsaw*. A director of the Polish section of Radio Free Europe for many years after the war and one of the most important
Poles in exile, Nowak is the last surviving actor and witness of the events described here.

27. Nowak, *Courier*, p. 333. See p. 122, fn. 21.

28. Details in Kunert, *Słownik*, vol. 1, pp. 45–46. The statements of Bokszczanin are also given in detail by Steiner, *Varsovie.*

29. These data, which served national Polish historiography in the 1960s as
an explanation for the abandonment of the Soviet offensive at the moment the
uprising erupted, are now constrained for the same purpose by Russian post-
Soviet historiography; see Lew Besymenski, "Der sowjetische Vorstoß auf die
Weichsel," in Martin and Lewandowski (eds.), *Warschauer Aufstand*, pp. 90–99.
However, there are no references that can suggest another context.

According to other data (quoted in Antoni Przygoński, *Stalin a powstanie
warszawskie*, Warsaw 1994), between July 20 and August 6, the Second Tank Army
lost 425 tanks (53 percent of the original stock), 116 of them in the battle between
August 1 and August 6. For the current debates in Polish historiography about
the objectives of the Soviet offensive at the end of July and the beginning of August, see Stanisław Jaczyński, "Die Rote Armee an der Weichsel: Politischer oder
militärischer Attentismus?" in Martin and Lewandowska (eds.), *Warschauer
Aufstand*, pp. 195–209; here, pp. 195–202.

30. The article cited in detail by Mazur, *Biuro Informacji*, pp. 303–4; Tomasz
Szarota, *Niemcy i Polacy. Wzajemne postrzeganie i stereotypy*, Warsaw 1996, p. 170.
Ibid., pp. 134–84, offers a detailed description of the evolution of the Polish
image of the Germans of 1939–1944.

31. For Nazi propaganda, see esp. Eugeniusz C. Król, *Propaganda i indoktry-
nacja narodowego socjalizmu w Niemczech 1939–1945*, Warsaw 1999, pp. 526–69.

32. See Przemyski, *Ostatni komendant*, pp. 143–44.

33. See Ciechanowski, *Rising*, pp. 239–41.

34. See an excerpt from his memorandum on this subject in Ciechanowski,
"Die Genese des Aufstands: Zum Entscheidungsprozeß auf polnischer Seite," in
Martin and Lewandowska (eds.), *Warschauer Aufstand*, pp. 100–117; here
pp. 115–16.

6. Attack and Mass Murder

1. Stanisław Płoski, "Niemieckie materiały do historii powstania warszawskiego," *Najnowsze Dzieje Polski* 1 (1957): 155–212; here, p. 180.

2. Ney, *Komenda*, pp. 321–22.

3. See the evidence of Krannhals, *Aufstand*, pp. 101–6, whose image of a
"prepared, armed, alarmed, and expectant" enemy seems somewhat overdone.

4. Borkiewicz, *Powstanie*, p. 50; ibid., pp. 48–56, for a precise description of the mobilization.

5. A precise description of the first and subsequent days of the uprising is in Andrzej K. Kunert, *Rzeczpospolita walcząca. Powstanie Warszawskie 1944*, Warsaw 1994, see pp. 1–12.

6. *Grupa bojowa "Krybar" w walce o Powiśle i Uniwersytet Warszawski*, Warsaw 1995, p. 29.

7. Many AK troops in the city center were supplied with these uniforms.

8. Although some 3,500 soldiers could be mobilized, only a few attacks succeeded in the northern part of Praga, where, on August 1, one of the sites occupied was the big building of the railroad administration. In a few parts of the eastern quarter no battle took place at all since parts of those Wehrmacht and Waffen-SS units that had taken part in the battle east of Warsaw were here.

9. On August 5, the AK liberated the camp on Gęsia Street, where almost 350 Jews (including twenty-four women) were held prisoner.

10. Quoted in Płoski, "Niemickie materiały," p. 181.

11. See, among others, Borkiewicz, *Powstanie*, pp. 89–90.

12. Quoted in Kunert, *Rzeczpospolita walcząca*, Warsaw 1994, pp. 20, 27.

13. Quoted in Płoski, "Niemickie materiały," p. 181. Several German documents of the first days are reprinted in the appendix of Krannhals, *Aufstand*, pp. 351–59.

14. Frank, *Diensttagebuch*, p. 895.

15. See Marek Getter, "Die Zivilverwaltung während des Warschauer Aufstandes," in Martin and Lewandowski (eds.), *Aufstand*, pp. 153–63; and chapter 11 of this book.

16. Basic to that: Helmut Auerbach, "Die Einheit Dirlewanger," *VfZ* 10 (1962): 250–63; quotation from Hans Umbreit, "Wehrmachtsverbände und Sondereinheiten im Kampf gegen die Aufständischen und die Zivilbevölkerung: Planloser Terror oder militärisches Kalkul?" in Martin and Lewandowska (eds.), *Aufstand*, pp. 141–52; here, p. 147.

17. Umbreit, "Wehrmachtsverbände," pp. 149–50; Zenon Budny, "Kontrowersje wokół Brigadeführera Bronisława Kamińskiego," in *Dzieje Najnowsze* 38, nos. 3–4 (1996): 87–97, demonstrates that against the widely held opinion ("Ukrainian" or "Russian nationalists," "Kalmuks") nothing certain can be said about Kamiński's national identity or that of his subordinates—except that they were former Soviet citizens.

18. *Archiwum Akt Nowych*, 214-I-7, Correspondence of the GG administration of July 1944.

19. Krannhals, *Aufstand*, p. 127.

20. At the turn of the year 1939–40, there was even an idea to blow up the royal palace, which had been damaged in September 1939. There is a detailed description in Michael G. Esch, "'Ohne Rücksicht auf historisch Gewordenes.' Raumplanung und Raumordnung im besetzten Polen," in *Modelle für ein deutsches Europa. Ökonomie und Herrschaft im Großwirtschaftsraum*, Berlin 1992, pp. 77–123.

21. Quoted in Władysław Bartoszewski, "Mit polnischen Augen gesehen," in Joe J. Heydecker, *Die Stille der Steine*, Berlin 1994, pp. 8–9; here, p. 8.

22. Krannhals, *Aufstand*, pp. 308ff., 327ff., 420–21.

23. *Kedyw,* abbreviation of Kierownictwo Dywersji, the special units of the AK mentioned in chapter 3, which were directly under the high command and, from 1943 on, carried out assaults, assassinations, and so on; elite of the Warsaw AK troops.

24. Quoted in Krannhals, *Aufstand*, p. 312. The losses of the Reinefahrt combat group amounted to six dead and thirty wounded.

25. The ambiguity of von dem Bach, who was no doubt responsible for many war crimes, but who unequivocally saved human life in Warsaw, is perhaps best grasped in the narrative of Kazimierz Brandys, "Wywiad z Ballmayerem," in Brandys, *Opowiadania*, Warsaw 1973, pp. 148–79.

26. This is correctly emphasized by Hanson, *Population,* end of chapter 1.

27. Quoted in Krannhals, *Aufstand*, pp. 372–73.

28. Ibid., p. 325.

7. Refusal from Moscow

1. *Dokumenty i materiały do historii stosunków polsko-radzieckich,* vol. 8, Jan. 1944–Dec. 1945 (henceforth cited as *DiM*), Warsaw 1974, p. 160.

2. See the essays by Bernd Martin and Jost Dülffer in Martin and Lewandowska (eds.), *Warschauer Aufstand,* pp. 39–56, 177–94.

3. Aleksander Kochański, "Stalin a polscy partyzanci," *Polityka* 37 (1991). The order was based on the fact that the AK units "certainly have German spies in their ranks."

4. Tadeusz Żenczykowski, *Samotny bój Warszawy,* Lublin-Paris 1990, pp. 30–35.

5. See Żenczykowski, *Samotny,* p. 59.

6. See Tadeusz Sawicki, *Wyrok na miasto. Berlin i Moskwa wobec powstania warszawskiego,* Warsaw 1993, pp. 24–25.

7. *DiM*, p. 183.

8. See Żenczykowski, *Samotny,* p. 39.

9. *DiM*, pp. 184–85, 189, 192–93.

10. Antoni Przygoński, *Stalin a powstanie warszawskie,* Warsaw 1994; *Na oczach Kremla. Tragedia walczącej Warszawy w świetle dokumentów rosyjskich,* Warsaw 1994.

11. Quoted in Andrzej Korzon, "ZSRR a Powstanie Warszawskie," in *Powstanie warszawskie z perspektywy,* pp. 166–84; here, p. 169.

12. *DiM*, pp. 193–94.

13. *DiM*, pp. 197–98. Soviet press reports from this time were collected by Korzon, "ZSRR," pp. 171ff.

14. For the British attitude toward the Uprising and the air drops, see Jan Ciechanowski, "Stosunek rządu brytyjskiego do Powstania Warszawskiego," in *Powstanie z perspektywy,* pp. 203–27; here, p. 212. Of the eighteen crews of the Polish squadron in Italy (on August 1, 1944), only two remained.

15. Detailed description in Kajetan Bieniecki, *Lotnicze wsparcie Armii Krajowej,* Crakow 1994. And see Dülffer, *Hilfloses Zögern,* pp. 188–89.

16. Quoted in Kunert, *Powstanie,* p. 233.

17. For the press debate in Great Britain, see Kunert, *Powstanie*, passim; and P. M. H. Bell, *John Bull and the Bear: British Public Opinion, Foreign Policy and the Soviet Union, 1941–1945,* London et al. 1990, pp. 164, 152.

18. "Highest authorities are interested," according to General Carl Spaatz, head of the American strategic air force in Europe, on August 13, 1944, to the American military mission in Moscow; quoted in Bieniecki, *Lotnicze wsparcie,* pp. 299–300. For the characteristic assessment of the situation in the discussion of Spaatz's deputy with the president's advisor: "We have been used as tools by the British in this matter to the detriment of our relationship between Russia and the United States. Even if the Russians permitted us to conduct this operation, our chances of contributing to the Poles in Warsaw were very small."

19. George Kennan, *Memoirs, 1925–1950,* Boston 1967, pp. 210–11. And see W. Larch, "Averell Harriman and the Polish Question, December 1943–August 1944," *East European Politics and Society* 7, no. 3 (1993).

8. German Counteroffensive and Battle for the Old City

1. See Jacek Zygmunt Sawicki, "Na przedpolach Warszawy," in *Powstanie,* pp. 130–37; here pp. 134–35.

2. Biographical details in Kunert, *Słownik,* vol. 1, pp. 167–68.

3. More precise details in Borkiewicz, *Powstanie,* pp. 160–65; Krannhals, *Aufstand,* pp. 124–28, 359–64.

4. Quoted in Stanisław Płoski, "Niemieckie materiały do historii powstania warszawskiego," *Najnowsze Dzieje Polski* 1 (1957): 155–212; here p. 171.

5. A minute description of the battle for the Old City is given by Piotr Stachiewicz, *Starówka 1944. Zarys organizacji i działań bojowych Grupy "Północ" w powstaniu warszawskim,* Warsaw 1983.

6. Borkiewicz, *Powstanie,* p. 177.

7. Ibid., p. 206.

8. "Instruction Leaflet" and "Report" are quoted in Płoski, "Niemickie materiały," pp. 173–76, 183–84.

9. For details, see Marszalec, *Ochrona,* pp. 200–203.

10. Von dem Bach to the supreme commander of the Ninth Army, reproduced in Krannhals, *Aufstand,* pp. 386–87.

11. See the description of the nearly five-hour march in Ney-Krwawicz, *Komenda,* pp. 336ff.

9. In the Shadow of the Old City

1. The excerpt from the diary of Kurt Heller was published in *Warszawa Walczy,* August 22, 1944. I thank Marcin Kula for the original of the reprint by Witold Kula, an officer of the BIP and later a distinguished historian.

2. See *Grupa bojowa "Krybar" w walce o Powiśle i Uniwersytet Warszawski,* Warsaw 1995, esp. pp. 49ff.

3. Borkiewicz, *Powstanie*, p. 326, estimates the total losses of the AK in the city center in the period August 5–31 at 200 dead and 750 wounded.

4. Maciej Józef Kwiatkowski, "Niemcy wobec Powstania Warszawskiego," in *Powstanie warszawskie z perspektywy*, pp.149–65, here p. 156, thinks correctly that this chapter should have been investigated more closely and demonstrates that the Germans even thought of an enforced disarmament of their dubious allies.

5. Quoted in Borkiewicz, *Powstanie*, p. 351.

6. The text of the statement was published in the *Times* (London), August 30, 1944.

7. Krannhals, *Aufstand*, pp. 192–93.

8. Marszalec, *Ochrona*, pp. 270–81, 293–306, shows that a precise compilation of the number of those imprisoned and interned is virtually impossible; but at least 160 prisoners were killed by German bombs and artillery. The number of those executed is unknown; in the city center alone, seventy were condemned to death.

10. September: Struggle for Surrender

1. Article in the socialist *Robotnik*, quoted in Borkiewicz, *Powstanie*, p. 326.

2. Borkiewicz, *Powstanie*, p. 355.

3. Quoted in Kwiatkowski, *Niemcy*, p. 157.

4. Quoted in Borkiewicz, *Powstanie*, p. 373.

5. Dispatch of September 6, quoted in *AK*, vol. 4, p. 283. Similar fears in the next dispatches of September 6 and September 7, ibid., pp. 284–86, 289–90.

6. The dispatches of the prime minister and the supreme commander are reprinted in *AK*, vol. 4, pp. 293–95.

7. Borkiewicz, *Powstanie*, pp. 397–98; Komorowski initialed the text; *AK*, vol. 4, pp. 300–301.

8. Borkiewicz, *Powstanie*, p. 400.

9. "It seems that they [the Germans] will accept our conditions. We are delaying." Komorowski to London, September 10, 1944, *AK*, vol. 4, pp. 306–7; similarly the dispatch of September 11, p. 309.

10. A few remarks on this question in Korzon, *ZSRR*, pp. 175ff.

11. See Tomasz Strzembosz, *Stalin a Powstanie Warszawskie*, Warsaw 1994, pp. 14–15, 45–46, 70–71.

12. Details on this question in Strzembosz, *Powstanie*, pp. 16–20.

13. For this and the following, see Antoni Przygoński, *Stalin i powstanie warszawskie*, Warsaw 1994, pp. 58–59.

14. In Roman Bratny's *Kolumbowie, rocznik 20*, under his nom de guerre, Andrzej Morro.

15. Przygoński, *Stalin* (relying on the memoirs of General Sergei Stemienko), p. 59.

16. Detailed description of the landing operations of September 16–19 in Strzembosz, *Powstanie*, pp. 21–28. And see below (Żoliborz).

17. Bieniecki, *Lotnicze wsparcie*, pp. 306–7, has recently checked that even

fewer—that is, only 1,170 containers—had been dropped; of them, only about 25 percent over the parts of the city controlled by the rebels. But, since in all probability, individual AK troops were not eager to register the goods they received—and to share them with other units—there will certainly never be precise data on this issue.

18. Quoted in Płoski, "Niemickie materiały," pp. 191–92.

19. Details in Borkiewicz, *Powstanie*, p. 422.

20. Quoted in ibid., p. 500.

21. The screenplay was written by Jerzy Stefan Stawiński, who had taken part in the battles and evacuation in Mokotów.

22. Borkiewicz, *Powstanie*, pp. 500–501.

23. The text of the surrender agreement is in Krannhals, *Aufstand*, pp. 404–7; quotation p. 406.

24. Thus, on September 9, he presented to the representative of the Warsaw Diocese, Bishop Antoni Szlagowski, the heart of Frederic Chopin, which had been found by German troops in the ruins of Holy Cross Church. Several attempts to win over the highest Warsaw clergy of the Roman Catholic Church, at least as mediators, is documented in the report of Stanislaw Markowski in *Kościół a powstanie*, pp. 85–89.

11. The Civilian Population

1. Joan K. M. Hanson, *The Civilian Population and the Warsaw Rising of 1944*, Cambridge 1982. Unless otherwise indicated, the following quotations are from Hanson's book. And see the survey by Stanisława Lewandowska, "Die Zivilbevölkerung im Warschauer Aufstand," in Martin and Lewandowska (eds.), *Aufstand*, pp. 164–76.

2. See *Exodus Warszawy. Ludzie i miasto po powstaniu 1944*, Warsaw 1992, vol. 1, p. 36.

3. More precise data on this subject is in Marek Getter, "Die Zivilverwaltung während des Warschauer Aufstands," in Martin and Lewandowska (eds.), *Aufstand*, pp. 153–63. For the police services, see Janusz Marszalec, *Ochrona porządku i bezpieczeństwa publicznego w Powstaniu Warszawskim*, Warsaw 1999.

4. The distinguished Szczepański who commanded the rearguard of the AK troops in the Old City was wounded on September 1 and died ten days later.

5. Quoted in *Kościół a powstanie*, pp. 180–81.

6. Quoted in ibid., pp. 37–38.

7. Described in detail in Marszalec, *Ochrona*, passim; here esp. pp. 140–41, 250–53, 257–61. Two of the murderers were shot, the other two probably went underground—despite the investigations of the military police.

8. Most of the Warsaw residents (about 330,000 to 350,000) left the city through the camp in Pruszków. The others went through the smaller transit camps of Ożarów, Ursus, Piastów, Włochy, and Grodzisk Mazowiecki; see *Exodus*, vol. 1, pp. 9–10, 36. Ibid., *Erlebnisberichte der Flüchtlinge und Vertriebenen* (Reports on the experiences of refugees and exiles).

9. See also the characteristic essay of the "Tygodnik Katolicki" in *Kościół a powstanie*, pp. 69–70.

10. Estimate in *Exodus*, vol. 1, p. 36.

11. For Żoliborz, see Marszalec, *Ochrona*, p. 100; Chruściel quotation in Hanson, p. 151.

12. Quoted in Hanson, p. 156; Magdalena Michalska, "Całe życie w węzełku," *Polityka* 40 (1999).

Epilogue

1. The article "Po walce" (After the battle) is reprinted in *Kościół a powstanie*, pp. 81–82.

2. See Andrzej Lechowski, *Frontowe dni Pragi. Wrzesień 1944—styczeń 1945*, Pruszków 1995, pp. 57, 63–68, 109–10.

3. *Exodus*, vol. 1, pp. 37, 12, 15–16. Higher, but less convincing details on the dimensions of the exodus, ibid., vol. 3, pp. 12–13. According to Magdalena Michalska, "Całe życie w węzełku," 165,000 were taken for forced labor, and 50,000 were sent to concentration camps.

4. Władysław Szpilman, *The Pianist: The Extraordinary True Story of One Man's Survival in Warsaw, 1939–1945*, London 1999.

5. Joe J. Heydecker, *Die Stille der Steine*, Berlin 1994, pp. 18–20. This book also contains many impressive pictures of Warsaw in November 1944.

6. Krannhals, *Aufstand*, pp. 329–32; Esch, "Ohne Rücksicht," pp. 113ff.

7. Altogether, in the period 1939–1945, some two-thirds of the Polish library collections were lost. See Andrzej Mężyński, "Die Verluste der polnischen Bibliotheken während des Zweiten Weltkriegs im Lichte neuer Archivforschungen," in *Displaced Books. Bücherrückgabe aus zweierlei Sicht*, Hannover 1999, pp. 34–39.

8. Quoted in Krannhals, *Aufstand*, pp. 332, 419.

9. *Exodus*, pp. 14–15.

10. *Głos Ludu* (central organ of the PPR), February 6, 1945, p. 3: "Zza kulis powstania w Warszawie."

11. The artist's striking blindness to this connection is documented in his memoirs: *Art of Memory: Holocaust Memorials in History*, James Young (ed.), New York 1994.

12. When the Polish editors of the Voice of America called attention to this official "control of the dates," the party organ, *Trybuna Ludu*, countered with the argument: "This is no place for the additional charge of all those truths of the Uprising that have so often been enumerated." *Trybuna Ludu* (henceforth *TL*), August 3, 1955, p. 2.

13. In the period 1956–1988, celebrations took place in several places, including cemeteries, at the grave of the Unknown Soldier, and at the memorial for the heroes of Warsaw 1939–1945 ("Nike").

14. These and the following data are from the seminar paper of Monika Matusik on the commemorations of August 1 in the Polish People's Republic, 1998.

15. Ceremonial address of Zenon Kliszko is reproduced in *TL*, August 1, 1964, p. 1. The revision of the official image of the Uprising is documented in Kliszko, *Powstanie warszawskie. Artykuły, przemówienia, wspomnienia, dokumenty*, Warsaw 1967.

16. *TL*, August 1, 1968, p. 4.

17. *TL*, August 1, 1974, p. 3.

18. *TL*, August 1, 1971, p. 1.

19. The memorial (which is aesthetically controversial to this day) was first dedicated in 1989, even though its formation was announced as early as 1982.

20. Thus the basic tone of the articles in *Powstanie warszawskie z perspektywy półwiecza*, Warsaw 1995. In subsequent years, this trend has become even stronger.

21. Lena Kolarska-Bobińska, Marcin Głowacki, "Powstanie Warszawskie w świadomości społecznej," in *Powstanie z perspektywy*, pp. 449–65.

22. The German text of the speech is documented in *Dialogue* 1–4 (1994).

23. Tomasz Łubieński, *Bić się czy nie bić? O polskich powstaniach*, Warsaw 1997, pp. 137–88; here, p. 169.

24. Tzvetan Todorov, "Skazani na heroizm," in *Gazeta Wyborcza* April 18/19, 1998.

Bibliography

Primary Sources

Archiwum Akt Nowych, 214-I-7. *Correspondence of the GG Administration of July 1944.*

Armia Krajowa w dokumentach 1939–1945. Vols. 1–6. 1939–1945. London 1970–1981.

Boradyn, Zygmunt, Andrzej Chmielarz, and Henryk Piskunowicz, eds. *Armia Krajowa na Nowogródczyźnie I Wileńszczyźnie (1942–1944) w świetle dokumentów sowieckich.* Warsaw 1997.

Dokumenty i materiały do historii stosunków polsko-radzieckich. Vol. 8, styczeń 1944–grudzień 1945. Warsaw 1974.

Drozdowski, Marian Marek, ed. *Kościół a powstanie warszawskie. Dokumenty, relacje, poezja.* Warsaw 1994.

Exodus Warszawy. Ludzie i miasto po powstaniu 1944. Vols. 1–5. Warsaw 1992–1995.

Heydecker, Joe J. *Die Stille der Steine.* Berlin 1994.

Hułas, Magdalena, ed. "Memorandum Stafforda Crippsa z 22 października 1940 r. Polskie aspekty." *Dzieje Najnowsze* 25, 4 (1993): 81–93.

———. "Wojenna współpraca SOE i NKWD oraz miejsce w niej Polski w świetle dokumentów SOE." In *Polska między Niemcami a Rosją. Studia ofiarowane Marianowi Wojciechowskiemu w 70 rocznicę urodzin,* ed. Włodzimierz Borodziej and Pawel Wieczorkiewicz. Warsaw 1997, pp. 60–72.

Kennan, George. *Memoirs 1925–1950.* Boston 1967.

Kliszko, Zenon. *Powstanie Warszawskie. Artykuły, przemówienia, wspomnienia, dokumenty.* Warsaw 1967.

Kunert, Andrzej K., ed. "Protokoły posiedzeń Rady Jedności Narodowej (7 XI 1949–1 VII 1945)." *Archiwum Polski Podziemnej. Dokumenty i materiały 1939–1956.* Vol. 3. Warsaw 1995, pp. 5–87.

Ludność cywilna w postaniu warszawskim. Vols. 1–3. Warsaw 1974.

Madajczyk, Czesław, ed. *Vom Generalplan Ost zum Generalsiedlungsplan.* Munich 1994.

Bibliography

Materski, Wojciech, ed. *Armia Polska w ZSRR*. Warsaw 1992.
———. *Polscy jeńcy wojenni w ZSRR 1939–1941*. Warsaw 1992.
———. *Katyn: Documents on Genocide*. Warsaw 1993.
Michalska, Magdalena. "Całe życie w węzełku." *Polityka* 40 (1999).
Na oczach Kremla. Tragedia walczącej Warszawy w świetle dokumentów rosyjskich. Warsaw 1994.
Nowak, Jan. *Courier from Warsaw*. Detroit 1982.
Płoski, Stanisław, ed. "Niemieckie materiały do historii powstania warszawskiego." *Najnowsze Dzieje Polski* 1 (1957): 155–212.
Präg, Werner, and Wolfgang Jacobmeyer, eds. *Das Diensttagbuch des deutschen Generalgouverneurs in Polen 1939 bis 1945*. Stuttgart 1975.
Przygoński, Antoni, ed. *Stalin a Powstanie Warszawskie*. Warsaw 1994.
Roszkowski, Wojciech, ed. *Konflikty polsko-sowieckie 1942–1944*. Warsaw 1993.
"Rozmowy PPR z Delegaturą Rządu." *Archiwum Ruchu Robotniczego*. Vol. 9. Warsaw 1984, pp. 5–24.
Steiner, Jean-François. *Varsovie*. Paris 1975.
Strzembosz, Thomasz, ed. *Bohaterowie "Kamieni na szaniec" w świetle dokumentów. Wstęp, opracowanie i wybór tekstów Tomasz Strzembosz*. Warsaw 1994.
Szpilman, Władysław. *The Pianist: The Extraordinary True Story of One Man's Survival in Warsaw, 1939–1945*. London 1999.
Teczka specjalna Stalina. Raporty NKWD z Polski 1944–1946. Warsaw 1998.
Wańkowicz, Melchior. *Ziele na kraterze*. New York 1955.
Wyka, Kazimierz. *Życie na niby*. 2nd ed. Warsaw 1959.

Secondary Sources

Auerbach, Helmut. "Die Einheit Dirlewanter." *VfZ* 10 (1962): 250–63.
Baliński, Wojciech. *Czlowiek w cieniu : Tadeusz Pełczyński: zarys biografii*. Kraków 1994.
Bell, Philip M. H. *John Bull and the Bear: British Public Opinion, Foreign Policy and the Soviet Union, 1941–1945*. London 1990.
Bieniecki, Kajetan. *Lotnicze wsparcie Armii Krajowej*. Kraków 1994.
Błażyński, Zbigniew, ed. *Władze RP na obczyźnie podczas II wojny światowej*. London 1994.
Boradyn, Zygmunt, Andrzej Chmielarz, and Henryk Piskunowicz, eds. *Z dziejów Armii Krajowej na Nowogródczyźnie i Wileńszczyźnie (1941–1945)— Studia*. Warsaw 1997.
Borkiewicz, Adam. *Powstanie warszawskie 1944: zarys działań natury wojskowej*. 3rd ed. Warsaw 1969.
Borodziej, Włodzimierz. *Terror und Politik. Die Deutsche Polizei und die polnische Widerstandsbewegung im Generalgouvernement 1939–1944*. Mainz 1999.
Borodziej, Włodzimierz, and Klaus Ziemer, eds. *Deutsch-polnische Beziehungen 1939–1945–1949. Eine Einführung*. Osnabrück 2000.
Brandes, Detlev. *Großbritannien und seine osteuropäischen Alliierten 1939–1943*. Munich 1988.

Bibliography

Brandys, Kazimierz. "Wywiad z Ballmayerem." In *Opowiadania*. Warsaw 1973, pp. 148–79.

Broszat, Martin. *Nationalsozialistische Polenpolitik 1939–1945*. Stuttgart 1961.

Budny, Zenon. "Kontrowersje wokól Brigadeführera Bronisława Kamińskiego." *Dzieje Najnowsze* 38, nos. 3–4 (1996): 87–97.

Ciechanowski, Jan M. *The Warsaw Rising of 1944*. Cambridge 1974.

Davies, Norman. *White Eagle—Red Star: The Polish-Soviet War, 1919–1920*. London 1972.

Duraczyński, Eugeniusz. "Powstanie warszawskie—badań i sporów ciąg dalszy." *Dzieje Najnowsze* 27, no. 1 (1995): 71–88.

Esch, Michael G. "'Ohne Rücksicht auf historisch Gewordenes.' Raumplanung und Raumordnung im besetzten Polen." In *Modelle für ein deutsches Europa. Ökonomie und Herrschaft im Großwirtschaftsraum*. Berlin 1992, pp. 77–123.

Forster, Alan J. "Die britische Presse und Osteuropa in der Anfangsphase des Kalten Krieges." In *Kommunismus und Osteuropa. Konzepte, Perspektiven und Interpretationen im Wandel*, ed. Eva Schmidt-Hartmann. Munich 1994, pp. 101–33.

Fijałka, Michał. *27. Wołyńska dywizja piechoty AK*. Warsaw 1986.

Fitzgibbon, Louis. *Katyn. A Crime without Parallel*. London 1972.

Graml, Hermann. *Europas Weg in den Krieg. Hitler und die Mächte 1939*. Munich 1990.

Giżejewska, Małgorzata, and Tomasz Strzembosz, eds. *Społeczeństwo białoruskie, litewskie i polskie na ziemiach północno-wschodnich II Rzeczypospolitej w latach 1939–1941*. Warsaw 1995.

Gross, Jan T. *The Revolution from Abroad: The Soviet Conquest of Poland's Western Ukraine and Western Belorussia*. Princeton 1988.

———. *Polish Society under German Occupation: The Generalgouvernement 1939–1944*. Princeton 1979.

Grupa bojowa "Krybar" w walce o Powiśle i Uniwersytet Warszawski. Warsaw 1995.

Hanson, Joan K. M. *The Civilian Population and the Warsaw Rising of 1944*. Cambridge 1982.

Jacobmeyer, Wolfgang. "Die polnische Widerstandsbewegung im Generalgouvernement und ihre Beurteilung durch deutsche Dienststellen." *VfZG* 25 (1977): 658–81.

———. *Heimat und Exil. Die Anfänge der polnischen Untergrundbewegung im Zweiten Weltkrieg*. Hamburg 1973.

Jasiewicz, Krzysztof, ed. *Europa nie prowincjonalna*. Warsaw 2000.

Kirchmayer, Jerzy. *Powstanie warszawskie*. Warsaw 1959.

Kleßmann, Christoph. *Die Selbstbehauptung einer Nation. NS-Kulturpolitik und polnische Widerstandsbewegung im Generalgouvernement 1939–1945*. Düsseldorf 1971.

Kochański, Aleksander. "Stalin a polscy partyzanci." *Polityka* 37 (1991).

Komorowski, Krzysztof, ed. *Armia Krajowa. Rozwój organizacyjny*. Warsaw 1996.

Korab-Żebryk, Roman. *Operacja wileńska AK*. Warsaw 1985.

Krannhals, Hanns von. *Der Warschauer Aufstand 1944*. Frankfurt am Main 1962.

Kunert, Andrzej K. *Ilustrowany przewodnik po Polsce Podziemnej 1939–1945*. Warsaw 1996.

Bibliography

————. *Rzeczpospolita walcząca. Powstanie Warszawskie 1944.* Warsaw 1994.
————. *Słownik biograficzny konspiracji warszawskiej 1939–1944.* Vols. 1–3. Warsaw 1987–1991.
Larch W. "Averell Harriman and the Polish Question, December 1942–August 1944." *East European Politics and Society* 7/3 (Fall 1993).
Lechowski, Andrzej. *Frontowe dni Pragi. Wrzesień 1944-styczeń 1945.* Pruszków 1995.
Lewandowska, Stanisława. *Życie codzienne Wilna w latach II wojny światowej.* Warsaw 1997.
Łossowski, Piotr. *Litwa a sprawy polskie 1939–1940.* Warsaw 1985.
Łubieński, Tomasz. *Bić się czy nie bić? O polskich powstaniach.* Warsaw 1997.
Madajczyk, Czesław. *Die Okkupationspolitik Nazideutschlands in Polen 1939–1945.* Berlin 1987.
Marszalec, Janusz. *Ochrona porządku i bezpieczeństwa publicznego w Powstaniu Warszawskim.* Warsaw 1999.
Martin, Bernd, and Stanisława Lewandowska, eds. *Der Warschauer Aufstand 1944.* Warsaw 1999.
Matusik, Monika. *Obchody rocznic Powstania Warszawskiego w latach 1956–1989.* Seminar paper 1998.
Mężyński, Andrzej. "Die Verluste der polnischen Bibliotheken während des Zweiten Weltkriegs im Lichte neuer Archivforschungen." In *Displaced Books. Bücherrückgabe aus zweierlei Sicht.* Hannover 1999, pp. 34–39.
Motyka, Grzegorz. "Ukraińska orientacja." *Karta* 23 (1997): 54–73.
Ney-Krwawicz, Marek. *Powstanie powszechne w koncepcjach i pracach Sztabu Naczelnego Wodza i Komendy Głównej Armii Krajowej.* Warsaw 1999.
————. *Komenda Główna Armii Krajowej 1939–1945.* Warsaw 1990.
Pobóg-Malinowski, Władysław. *Najnowsza historia polityczna Polski.* Vol. 2/2. London 1960.
Polski Siły Zbrojne w II wojnie światowej. Vol. 3: *Armia Krajowa.* London 1950.
Powstanie warszawskie 1944 r. Bibliografia selektywna, 3 vols. Warsaw 1994.
Powstanie warszawskie z perspektywy półwiecza. Warsaw 1995.
Przemyski, Andrzej. *Ostatni komendant—Generał Leopold Okulicki.* Lublin 1990.
Sawicki, Tadeusz. *Wyrok na miasto. Berlin i Moskwa wobec powstania warszawskiego.* Warsaw 1993.
Siemaszko, Zbigniew S. *Działalność Generała Tatara (1943–1949).* London 1999.
Stachiewicz, Piotr. *Starówka 1944. Zarys organizacji i działań bojowych Grupy "Północ" w powstaniu warszawskim.* Warsaw 1983.
Stafford, David. *Britain and European Resistance: A Survey of the Special Operations Executive, with Documents.* Toronto/Buffalo 1980.
Strzembosz, Tomasz. "Refleksje o polskim podziemiu." *Zeszyty Studium Społecznej Nauki Kościoła* 14 (1988): 21–47.
————. *Akcje zbrojne podziemnej Warszawy 1939–1944.* Warsaw 1983.
————. *Stalin a Powstanie Warszawskie.* Warsaw 1994.
Szarota, Tomasz. *Warschau unter dem Hakenkreuz. Leben und Alltag im besetzten Warschau, 1.10.1939 bis 31.7.1944.* Paderborn 1985.
————. *Stefan Rowecki "Grot."* Warsaw 1983.

Bibliography

Terej, Jerzy Janusz. *Na rozstajach dróg. Ze studiów nad obliczem i modelem Armii Krajowej.* Wrocław et. al. 1978.

Terry, Sarah Meikeljohn. *Poland's Place in Europe: General Sikorski and the Origins of the Oder-Neisse-Line, 1939–1943.* Princeton 1983.

Todorov, Tzvetan. "Skazani na heroism." *Gazeta Wyborcza*, April 18–19, 1998.

Tomaszewski, Bolesław, and Jerzy Węgierski. *Lwowska AK.* Warsaw 1987.

Torzecki, Ryszard. *Polacy i Ukraińcy. Sprawa ukraińska w czasie II wojny światowej na terenie II Rzeczypospolitej.* Warsaw 1993.

Węgierski, Jerzy. *W lwowskiej Armii Krajowej.* Warsaw 1989.

Young, James E., ed. *Art of Memory: Holocaust Memorials in History.* New York 1994.

Żenczykowski, Tadeusz. *Samotny bój Warszawy.* Lublin, Paris 1990.

Index

air drops. *See* Allied air drops
air forces: American, 93, 94–95, 118, 121,
133, 162n18; British, 92; German, 79, 103,
116, 117, 122; Polish, 43, 69, 92, 93;
Soviet, 116, 117, 118, 121, 122, 123
airports, 8, 75, 77
AK. *See* Armia Krajowa
AL. *See* Armia Ludowa
Allied air drops: in Galicia, 59; to German-
occupied areas, 121; planes lost, 92, 93,
121; pre-Uprising, 34; psychological
effects, 121; requests from AK leadership, 77, 115–16; risks, 92; Soviet refusal
of landing rights, 94–95, 118; by Soviets,
118, 122; to Warsaw, 89, 92–93, 98, 108,
121, 133, 163–64n17; of weapons, 85, 98,
108, 122
Allies: lack of attention to Burza campaign, 60; level of support for Uprising,
34, 38, 40, 43, 69, 88–89, 92–95; need for
support from, 39; Poland as member of,
148; recognition of AK's combatant status, 112. *See also* Britain; Soviet Union;
United States
Anders, Władysław, 30–31, 63, 148
anniversaries of Uprising, 142, 143, 144–
45, 146, 147–48
archives: Polish, 142; Soviet, 90
Armia Krajowa (AK; Home Army): anti-
Soviet fight, 140; authority, 22; casualties,
3, 75, 76, 80–81, 106, 130; combatant status, 94, 112–13, 117, 127; counterterror,
41; espionage, 66; headquarters during

Uprising, 66, 96, 97, 157n12; Komorowski's command of, 43, 44; lack of Allied
support, 34; leaders, 62–63, 66; "Nie"
organization, 63; number of soldiers, 22,
98; oath-taking ceremonies, 86; prisoners of Germans, 123, 125, 126, 128, 140;
relationship with Red Army, 46, 50, 51,
56, 58, 59–60; relations with other underground groups, 22, 23; Soviet view
of, 34, 35, 67–68; treatment by postwar
Communist regime, 143, 144; units disarmed by Soviets, 52, 56–57, 58, 60, 67–
68, 87, 94; in Warsaw, 67, 68, 71, 74–75,
77, 115. *See also* Warsaw Uprising of
1944; weapons
Armia Ludowa (AL; People's Army):
attempts to contact Red Army, 118; in
Lublin, 57; relations with AK, 23; retreat
from Old City, 103, 112; role in resistance, 142; in Warsaw, 23
armies. *See* First Polish Army; military,
Polish; Red Army; Wehrmacht
arson, 40
art objects, stolen by Germans, 142
assassinations, 40, 41
Austria, Polish revolts against rule of, 4

Bach, Erich von dem. *See* von dem Bach,
Erich
barricades, 77, 78, 83, 85, 98, 99
Bartoszewski, Władysław, 77
Baszta regiment, 111
Beaverbrook, Lord William M., 26

173

PRAGA

Wisła

Żoliborz

Powązki

Śródmieście

Cmentarz Powązkowski

Cmentarz Żydowski

Cmentarz Ewangelicki

Puszcza Kampinoska

Lotnisko Bielany

Dworzec Gdański

Fabryka Kamlera

Most Gdański

PWPW

Ratusz

Katedra

Most Kierbedzia

Pałac Bruechla

PAST

Uniwersytet

Elektrownia

Most Średnicowy

Dworzec Główny

Muzeum Narodowe

Most Poniatowskiego

O - Włazy do kanałów
········ - Trasy kanałowe

0   200   400   600   800   1000 m